THE GREATEST REVUE SKETCHES

Compiled and Edited by
DONALD OLIVER

 A BARD BOOK/PUBLISHED BY AVON BOOKS

THE GREATEST REVUE SKETCHES is an original publication of Avon Books. This work has never before appeared in
book form.

AVON BOOKS
A division of
The Hearst Corporation
959 Eighth Avenue
New York, New York 10019

Copyright © 1982 by Donald Oliver
Additional Copyright notices appear at the end of this book
and shall constitute an extension of this copyright page.
Published by arrangement with the author
Library of Congress Catalog Card Number: 81-65088
ISBN: 0-380-79194-3

First Bard Printing, January, 1982

BARD TRADEMARK REG. U. S. PAT. OFF. AND IN
OTHER COUNTRIES, MARCA REGISTRADA, HECHO EN
U. S. A.

Printed in the U. S. A.

OP   10 9 8 7 6 5 4 3 2 1

This book is dedicated, with love, to
Howard Dietz
and
Lucinda Ballard Dietz
for bringing their past into my present.

TABLE OF CONTENTS

Contents

PREFACE

Florenz Ziegfeld is generally credited with being the major force in the development of the twentieth century form of entertainment known as the "revue." From its origins in English music halls, vaudeville, burlesque, and the extravaganzas of the previous century (not to mention the Parisian *Folies Bergere*), he created the *Follies of 1907*, which "Glorified the American Girl" in a series of unrelated songs, skits, dances, and tableaux using the same cast throughout.

Prior to Ziegfeld, revues had been loose-jointed evenings satirizing current events. But it was Ziegfeld who codified the form, hiring top-notch writers to create original material spoofing or lampooning the easily recognizable figures (and foibles) of the day. He was the first to produce this type of show on a strict annual basis, and with each succeeding year became increasingly concerned with the physical beauty of the productions. For the 1915 edition, Joseph Urban was hired to design the scenery. Urban was a true artist, and his innovations in the use of color and form made the shows spectacularly beautiful to watch while at the same time highlighting and complementing the glamour of the girls. Ziegfeld also hired stellar comedians to perform—Fannie Brice, W.C. Fields, Eddie Cantor, Will Rogers, Ed Wynn, Leon Errol, and Ina Claire—all appeared in one or more editions of the *Follies*.

Many others imitated Ziegfeld's formula. In quick succession there were the Shubert's *Passing Show* series, the *Greenwich Village Follies*, *George White's Scandals*, the *Earl Carroll Vanities*, *Artists and Models,* and Irving Berlin's *Music Box Revues,* and many others.

Since many different writers contributed material to a show, it was up to the individual producers to set the style and tone. Although the undraped female form was the most important element in all of these shows, the amounts of nudity, and the taste with which it was done, varied. Thus, the *Follies* were lavish and tasteful, the *Scandals* snazzy, and the *Vanities* tough and somewhat vulgar. These shows were presented in opulent annual editions and were reasonably successful, resulting in what seems to have been a "Golden Age" of revues, which lasted from about 1915 to about 1930.

But with the advent of talking pictures and the deepening Depression, the public tired of gargantuan girlie-shows. And since Ziegfeld died in 1932 and George White left New York for Hollywood (to produce films), only Earl Carroll was left to continue the type of show that had been a staple of the theatre for over twenty years. But because he was not able to sustain the level of success in the 1930's (in New York) that he had achieved in the previous decade, he too moved to Los Angeles.

In the 1920's a subgenre was formed and labeled the "intimate revue" (although the casts of these shows were often quite large and the production values elaborate). What differentiated them was their stress on the material rather than on the girls. The sketches and songs were more literate, the humor and satire sharper, and the shows as a whole more cohesive. The first of this kind was *The 49ers* in 1922, but it was with the success of *Andre Charlot's Revue of 1924* (imported from England) that intimate revues proliferated.

Particularly striking results occurred when one writer, or a team of writers, wrote all of the material in a show. Most notable in America was the work of Howard Dietz and Arthur Schwartz, whose 1931 show *The Band Wagon* starring Fred and Adele Astaire was classy and elegant. With its incredibly high entertainment value, it set the standard by which every succeeding show of this type was measured.

Intimate shows often had a unifying theme. For *As Thousands Cheer*, the sketches and songs were inspired by headlines of the day; for *At Home Abroad*, it was a world tour; for *The Show Is On*, the entertainment world; and for *Pins and Needles*, the labor movement.

Although audiences shrank because of the Depression, the people who were then able to afford ticket prices were very much "in the know" and therefore for the only time in history, shows were able to be aimed at specific audiences—those who caught even the most obscure reference and understood "inside" jokes.

During the war years, there were more people traveling through New York, bringing a wider audience to the theatre, and "book shows" (those with a plot) flourished. But all it took was one more hit, *Call Me Mister* (in 1946), which not-so-coincidentally was a theme revue about returning to civilian life, to prompt other producers to try revues again. There was a brief resurgence in the late 1940's and early 1950's until television variety shows gave the public similar entertainment for free, signaling the end of revues on Broadway.

By using only a handful of performers and eliminating any scenic requirements, such producers as Julius Monk and Ben Bagley placed their shows in cabarets, thus carrying on the tradition of the more intimate revue from the late 1950's to the mid-1960's.

In recent years, the Broadway revue has resurfaced in shows like *Ain't Misbehavin'*, *Side By Side By Sondheim*, and *Sophisticated Ladies*. These shows are merely song-fests with little or no spoken material of any kind, and although different in form and character, they are still lineal descendants of Ziegfeld's productions.

Even though many of the revues prior to 1915 had the flimsiest sort of story line to carry them along, the self-contained revue sketch was an indispensable ingredient. Revue sketches were (and are) comedy scenes, of varying length—the only rule governing them was that they end with a blockbuster laugh. Sketches were necessary chiefly because they provided the audience with respites from the parades of chorus girls, simultaneously giving the girls time to change costumes between musical numbers, and they furnished generous amounts of humor throughout the evening.

A great many of these sketches were written specifically for personalities on the order of Fannie Brice, Bert Lahr, Willie and Eugene Howard, and Beatrice Lillie. I have tried to select sketches for the book for which knowledge of the player's personality was not a prerequisite to enjoyable reading.

The most popular idea for sketches was that of the eternal triangle—husband, wife, and lover. It is a tribute to the ingenuity of the writers that so many fresh variations on that theme were invented. I have included several examples of this type: "The Yellow Peril," "My," "Triangle," "The Age in Which We Live!"

The sketches were often topical, as in *As Thousands Cheer,* and as noted earlier, Moss Hart's sketches in that show were inspired by headlines of the day. However, Mr. Hart was able to create situations in the scenes that were intrinsically funny, so the topicality wasn't the only thing to laugh at.

A sketch, entitled "And Thereby Hangs a Tail," written by Morrie Ryskind and Phillip Loeb for the 1925 *Garrick Gaieties* was a satire on the Scopes trial. It was set in a simian courtroom with Charles Darwin on trial for spreading the insulting theory that man was descended from apes. Despite that clever premise, most of the humor in it depended upon the audience's thorough knowledge of William Jennings Bryan's idiosyncrasies. Although that fact made it enormously successful in 1925, modern readers would find it difficult to understand.

For examples of topical sketches that transcend their original era, this collection includes two from a left-wing show of 1935 called *Parade.* Produced by the Theatre Guild, it was the first commercial musical to take such a strongly leftist point of view. People walked out during the opening night performance, the critics roasted the show the next day, and it ran only forty performances. It was a show clearly ahead of its time, for the sketches in *Parade* are remarkably similar to the type of material used on TV's *Saturday Night Live.*

Black humor was popular in the 1930's. "Mourning Becomes Impossible," "On the American Plan," and the aforementioned selections from *Parade* demonstrate this type.

Revues provided a unique training ground for writers

and composers. They were able to contribute a single song or sketch to a show and prove their mettle before being entrusted with the writing of an entire show.

Most of the great comedy writers of this century have tried their hand at revue sketches. Not surprisingly, the three most successful creators of comedy today, Woody Allen, Mel Brooks, and Neil Simon had their early work produced in revues in the 1950's.

The organization of the book is chronological, the date taken from the official opening night in New York. "Abend di Anni Nouveau" is placed according to its copyright date, as is "The Will." All the cast lists come from the opening night playbills of the shows—or the date closest to opening night where no premiere playbill survives.

In this book, proper credit is rightfully being given to certain authors who surreptitiously contributed material to shows bearing other authors' names. Moss Hart and George S. Kaufman were the producers of *Sing Out the News* (as associates to Max Gordon) and when the show needed strengthening, Hart and Kaufman pitched in and wrote two sketches, one of which was "Gone with the Revolution." Similarly, David Freedman wrote "Speed" and "A Smoking Car" for *Strike Me Pink,* although his name never appeared in any playbills.

Part of the excitement of doing research is the thrill of discovery. I had the immense fortune to "discover" the work of two writers with whom I had, previously, only a passing familiarity. One is Billy K. Wells, a brilliant and inventive writer who wrote so many famous vaudeville routines and sketches that were, and still are, copied so frequently that their origins have been forgotten. For example, Mr. Wells was the originator of Smith and Dale's "Dr. Kronkeit" routine. He wrote most of the sketches used in most of the editions of *George White's Scandals* and also achieved great success writing for radio, creating for the character of Modern Baron Munchausen the now-famous and still-quoted line "Vas you dere, Sharlie?"

The other writer is David Freedman, an incredibly prolific sketch and gag writer who created Fannie Brice's memorable character, Baby Snooks. He was quite articulate about his technique. He had formulas for his jokes, as rigid as quadratic equations, but when told, had the ring of spontaneity. Believing that there were no new jokes in the world, he was a master at taking old themes and inventing new twists. A typical David Freedman joke is his variation on the "Who was that lady I saw you with last night" idea.

FIRST CANNIBAL: Who was that lady I saw you with last night?
SECOND CANNIBAL: That was no lady. That was my supper.

He once wrote that "real humor has its basis in the idea of incongruity. Given a perfectly logical and regular sequence of ideas, we can so introduce a thought that it will seem wholly incongruous, ludicrous or ridiculous and will stimulate laughter." His technique allowed him to write for as many as five radio programs a week—the equivalent of writing two full-length plays every seven days. I am grateful that so much of the works of such writers as Wells and Freedman survive, and are now available to new audiences.

In collecting the material for this book, I became a detective as well as a researcher. Complete scripts of revues were not published and the rental libraries that specialize in handling production materials for book shows do not handle revues. Going to the writers themselves was not always helpful either, for even though most writers kept up-to-date scripts of their book shows, they didn't seem to have scripts of the revues they worked on. The reasons for this are actually simple. Since, as mentioned earlier, a single revue was generally written by many writers, only the stage manager had an accurate and complete prompt book. In addition, as the late lyricist E. Y. Harburg explained to me, writers of his era never thought that there would be any interest in the sketches beyond the initial Broadway run—and tour—of the show. (The songs, however, were designed to outlive their context.)

He added that once they finished one show, they were on to the next. Hit shows—prior to *Oklahoma!* in 1943—rarely ran more than one season. New product was needed continuously. This was especially true in the cases of the topical revues, whose humor dated quickly.

As a result of the authors' lack of concern for the documentation of their works, a great many sketches seem to be "lost." I have been unable to locate any of the playing scripts for any of the *Follies* that were produced under Ziegfeld's supervision; and no one seems to have a script of *Seven Lively Arts*—meaning that the Moss Hart material in that show is nowhere to be found. And this brings to mind a bigger question and concern—if major works, such as the *Follies* and *Seven Lively Arts* are "lost," how can we hope to find more obscure material? For example, where is the sketch called "The Great Barrington" written by George S. Kaufman, which was in *The Show Is On* during its out-of-town tryout but dropped before the show got to New York? The concern for and need to see this type of material comes from the knowledge that dropping a sketch did not necessarily mean that it was less effective than the surviving material. The show could have been overlong; in this particular case, the Kaufman piece was one of only two sketches not written by David Freedman; and *The Show Is On* had exceptionally strong material, so being that there was an embarrassment of riches. . . . Perhaps some of these works will be found through further research.

Notwithstanding what was unavailable, there was a great wealth to choose from in compiling this book, and a great many people were incredibly helpful in locating material. Sketches were found in old filing cabinets; in boxes that had been stored in libraries and not opened for thirty years; in attics and in closets; and occasionally, on shelves. In addition to the writers or their estates and families whose works are represented herein, my boundless gratitude is extended to the following people for their assistance:

Ben Bagley, Carmine M. Barcia, Ken Bloom, Joe Cantlin, Emmett D. Chisum [with the University of Wyoming—Division of Rare Books and Special Collections], Mike Dwyer [with the Library of Congress], Roger duBois, Carl Fleming, Maxine Fleckner [Director of the film archive at the Wisconsin Center for Film and Theatre Research], Beatrice, Ben and Nancy Freedman, Matthew Garey, Jack Gilford, Stanley Green, Jay Harnick, Kitty Carlisle Hart, Herbert Hartig, Joanne Horwitt, Miles Kreuger and the Institute of the American Musical, Bruce Laffee, the helpful and knowledgeable staff at the Lincoln Center Library, Milt Larsen [the director of the Variety Arts Center in California], Ken Murray, George Nestor, Kathryn Lynch, Roger Richman, Peter Rinearson, David Rogers, Robert Sher, Arthur Siegel, Elliot Sirkin, Sheila Smith, Jeffrey Spencer, Michael Stewart, Andy Teitel, Wendy Warnken [with the Museum of the City of New York Theatre Collection], and Eric Zengota. Special thanks are due to the people whose interest and encouragement helped form the backbone of this project, and they are: Lucinda Ballard Dietz, Bill Gile, and David Grossberg. Thanks are also due to Hector Baez for the hours spent digging through card catalogs at the Library of Congress. Lastly, because of Marc Schwartz' ingenuity and resourcefulness, we were able to research two projects simultaneously, and for that I am deeply indebted.

THE TREASURER'S REPORT

by Robert Benchley

First produced in *No Sirree!* at the 49th Street Theatre, for a limited engagement of a single performance, on April 20, 1922. The "Report" was delivered by Mr. Benchley who subsequently performed it in the *Third Music Box Revue*, at the Music Box Theatre, on September 22, 1923. In addition, "The Treasurer's Report" was filmed as a one-reel short by the Fox Film Corporation in 1927, once again, with Mr. Benchley.

Characters

ASSISTANT TREASURER

The report is delivered by an ASSISTANT TREASURER *who has been called to pinch-hit for the regular treasurer who is ill. He is not a very good public speaker, this assistant, but after a few minutes of confusion is caught up by the spell of his own oratory and is hard to stop.*

ASSISTANT TREASURER: I shall take but a few moments of your time this evening, for I realize that you would much rather be listening to this interesting entertainment than to a dry financial statement ... but I *am* reminded of a story—which you have probably all of you heard.

It seems that there were these two Irishmen walking down the street when they came to a—oh, I should have said in the first place that the parrot which was hanging out in *front* of the store—or rather belonging to one of these two fellows—the *first* Irishman, that is—was—well, *any*way, this parrot—

[*After a slight cogitation, he realizes that, for all practical purposes, the story is as good as lost; so he abandons it entirely and, stepping forward, drops his facile, story-telling manner and assumes a quite spurious business-like air.*]

Now, in connection with reading this report, there are one or two points which Dr. Murnie wanted brought up in connection with it, and he has asked me to bring them up in connec—to bring them up.

In the first place, there is the question of the work which we are trying to do up there at our little place at Silver Lake, a work which we feel not only fills a

3

very definite need in the community but also fills a very definite need—er—in the community. I don't think that many members of the society realize just how big the work is that we are trying to do up there. For instance, I don't think that it is generally known that most of our boys are between the age of fourteen. We feel that, by taking the boy at this age, we can get closer to his real nature—for a boy *has* a very real nature, you may be sure—and bring him into closer touch not only with the school, the parents, and with each other, but also with the town in which they live, the country to whose flag they pay allegiance, and to the—ah—[*trailing off*] town in which they live.

Now the fourth point which Dr. Murnie wanted brought up was that in connection with the installation of the new furnace last fall. There seems to have been considerable talk going around about this not having been done quite as economically as it might—have— been—done, when, as a matter of fact, the whole thing *was* done just as economically as possible—in fact, even *more* so. I have here a report of the Furnace Committee, showing just how the whole thing was handled from start to finish.

[*Reads from report, with considerable initial difficulty with the stiff covers.*]

Bids were submitted by the following firms of furnace contractors, with a clause stating that if we did not engage a firm to do the work for us we should pay them nothing for submitting the bids. This clause alone saved us a great deal of money.

The following firms, then, submitted bids:

Merkle, Wybigant Co., the Eureka Dust Bin and Shaker Co., The Elite Furnace Shop, and Harris, Birnbauer and Harris.

The bid of Merkle, Wybigant being the lowest, Harris Birnbauer were selected to do the job.

[*Here a page is evidently missing from the report, and a hurried search is carried on through all the pages, without result.*]

Well, that pretty well clears up that end of the work.

Those of you who contributed so generously last year to the floating hospital have probably wondered what became of the money. I was speaking on this subject only last week at our up-town branch, and, after the meeting, a dear little old lady, dressed all in lavender, came up on the platform, and, laying her hand on my arm, said: "Mr. So-and so (calling me by name) Mr. So-and-so, what the hell did you do with all the money we gave you last year?" Well, I just laughed and pushed her off the platform, but it has occurred to the committee that perhaps some of you, like that little old lady, would be interested in knowing the disposition of the funds.

Now, Mr. Rossiter, unfortunately our treasurer—or rather Mr. Rossiter, our *treasurer, unfortunately* is confined at his home tonight with a bad head-cold and I have been asked—

[*He hears someone whispering at him from the wings, but decides to ignore it.*]

and I have been asked if I would—

[*The whisperer will not be denied, so he goes over to the entrance and receives a brief message, returning beaming and laughing to himself.*]

Well, the joke seems to be on *me!* Mr. Rossiter has *pneumonia!*

Following, then, is a summary of the Treasurer's Report:

[*Reads, in a very business-like manner*]

During the year 1921—and by that is meant 1920—the Choral Society received the following in donations:

B. L. G.	$500
G. K. M.	500
Lottie and Nellie W——	500
In memory of a happy summer at Rye Beach	10
Proceeds of a sale of coats and hats left in the boat-house	14.55
And then the Junior League gave a performance of *Pinafore* for the benefit of the Fund which, unfortunately, resulted in a deficit of	$300
Then, from dues and charges	2,354.75

And, following the installation of the

new furnace, a saving in coal amounting to $374.75—which made Dr. Mur-
nie very happy, you may be sure.
Making a total of receipts amounting to $3,645.75

This is all, of course, reckoned as of June.

In the manner of expenditures, the club has not been
so fortunate. There was the unsettled condition of business, and the late spring, to contend with, resulting in
the following—er—rather discouraging figures, I am
afraid.

Expenditures	$23,574.85
Then there was a loss, owing to—sev- eral things—of	3,326.70
Car-fare	4,452.25

And then, Mrs. Rawlins' expense account, when she went down to see the
work they are doing in Baltimore,
came to $256.50, but I am sure that
you will all agree that it was worth it
to find out—er—what they are doing
in Baltimore.

And then, under the general head of Odds and Ends	2,537.50
Making a total disbursement of [*Hurriedly*]	$416,546.75

Or a net deficit of—ah—several thousand dollars.

Now, these figures bring us down only to October.
In October my sister was married, and the house was
all torn up, and in the general confusion we lost track
of the figures for May and August. All those wishing
the *approximate* figures for May and August, however,
may obtain them from me in the vestry after the dinner,
where I will be with pledge cards for those of you who
wish to subscribe over and above your annual dues,
and I hope that each and every one of you here tonight
will look deep into his heart and [*Archly*] into his
pocketbook, and see if he can not find it there to help

us to put this thing over with a bang [*Accompanied by a wholly ineffectual gesture representing a bang*] and to help and make this just the biggest and best year the Armenians have ever had. . . . I thank you.
[*Exits, bumping into proscenium*]

THE TRIDGET OF GREVA

**Translated from the Squinch
by Ring Lardner**

First produced in *The 49ers*, at the Punch and Judy Theatre, on November 7, 1922.

Characters

LOUIS BARHOOTER, the tridget
DESIRE CORBY, a corn vitter
BASIL LAFFLER, a wham salesman

The show ran for only two weeks, and since no program survives, it is impossible to determine the original cast

At the rise of the curtain, BARHOOTER, CORBY *and* LAF-
FLER *are seated in three small flat-bottomed boats. They
are fishing.*

LAFFLER: Well, boys, any luck? [*He looks from one to
the other. Neither pays any attention.*]
CORBY: [*After a pause, to* BARHOOTER] How's your wife,
Louis?
BARHOOTER: She in pretty bad shape.
CORBY: [*Who has paid no attention to the reply*] That's
fine.
BARHOOTER: By the way, what was *your* mother's name
before she was married?
CORBY: I didn't know her then.
LAFFLER: Do they allow people to fish at the Aquarium?
[BARHOOTER *and* CORBY *ignore him.*]
BARHOOTER: You must know her first name.
CORBY: I don't. I always called her mother.
BARHOOTER: But your father must have called her some-
thing.
CORBY: Everything he could think of.
[LAFFLER's *and* BARHOOTER's *fishlines become entan-
gled.* BARHOOTER *gets out of his boat, untangles the
lines, and resumes his place in the boat.*]
BARHOOTER: [*To* CORBY] I wanted to ask you something
about your sister, too.
CORBY: What about her?
BARHOOTER: Just anything. For instance, what's the mat-
ter with her?
CORBY: Who?

11

BARHOOTER: Your sister.

CORBY: I'm not married.

[*After a pause,* BARHOOTER *and* CORBY *both laugh.*]

BARHOOTER: [To LAFFLER] Do you know what we were laughing at?

LAFFLER: I have no idea.

BARHOOTER: I wish I knew who to ask.

CORBY: [To BARHOOTER] Which way is the wind from?

BARHOOTER: [*Moistens his finger and holds it up*] It's from offstage. [*He draws in his line, discovers the bait is gone.*] That fellow got my bait. [*He throws his line out again without rebaiting it.*]

CORBY: [To BARHOOTER] I understand you're an uncle.

BARHOOTER: Yes, but do you want to know what happened?

CORBY: No.

BARHOOTER: Well, two days before the baby was born, Bertha and her husband were out driving.

LAFFLER: Who's Bertha?

BARHOOTER: [*Paying no attention*] They were going up a steep hill and Harry tried to change into second speed.

LAFFLER: Who's Harry?

BARHOOTER: But he made a mistake and shifted into reverse and the car went clear to the bottom of the hill.

CORBY: In reverse?

BARHOOTER: Yes. And the baby is very backward.

CORBY: It seems to me there is something wrong with all your sister's children. Look at Julia!

[BARHOOTER *and* LAFFLER *look in all directions, as if trying to locate Julia.*]

BARHOOTER: [To CORBY] Can you imitate birds?

CORBY: No. Why?

BARHOOTER: I'm always afraid I'll be near somebody that can imitate birds.

CORBY: [*To* BARHOOTER] That reminds me, Louis—Do you shave yourself?

BARHOOTER: Who would I shave?

CORBY: Well, when you shave, what do you do with your old whiskers?

BARHOOTER: I don't do anything with them.

CORBY: Will you save them for me?

BARHOOTER: What do you do with them?

CORBY: I play with them.

BARHOOTER: [*With no apparent interest*] You're a scream, Corby.

LAFFLER: [*To* BARHOOTER] Is your first wife still living?

BARHOOTER: I'm not sure. I haven't been home for a long while. But I heard she was dead.

LAFFLER: What did she die of?

BARHOOTER: I think she got her throat caught between my fingers.

LAFFLER: Mr. Corby—

CORBY: Well?

LAFFLER: I often wonder how you spell your name.

CORBY: A great many people have asked me that. The answer is, I don't even try. I just let it go.

LAFFLER: I think that's kind of risky.

CORBY: I'm getting hungry. I wish we could catch some fish.

BARHOOTER: I'm hungry, too, but not for fish.

LAFFLER: I can't eat fish either. I've got no teeth. [*Opens his mouth and shows his teeth*] About all I can eat is broth.

BARHOOTER: Well, let's go to a brothel.

BLACKOUT

IF MEN PLAYED CARDS
AS WOMEN DO

by George S. Kaufman

First produced in Irving Berlin's *Third Music Box Revue*, at the Music Box Theatre, on September 22, 1923, with the following cast:

JOHN Joseph Santley
BOB Phil Baker
GEORGE Hugh Cameron
MARC Solly Ward

The sketch was also used in the Paramount film, *Star-Spangled Rhythm,* performed by RAY MILLAND, FRED MACMURRAY, FRANCHOT TONE, and LYNNE OVERMAN.

it. [*Another critical look*] And if you had these chairs reupholstered in blue—

JOHN: Well, what do you think of a plain chintz?

GEORGE: That would be nice. Oh, say! I've got a T.L. for you, Bob.

BOB: Oh, good! What is it?

GEORGE: Well, you owe me one first.

BOB: Oh, tell me mine! Don't be mean!

GEORGE: Well, all right. Frank Williams said you looked lovely in your dinner coat.

BOB: That *is* nice.

JOHN: How's the baby, George?

GEORGE: Awfully cranky lately. He's teething. I left him with the nurse tonight—first chance I've had to get out. [*Takes a seat at the table*] Who else is coming?

JOHN: Just Marc.

GEORGE: [*With meaning*] Oh, is he? I want to speak to you boys about Marc. Don't you think he's been seeing a lot of that Fleming woman lately?

BOB: He certainly has. He was at the Biltmore, having tea with her yesterday—I know because a cousin of Tom Hennessey's saw him.

JOHN: Which cousin is that?

BOB: I don't know whether you know him—Ralph Wilson. He married that Akron girl—they have two children.

GEORGE: *You* remember—one of them is backward.

JOHN: Oh, yes! I heard that. [*Another knock on the door*] Come in! [MARC *enters.*]

MARC: Hello, everybody!

GEORGE, JOHN *and* BOB: Hello, Marc!

MARC: I'm sorry to be the last, but we have a new maid, and you know what that means.

JOHN: That's all right. Say, I like the cut of that vest, Marc. Look, boys! Don't you like that vest?

MARC: It is nice, isn't it?

GEORGE: Oh, lovely! Turn around and let's see the back. [GEORGE *and* JOHN *both get up and examine his clothes, pull down his trousers, etc.*]

MARC: I had it made right in the house—I have a little tailor that comes in. Four dollars a day.

GEORGE: Excuse me—there's a little spot—
[*He moistens a finger and rubs* MARC's *lapel.*]

JOHN: Well, shall we play a little poker?

MARC: [*Sitting*] Yes, sure. Oh, John, may I trouble you for a glass of water?

JOHN: Why, of course, Marc.
[GEORGE *and* BOB *sit again.*]

MARC: I'll get it myself if you'll tell me where—

JOHN: Oh, no—that's all right.
[*He goes out. A pause. The men look at each other, meaningfully. Their heads come together.*]

MARC: John doesn't look well, does he?

BOB: No. Did you notice those lines? He can't hide them much longer.

MARC: He was very good-looking as a boy.

GEORGE: Isn't this room the most terrible thing you ever saw?
[MARC *goes to the table upstage; picks up a cigar and shows it to the others. They are scornful.*]

MARC: Huh! Ten cents. [*Pause*] I really wanted to get that water myself. I'd like to see his kitchen. [JOHN *reenters with the water.*] Oh, thanks, John. [MARC *drinks.*]

JOHN: Is it cold enough, Marc?

MARC: [*Indicating that it isn't*] Oh, yes. Of course, I generally put ice in, myself. [*Sits*]

GEORGE: Say, we had the loveliest new dessert tonight!

BOB: Oh! What was it? It's awfully hard to find a new dessert.

MARC: [*With emphasis*] *Is* it?

GEORGE: Well, it was a sort of prune whip. You make it out of just nothing at all. And then, if company comes when you don't expect them—

BOB: I want the recipe.

MARC: How many eggs?
[JOHN *up at the rear table. Turns on this speech*]

JOHN: Does it take much butter?

GEORGE: Oh, no—very little. I'll bring you the recipe Tuesday afternoon.
[MARC *feels a rough place on his chin. Rubs it, then takes a good-sized mirror out of his pocket and stands it on the table. Examines his chin. Then takes out a safety razor and starts to shave. After that he takes out*

two military brushes and combs his hair. The others pay no attention to this. JOHN *is at the rear table, with his back to the audience;* BOB *is seated, fooling with the cards;* GEORGE *is seated, calmly smoking. After* MARC *has put everything away,* BOB *breaks the silence.*]

BOB: Are we ready?

JOHN: No! Wait just a minute. [*He brings down the fancy table cover, which he spreads on the table.*] There we are!

MARC: [*Feeling it*] That's nice, John. Where'd you get it?

JOHN: Why, I bought a yard of this plain sateen down at Macy's—

GEORGE: Really? How much was it?

JOHN: A dollar sixty-three. It was reduced. Then I had this edging in the house.

BOB: Awfully nice!

MARC: Oh, say! Walter Sharp just got back from Paris—

GEORGE: He did?

MARC: Yes. And *he* says they're wearing trousers longer over there.

GEORGE: Really?

[*There is quite a fuss about it.*]

JOHN: [*Brings chips and takes his seat*] What'll we play for?

BOB: Oh, what's the difference? One cent limit?

GEORGE: Does it matter who deals?

[*Takes the cards from* BOB]

MARC: Say, did you hear about Eddie Parker?

JOHN: No.

MARC: Well, it seems he saw these advertisements about how to get thin, and he thought he'd try them. You know Eddie's taken on a lot of weight since his marriage.

GEORGE: Twenty pounds—absolutely.

MARC: Well, they sent him some powders and he began taking them, and what do you think?

GEORGE: Well? [MARC *whispers to him.*] You don't say so?

JOHN *and* BOB: [*Excited*] What was it? What was it?

[GEORGE *whispers to* JOHN, *who whispers to* BOB; *great excitement.*]

MARC: Who has the cards?

GEORGE: Here they are. [*Starts to deal—poker hands*]

MARC: I don't want to play late. I've been shopping all day.

GEORGE: And I have an appointment at the barber's tomorrow. I'm going to try a new way of getting my hair cut. [*The deal is completed.*]

BOB: [*Picking up a few cards*] Which is higher—aces or kings?

GEORGE: Now, who bets first?

JOHN: Are these funny little things clubs?

MARC: What are the chips worth?

JOHN: Let's have them all worth the same thing.

BOB: A penny apiece. . . .

GEORGE: Say, Lord & Taylor are having a wonderful sale of nightgowns!

MARC: What do you pay your maid?

BOB: Sixty-five, but she isn't worth it.
[*The three start talking at once about maids, and* JOHN *has a hard time being heard.*]

JOHN: [*Excited*] Boys! Boys! Listen to this! Boys!

ALL: Well?

JOHN: [*Excited*] I *knew* there was something I wanted to tell you!

ALL: [*They must not speak together.*] What is it?

JOHN: Well, now in the first place you must promise not to breathe a word of it to anybody, because I got it in absolute confidence and I promised I wouldn't tell.

GEORGE: What is it?

MARC: Well?

BOB: Well?

JOHN: It's about Sid Heflin! Now, you won't tell anybody? At least, don't let on you got it from me!

ALL: No!

JOHN: Well, I'm told—and I got this pretty straight, mind you—I'm told that he's going to—ah—[*He puts the message across with his eyes.*]

MARC: I don't believe it!

BOB: What do you mean?

GEORGE: When?

JOHN: In April!

MARC: April!
[*They count on their fingers, up to four.*]

GEORGE: What do you mean?

JOHN: Exactly! They were married late in January!

   [*They all throw down their hands and begin talking at once.*]

CURTAIN

THE YELLOW PERIL

by Paul Gerard Smith

First produced in *Keep Kool,* at the Morosco Theatre, on May 22, 1924.

The characters in this sketch bear little resemblance to the list of characters in the playbills for *Keep Kool.* So, rather than print possibly inaccurate information, I have not included an original cast list for this sketch. For the record, the star of the show was Hazel Dawn.

Characters

MAN
PROPERTY MAN
WOMAN
GENTLEMAN

SCENE: *A room, profusely decorated in goldenrod. A* MAN *walks out in his shirtsleeves. A* WOMAN *starts to tiptoe across the stage.*

MAN: [*Interrupting the* WOMAN] Wait a minute—wait a minute. Where's the property man?
[PROPERTY MAN *enters.*]
PROPERTY MAN: Here I am.
MAN: Say, what's the matter with you? Do you see this? It says here this scene is to be decorated with thousands of roses.
PROPERTY MAN: I know it.
MAN: Where are they?
PROPERTY MAN: I couldn't get none. The stores were closed. I done the best I could.
MAN: What are those yellow things?
PROPERTY MAN: Goldenrod. I'll get roses tomorrow night.
MAN: You bet you will, or you'll get a new job. All right.
[MAN *and* PROPERTY MAN *walk off. The* WOMAN *re-enters as the lights dim down. She is picked up by a spotlight. She tiptoes over to the window and whistles. She tiptoes to center of the room and sneezes. Window opens.* MAN *comes through.*]
MAN: Light the—[*Sneezes*] lights.
[*She lights the lights. He walks over to the table.*]
WOMAN: Did you—[*Sneezes*] get them?
MAN: Yes—[*Scatters jewels on table*] Here they are.
WOMAN: What about the—[*Sneezes*] papers?
MAN: They are with the—[*Sneezes*] child in—[*Sneezes*] London.
[*Noise offstage*]

27

WOMAN: Shhhhh—someone's [*Kerchoo*] coming.
[*She hides him behind the curtain. A* GENTLEMAN,
middle-aged, enters, very dignified.]

GENTLEMAN: Susette—what are you doing up at this
[*Sneezes*] hour?
[*His toupee falls off. She gives it back to him. He ad-
justs it.*]

WOMAN: I couldn't sleep—I was [*Sneezes*] afraid.

GENTLEMAN: Afraid—of what?

WOMAN: The house is being [*Sneezes*] watched.

GENTLEMAN: Non—[*Sneezes*] sense. Give me a drink.
[*She gives him glass of liquor. As she hands it to him
she sneezes and it spills. Pours another. He tosses it
into his face and starts a sneeze which won't materi-
alize. He drinks.*]

GENTLEMAN: Where are—the—[*Sneezes*] passports?

WOMAN: I—I—I—I—I—[*Sneezes*]

GENTLEMAN: And the jewels?

WOMAN: [*Opens table. Piles up jewels the other* MAN *gave
her*] Shall we divide them now?

GENTLEMAN: Divide them—don't be a [*Sneezes*] fool.
[*The* GENTLEMAN *grabs jewels—the* WOMAN *pulls a
gun on him.*]

WOMAN: Wait a minute—take your hands off, you [*Sneezes*]
double crosser. Think you can get away with that, you
big crook? Not on your life—back up—hands off or I'll
blow your brains [*Sneezes*] out!

GENTLEMAN: Put down that [*Sneezes*] gun.

WOMAN: Put down them [*Sneezes*] jewels. I'll give you
three. Come on—one—two—[*She starts to sneeze—he
takes the gun, holds it till she finishes—she sneezes—
he hands it back.*] three.

GENTLEMAN: [*He pulls the trigger and grabs himself as
if shot*] You've killed me—Good [*Sneezes*] God.
[*He falls on the floor, dead. The* MAN *comes from behind curtains.*]

MAN: Quick—we haven't a moment to [*Sneezes*] waste.

WOMAN: I've [*Sneezes*] killed him—I've murdered
[*Sneezes*] him. He was good to me—and I [*Sneezes*]
killed him.

MAN: [*Who has packed the jewels by this time*] Turn out
the lights. Don't make a [*Sneezes*] sound.

[*He opens window—she turns out lights. Spotlight picks up dead body.*]

WOMAN: I can't leave him like this—I can't—he was good to me.

MAN: I will take care of you, dearest. Come with me.

WOMAN: Do you love me?

MAN: There is no one in the world—[*Butchoo. Kisses her*] Come!

WOMAN: Just a moment, dear. [*She takes the goldenrod in her hands.*] Poor thing that once was a friend, fare—[*Sneezes*] well.

[*She sprinkles goldenrod over the* GENTLEMAN. *The* MAN *and the* WOMAN *exit. The dead body sneezes.*]

BLACKOUT

MY

by Billy K. Wells

First produced in the eighth edition of *George White's Scandals*, at the Apollo Theatre, on June 4, 1926, with the following cast:

WIFE Frances Williams
FRIEND Harry Richman
HUSBAND Jim Carty
OTHER MAN James Miller

SCENE: *A Boudoir. There is a chifforobe down stage left.*
WIFE *is discovered closing the doors of the chifforobe.*
She has a pair of trousers in her hand. FRIEND *enters.*

WIFE: [*Turning to* FRIEND] My goodness!
FRIEND: [*Arms extended*] My sweet!
WIFE: [*Arms extended*] My love!
FRIEND: [*Pointing to trousers in her hand*] My word!
WIFE: [*Nervously*] My husband's.
FRIEND: [*Smiling*] My friend.
WIFE: [*Disdainfully*] My fool!
  [*Throws trousers on bed*]
FRIEND: [*Embraces her*] My kiss?
WIFE: My weakness. [*They kiss*]
FRIEND: My queen!
WIFE: My king.
  [*They embrace again. Offstage, a door slams.*]
FRIEND: [*Surprised*] My lands!
WIFE: [*In fright*] My husband!
  [*Points under bed*]
FRIEND: My move! [*Crawls under bed*]
  [HUSBAND *enters.*]
HUSBAND: My wife!
WIFE: [*Pleading—standing in front of bed to hide* FRIEND]
  My dear—
HUSBAND: My eye!
  [*Grabs* WIFE *by her neck and swings her aside*]
WIFE: My neck!
HUSBAND: [*Pulls* FRIEND *from under bed*] My rival.

33

FRIEND: My finish!

HUSBAND: [*Aghast*] My friend!

FRIEND: My error!

HUSBAND: My home! My gun!
  [*Takes gun from his pocket*]

WIFE: My heavens!

FRIEND: My funeral!

WIFE: My fault!

HUSBAND: My foot!
  [*Points gun at* FRIEND]

FRIEND: My life!

HUSBAND: My price!
  [*Shoots* FRIEND, *who falls*]
    My end!
  [*He shoots himself and falls.*]

WIFE: My God!
  [*The chifforobe opens and the* OTHER FELLOW *comes
  out—dressed, wearing hat but minus pants.*]

OTHER FELLOW: My pants!
  [*Picks up pants from bed and exits*]

BLACKOUT

THE FEUD

by Lew Brown, Billy K. Wells
and George White

First produced in the eighth edition of *George White's Scandals,* at the Apollo Theatre, on June 14, 1926, with the following cast:

PINCUS Willie Howard
BECKY Dorothy McCarthy
LOUIS Eugene Howard
JAKE Jim Carty
IGNATZ Harry Morrissey
NATHAN Fred Lyon
JOHN MCGUIRE James Miller

The version of "The Feud" printed here is basically the one found in Mr. Wells' files—with emendations from the playing script of *George White's Scandals* found in the Library of Congress. The role of "Morris" is in the script but not in the cast list in the playbills, perhaps indicating that the part was eliminated to tighten the playing time of the sketch.

SCENE: *The Cabin of* PINCUS LENOWSKY, *somewhere in Old Kentucky. A fire glows in the fireplace and a lighted lamp is on the table.* BECKY *is discovered at the window—looking out.* PINCUS *is seated in a chair near the table. He has a long-barreled gun in his left hand and with his right, he pours tea from a small pot into a glass. As he squeezes lemon into the tea, a train is heard offstage. There is a whistle and a bell, then the train comes to a stop.*

PINCUS: [*Listening*] Dis must be der six-seventy-five hexpress from der junction, ain't it?

BECKY: Yes, Father.

PINCUS: Den dey'll soon be here. Morris from Los Angeles, Jake from Quebec, Ignatz from El Paso, Nathan from Panama and Louis from New York. Believe me, der Lenowsky family will be well represented in dis lokelity tonight.
[*He drinks.*]

BECKY: [*Crossing to table*] Why did you send for all your relatives, Father?

PINCUS: [*Rising and hitting table*] 'Ts' cause! For what rison and 'ts' why you will hearing when dey hev gotten here. Come, take away der disses. Already I hear foots-prints by der door.
[BECKY *picks up teapot and glass and places them in drawer of the bureau. There is a knock on the door.*]

BECKY: Careful, Father! It may not be them.

PINCUS: [*Crosses to the door—holds gun by the barrel with both hands*] Who comes dere?

37

MORRIS: [*From behind the door*] Morris.

JACOB: [*From behind the door*] Jacob.

IGNATZ: [*From behind the door*] Ignatz.

NATHAN: [*From behind the door*] Nathan.

LOUIS: [*From behind the door*] Louis.

PINCUS: No fooling?

ALL: [*From behind the door*] No fooling.

PINCUS: If dis ain't der true it will give bullets for such piple what proves difference. Becky! Uppen der door! [PINCUS *backs away, points the gun, closes his eyes and turns his head away from the door.* BECKY *crosses to the door and opens it.* MORRIS, JACOB, IGNATZ, NA- THAN *and* LOUIS *enter. Each one carries as many suit- cases and grips as he can possibly carry.* LOUIS, *who enters last, carries a small steamer trunk. They drop and lay them down all over the place. Each one dresses typical of the section he comes from. All greet* PINCUS, *either by name, or as "Uncle."*]

PINCUS: [*Drops gun and extends hands in greeting*] Well, well! If its haint mine brother Morris Lenowsky from Los Engle, 'n look! Jake, mine neffie from Quebec! 'N second cousin Ignatz Lenowsky from El Passy! And Nathan from Panama. And—mine goodness! Last but not most, seventh cousin Louis Lenowsky from New Yorik! All here. Fine, fine!

MORRIS: I received your telegram saying it was important for all living relatives to gather here as soon as possible so I got in touch with them, arranged to meet at Rock Ridge Junction, and—well, here we are.

JACOB: And very anxious to know what it's all about.

PINCUS: And why not? Sit down. [*He crosses to the table. The others sit, while* PINCUS *remains standing.*] Rela- tives, tirty-tree years I'm living here. Next to me is a neighbor—the McGuires! For eighteen years we was good friend like anything. Our ten children use to play with the eight McGuire kids. Den one day the Mc- Guires borried from us a jar of strawberry jam. When it came time to return it they sent us raspberry. *That*— started the feud.

ALL: Feud!

PINCUS: Yes. We sent our Benny back with the raspberry to get strawberry and they took from him the raspberry.

NATHAN: And he came back without any?

PINCUS: He didn't come back at all.

LOUIS: They killed him?

PINCUS: Absolutely. Mad like terrible I grabbed mine pistol and went out and shot two McGuires.

ALL: [*Applaud*] Bravo! Good for you. Good boy. [*Etc.*]

PINCUS: Next day the McGuires got four Lenowskys.

ALL: Four?

PINCUS: [*Affirms*] Six chickens, one cow and a duck! But we squared dot up by getting two geese, one dog and second cousin. So it has been going on for fifteen years. Up to date the score stands like dis:

[*He shows a board which reads as follows:*

We got	They got
Mike McGuire	Benny
Dan McGuire	Moe
1 Dog (small)	Issy
2 Geese	Bertha
1 Cousin	Uncle Max
2 Nephews	6 Chickens
1 Goat	1 Cow
Tim McGuire	1 Duck
Step-sister	Sarah
3 Aunts	Another cow
1 Grandfather	Aaron
	1 Dog (large)
	Oscar
	Solly
	Julius
	Uncle Abe
	Cousin Sam

PINCUS *can, if desired, read the score-card aloud.*]

PINCUS: Louis, you was always a good bookkeeper. Figure out how the account stands.

LOUIS: Roughly speaking, I'd say—they are two cows and one uncle to the good.

PINCUS: We're on the wrong side of the ledger! Relatives! Are we going to allow der McGuires to wipe the family of Lenowsky off the face of the universal? No! A thousand times mit interest, no! For dis reason I called you here. The seven of us must stick together and clean out the McGuires! They start shooting every night at eight o'clock.

[*A shot is heard from offstage. All rise—startled.* PINCUS *takes out a watch and looks at it.*]

They're a little early. As I was saying—the seven of us—

[*Another shot.* MORRIS *yells, reels and falls.*]

The six of us must stick together! Becky, pass the pistols.

[BECKY *takes a tray of revolvers from the bureau drawer, offers them to whoever is near and retains one for herself.*]

JACOB: Is that what you brought us here for? To fight your personal quarrel? To be shot down like a dog? Well, I refuse! I'm going!

PINCUS: You'll stay!

JACOB: I'll go!

[*He goes to the door.*]

PINCUS You'll stay!

JACOB: I'll go!

[*He opens the door—there is a shot from offstage. He reels, slams the door shut, reels, then falls.*]

PINCUS: You'll stay! Relatives, the five of us—

[*Shot from offstage.* IGNATZ *yells, reels and falls.*]

The four—

[*Another shot.* NATHAN *yells, reels and falls.*]

The three of us must stick together! Don't be afraid of them—they can't hit the side of a barn.

[*More shots from offstage*]

BECKY: [*Running to the window*] They got one of our cows!

PINCUS: Oy! Another one!

[*Goes to board and marks "Kow"*]

LOUIS: [*Shoots through the window*] I got a pig.

PINCUS: One pig! [*Marks "Peeg"*]

BECKY: [*Shoots*] Ah! I got a chicken!

PINCUS: Hurray! [*Marks "Cheeken." Shot from offstage*]

LOUIS: They got a duck!

PINCUS: Oy! [*Makes "2" out of "1" beside the word "duck." Shots from offstage*]

LOUIS: A calf!

PINCUS: Oy! Oy! [*Marks "Kaf." Shot offstage*]

LOUIS: A cow!

PINCUS: Oy, yoi, yoi! [*Marks "2" beside "Kow" then rubs out the "w" and puts "z." Shot offstage*]

BECKY: A goose!

[*Shot offstage before each of the following casualties*]

LOUIS: A dog!

BECKY: A cat!

LOUIS: A rooster!

BECKY: A hen!

LOUIS: A lamb!

PINCUS: [*Who has been trying to write as they call*] Wait! Wait! Tell dem to shoot slower—I can't write so fast! [*Shot offstage*]

LOUIS: They got another cow!

[PINCUS *groans and marks. Shot offstage*]

BECKY: A heifer! [*Shot offstage*]

LOUIS: Another cow! [*Shot offstage*]

BECKY: Another heifer!

PINCUS: For Gawds sake *you* get something! Get a horse! A jackass! Anything!

LOUIS: There's nothing stirring.

PINCUS: [*Runs to the window*] What are you talking? Dere is old man McGuire himself! See him? He's sneaking from behind dot barrel of apples—dere he goes behind dot barrel of nuts—now he's back by der apples—look! He jumps from the apples to the barrel of nuts. Git dot rat!

LOUIS: [*Shoots*] I got the rat!

PINCUS: By the apples?

LOUIS: No!

BECKY: [*Shoots*] I got a man!

PINCUS: Hurray! [*Runs and marks "Man"*]

LOUIS: [*Shoots*] And I got one!

PINCUS: Hurray!

[*Marks "X" beside "Man." Shot offstage.* LOUIS *yells, reels and falls*]

BECKY: They got Louis!

PINCUS: Hurray!

[*Marks "Louis." Shot offstage.* PINCUS *slaps his hand to his side and staggers*]

BECKY: [*Screams and runs to* PINCUS] Father! They got you!

PINCUS: [*Very weak*] Hurray! [*Falls*]

BECKY: Father!

PINCUS: [*Very weak*] Becky! Don't forget, Levi owes me two hundred dollars. Don't take a check! [*Falls*]

BECKY: [*On her knees beside* PINCUS] Father! Father! [*Shot offstage. A rock with a note attached is thrown through the window.*]

PINCUS: Whas dot?

BECKY: [*Picking up the rock and note*] A note.

PINCUS: Sixty or ninety days?

BECKY: It's a letter. Listen!
[*Reads*]
"Dear Little Girl,
   I know you are the only one left, the last of the Lenowskys and I am the last of the McGuires. You do not know me but I know you well. Day after day I have watched you and prayed that you would not fall in this terrible feud. Why? Because from the first time I saw you I've loved you. Loved you as only a great big man of the mountains can love. Let us call this feud off. Let us be friends and someday perhaps you will learn to love me as I love you and then you can face the future safe in the arms of a strong man who to please you would uproot giant trees of the forest with his bare hands! And fight for you as only the lone survivor of a fighting clan can fight. Say the feud is off by waving your handkerchief and I will come to you.
                              John, Last of the McGuires"
[*In ecstasy, she clasps the note to her heart.*]
Oh!

PINCUS: Thank goodness!

BECKY: What? Call the feud off?

PINCUS: Yes. I'm going fast but I'll die happy if I know you will be taken care of. Wave the handkerchief.

BECKY: Father! [*Runs to window, waves handkerchief*]

PINCUS: At last the feud is off! The feud is off!
[*There is a knock at the door.*]

BECKY: Come in!
[JOHN *enters.* BECKY *is startled.*]
Who are you?

JOHN: [*Very effeminate*] The Last of the McGuires!
PINCUS: [*Rises on elbow*] The feud is still on!
[*He shoots* JOHN, *who screams and falls.*]

BLACKOUT

ABEND DI ANNI NOUVEAU
A Play in Five Acts

by Ring Lardner

Characters

ST. JOHN ERVINE, an immigrant.

WALTER WINCHELL, a nun.

HEYWOOD BROUN, an usher at Roxy's.

DOROTHY THOMPSON, a tackle.

THEODORE DREISER, a former follies girl.

H. L. MENCKEN, a kleagle in the Moose.

MABEL WILLEBRANDT, secretary of the League of American Wheelmen.

BEN HECHT, a taxi starter.

JOHN ROACH STRATON, a tap dancer.

CARL LAEMMLE, toys and games, sporting goods, outing flannels.

ANNE NICHOLS, a six-day bicyclist.

ACT 1

SCENE: *A hired hall. It is twenty-five minutes of nine on New Year's Eve. A party, to which all the members of the cast were invited, is supposed to have begun at thirty-four minutes after eight. A* WAITER *enters on a horse and finds all the guests dead, their bodies riddled with bullets and frightfully garbled. He goes to the telephone.*

WAITER: [*Telephoning*] I want a policeman. I want to report a fire. I want an ambulance.
[*He tethers his mount and lies down on the hors d'oeuvres. The curtain is lowered and partially destroyed to denote the passage of four days. Two* POLICEMEN *enter, neither having had any idea that the other would come. They find the* WAITER *asleep and shake him. He wakes and smilingly points at the havoc.*]

WAITER: Look at the havoc.

FIRST POLICEMAN: This is the first time I ever seen a havoc.

SECOND POLICEMAN: It's an inside job, I think.

FIRST POLICEMAN: You WHAT?

WAITER: The trouble now is that we'll have to recast the entire play. Every member of the cast is dead.

FIRST POLICEMAN: Is that unusual?

SECOND POLICEMAN: When did it happen?

WAITER: When did what happen?

SECOND POLICEMAN: I've forgotten.

END OF ACT 1

ACT 2

SCENE: *The interior of an ambulance. Three men named*
LOUIE BREESE *are playing bridge with an* INTERNE. *The*
INTERNE *is* LOUIE BREESE's *partner.* LOUIE *leads a club.*
The INTERNE *trumps it.*

BREESE: Kindly play interne.
INTERNE: I get you men confused.
BREESE: I'm not confused.
THE TWO OTHER BREESES: Neither of us is confused.
  [*They throw the* INTERNE *onto Seventh Avenue. An*
  East Side GANGSTER, *who was being used as a card*
  table, gets up and stretches.]
GANGSTER: Where are we at?
BREESE: Was you the stretcher we was playing on?
GANGSTER: Yes.
BREESE: There's only three of us now. Will you make a
  fourt'?
GANGSTER: There's no snow.

END OF ACT 2

ACTS 3, 4 AND 5

SCENE: *A one-way street in Jeopardy. Two* SNAIL-GUNDERS *enter from the right, riding a tricycle. They shout their wares.*

FIRST SNAIL-GUNDER: Wares! Wares!

A NEWSBOY: Wares who?

FIRST SNAIL-GUNDER: Anybody. That is, anybody who wants their snails gunded.

[Three men suddenly begin to giggle. It is a secret, but they give the impression that one of them's mother runs a waffle parlor. They go off the stage still giggling. Two Broadway THEATRICAL PRODUCERS, *riding pelicans, enter almost nude.]*

FIRST PRODUCER: Have you got a dime?

SECOND PRODUCER: What do you think I am, a stage hand?

FIRST PRODUCER: Have you seen my new farce?

SECOND PRODUCER: No. I was out of town that night.

END OF ACTS 3, 4 AND 5

THE AMBULANCE CHASER

by Billy K. Wells

First produced in the ninth edition of *George White's Scandals*, at the Apollo Theatre, on July 2, 1928, with the following cast:

THE PATIENT Willie Howard
THE NURSE Frances Williams
THE LAWYER Eugene Howard

SCENE: *A hospital room. The bed is stage center. There is a table to its right upon which are bandages, safety pins, medicine bottles and a telephone.* PATIENT'S *hat and coat hang on a tree. There is a chair at the foot of the bed. The* PATIENT *is in the bed, attired in pajamas. Both legs are bandaged on a hurdle. Both arms are in splints and in slings. His head is bandaged. The* NURSE *is at the side of the bed holding* PATIENT'S *leg up, fastening bandage. At rise, the phone rings and the* NURSE *drops the* PATIENT'S *leg and picks up the phone.* PATIENT *yells, then groans.*

NURSE: Hello—yes—this is Mr. Finkelstein's room. Who? Just a moment. [*To* PATIENT] It's your brother. He's coming to see you and wants to know what kind of fruit you'd like.

PATIENT: My brother? Tell him to bring pineapples.

NURSE: [*Into phone*] Bring oranges. Good-bye. [*Hangs up*]

PATIENT: I said pineapple!

NURSE: [*Raising* PATIENT *to sitting position*] I don't like pineapples.

PATIENT: Who asked you? Who cares what you like?

NURSE: [*Removes pillows, supports* PATIENT] Now be nice and maybe I'll give you one of the oranges.

PATIENT: You're so good to me.
  [*Phone rings.* NURSE *drops* PATIENT *and picks up phone.* PATIENT *falls back with a yell and groans.*]

NURSE: Hello? Mr. Finkelstein's cousin? Oh, he's feeling fine. Yes . . . very comfortable. Good-bye.

53

PATIENT: Did I ask you to lie?

NURSE: [*Shakes pillows*] Oh, don't be a grouch. [*Lifts PATIENT*] I wasn't on duty when you were brought in. Are you seriously injured?

PATIENT: I can't tell till I see my lawyer.
[*Phone rings.* NURSE *drops* PATIENT *and picks up phone.* PATIENT *yells, falls back, groans.*]

NURSE: Hello? [*To* PATIENT] It's your brother calling again.

PATIENT: [*Loud*] Pineapples.

NURSE: [*Into phone*] What? I'll ask him. [*To* PATIENT] What kind of soup would you like?

PATIENT: Noodle.

NURSE: [*Into phone*] Clam chowder. [*Hangs up*]

PATIENT: Why do you ask me?

NURSE: [*Lifting* PATIENT] Don't you like clam chowder?

PATIENT: I hate it. Even if it's got clams in it I hate it.
[*Phone rings.* NURSE *drops* PATIENT *and picks up phone.* PATIENT *yells, falls back and groans.*]

NURSE: Hello? Oh, good morning, Doctor. Yes, he's doing very well—he's sitting up.

PATIENT: [*Wailing*] Sitting up.

NURSE: I'll see. [*To* PATIENT] Doctor wants to know if there is anything you'd like to have.

PATIENT: Yes, I'd like to have the telephone removed.

NURSE: [*Into phone*] I guess not, Doctor. Good-bye.
[*Hangs up.* LAWYER *knocks on door.*]
Come in.
[LAWYER *enters, crosses to bed and presents card to* PATIENT.]

LAWYER: My name is Marks and I'm a lawyer. Have a card.

PATIENT: This is no time to play Uncle Tom's Cabin.

LAWYER: I am serious. [*Sits on chair at the foot of the bed*] I would like to handle your case.
[NURSE *rearranges bandages on* PATIENT'*s head.*]

PATIENT: I don't know you. How do I know you are even a lawyer?

LAWYER: I got here credentials. [*Takes papers from pocket and shows them to* PATIENT] Look.
[*At this point* NURSE *covers* PATIENT'*s eyes with the bandage.*]

Here it is in black and white and now [*Puts papers away*] let's get down to business.

PATIENT: [*Pulls bandage from eyes*] What is this? Blind man's bluff?

NURSE: It slipped.

[*She rearranges bandages and covers* PATIENT's *mouth.*]

LAWYER: Give me the case and I'll get you a settlement in thirty days.

[PATIENT *tries to talk through the bandage.*]

LAWYER: What?

[PATIENT *tries to talk.*]

NURSE: [*Wraps* PATIENT's *face completely—leaving only his nose and one eye exposed. Pins the bandage*] I'm going downstairs. If you want anything, call me. [*Exits*]

[PATIENT *tries to talk.*]

LAWYER: [*Rises*] Wait—[*Looks off to where the* NURSE *went—then goes to* PATIENT *and removes face bandage*] What was you saying? [*Sits on chair*]

PATIENT: How do I know you are a good lawyer?

LAWYER: My dear man, in the last year I have handled sixty-six accident cases. Accidents is my middle name.

PATIENT: You're an ambulance-chaser.

LAWYER: What's the difference? I get results.

PATIENT: What do you charge?

LAWYER: Fifty percent.

PATIENT: What?

LAWYER: Twenty-five.

PATIENT: I'll give you ten percent—not a cent more.

LAWYER: Twenty is the best I can do. [*Rises*]

PATIENT: Fifteen—take it or leave it.

LAWYER: I'll take it. Excuse me, I'll use the phone. [*Goes to table and picks up phone*] Orchard 1—8—4—7. [*To* PATIENT] I'll get my partner busy on your case at once. [*In phone*] Hello, Moe? Is this Moe? This is Jack. Listen, Moe, I got Mr. Finkelstein's case—yes—alright—[*Hangs up*] My partner, Moe, is going to investigate at once and call me back. Let me see—[*He sits down, takes notebook from his pocket; reads and makes notes during the dialogue that follows.*] The accident happened at the corner of Ninety-Sixth Street and Broadway—

PATIENT: Between Ninety-sixth and Ninety-seventh—

LAWYER: I said it happened on the corner of Ninety-sixth.

PATIENT: I guess I know where it happened. It was between—

LAWYER: To cross a street in the middle of a block is against the law, so where did the accident happen?

PATIENT: On the corner of Ninety-sixth Street—how many times must I tell you? I was standing—

LAWYER: You was walking—

PATIENT: I was going to cross the street—

LAWYER: You was already half way over.

PATIENT: I just stepped off the curb—

LAWYER: You was nearly on the other side.

PATIENT: I saw the automobile coming—

LAWYER: You didn't see anything.

PATIENT: The chauffeur blew his horn—

LAWYER: He didn't! Without a warning he knocked you down.

PATIENT: When I was knocked down I jumped up—

LAWYER: You couldn't move.

PATIENT: I hollered for help—

LAWYER: You was unconscious. Now regarding your wife, when she heard of your accident—

PATIENT: She took charge of my store.

LAWYER: She went to bed with a nervous breakdown.

PATIENT: She didn't!

LAWYER: I'll arrange it. Regarding witnesses . . .

PATIENT: I haven't got any.

LAWYER: You got three coming from Chicago. I'll draw up the papers and bring suit for fifteeen thousand dollars.

PATIENT: Fifteen? What are you talking? I'm hurt at least eighteen thousand.

LAWYER: In that case, we'll sue for twenty.

PATIENT: Make it twenty-five thousand and be done with it.

LAWYER: What kind of a car was it?

PATIENT: A Rolls Royce.

LAWYER: A Rolls Royce! [*Scratching out last notation*] We are suing for fifty thousand dollars!

PATIENT: We might get twenty, maybe twelve—we'll take six but I'll settle for three hundred.

LAWYER: Stick to your story and the case is as good as

won. The important thing to remember is it was a Rolls Royce and the accident happened on the corner of Ninety-sixth Street and Broadway. Don't forget. [*Phone rings.*] Maybe it's Moe. [*Rises and picks up phone*] Hello, Moe? Yes, this is me, Moe. What's that, Moe? Mmm. Yes, Moe. No? Mmm. Yes, Moe. Mmm. I see, Moe. What you said, Moe. Alright, Moe. [*Hangs up*]

PATIENT: Who was that? Moe?

LAWYER: You liar you! What are you trying to do? Ruin my practice?

PATIENT: What are you talking?

LAWYER: What do you mean by telling me lies about your accident?

PATIENT: Lies?

LAWYER: Yes. I just learned it from Moe.

PATIENT: Ah—so that was Moe on the phone.

LAWYER: Yes, and he found out in the first place it wasn't a Rolls Royce—it was a Ford, in the second place the accident happened at Fifty-seventh Street not Ninety-sixth, in the third place it happened to your brother, not you, and in the fourth place you haven't got a case in the first place and can't collect a nickel!

PATIENT: Then the hell with it!

[*Rises and exits*]

BLACKOUT

SCHOOL DAYS

by W.C. Fields

First produced in the seventh edition of the *Earl Carroll Vanities*, at the Earl Carroll Theatre, on August 6, 1928, with the following cast:

TEACHER Martha Morton
1ST PUPIL Joey Ray
2ND PUPIL Gordon Dooley
3RD PUPIL W.C. Fields

rst produced in the seventh edition of the *Earl Carr*
nities, at the Earl Carroll Theatre, on August 6, 192
th the following cast:

IEF BIG SPEAR Edward Graham
TTLE SMALL BLANKET Gordon Dooley
AVELY W.C. Fields
S. SNAVELY Ray Dooley
ESTER Joey Ray

s sketch formed the basis for W.C. Fields' short fi
Fatal Glass of Beer, made for Mack Sennett's co
y in 1933.

SCENE: *Interior of a schoolroom. Three children's desks
and chairs are strung out across stage right, facing left.
Teacher's platform with small table and high stool is
stage left. An apple and an orange are on the desk. At
the back is a blackboard with childish figures of a cat,
a dog and a man drawn on it. At rise,* TEACHER *is on the
platform asking questions—pointer in her hand.*

TEACHER: Now, children, to what kingdom does the pea-
nut belong: animal, vegetable or mineral?
1ST PUPIL: [*Raising his hand*] I know, teacher. Animal!
TEACHER: No, you are thinking of the horse-chestnut.
[*She puts the pointer on her desk and knocks the apple
and the orange to the floor. She stoops to pick up the
apple.* 1ST PUPIL *laughs.* TEACHER *rises.*]
Well, Richard, why do you laugh?
1ST PUPIL: I saw your stocking garter.
TEACHER: Well, I never! Leave the room. Go home and
do not return to this school for a week. Do you understand? A week!
[1ST PUPIL *takes his books and exits snickering.*
TEACHER *leans over to pick up the orange.* 2ND PUPIL
laughs unrestrainedly.]
Well, Gordon, what are you laughing at?
2ND PUPIL: Oh, teacher, I saw your bare leg.
TEACHER: Merciful heavens! What next? Gordon Dooley,
you leave this room and do not return for a month—
2ND PUPIL: Oh, gee! But teacher—

61

TEACHER: Do you understand? Do not return for a month! [2ND PUPIL *exits with his books, grinning, with his hand over his mouth.* TEACHER *mounts stool, placing her feet on the rungs, arms akimbo and surveys the room defiantly.* 3RD PUPIL *laughs and tries to suppress it by placing his hand over his mouth.*]
Well, Willie, what is the matter with you?
3RD PUPIL: [*Rises—starts to leave*] My schooldays are over forever.
[TEACHER *looks at her dress and pulls it down.*]

BLACKOUT

STOLEN BONDS

by W.C. Fields

SCENE: *The interior of an old country farmhouse made of logs in the Canadian Northwest. There is a living room on the left—a small bedroom right. There is a window in the center of the living room and electric lights with chain attachment at each side of the window. An old lantern hangs on the wall. Several skins are thrown about the floor. A small table with two chairs is off center of the living room. Door stage right. Old fashioned telephone hung on wall near this door. In the bedroom there is a bed and a curtain hangs over doorway. A few sticks of firewood lie near the fireplace. On the table in living room are two plates, knives, forks, spoons, one trick spoon (for* SNAVELY*), and a long loaf of French bread. At rise, two Indians in blankets are seated by the fire. The wind howls outside. Snow is falling. Door at back opens and* SNAVELY *enters. As he opens the door, velocity of wind can be heard more plainly and a quantity of snow is blown into the living room. Dogs can be heard howling outside. The room is dimly lighted.* SNAVELY *is carrying one gold nugget about the size of a human skull, which he carefully deposits on the table with a thud.*

SNAVELY: It ain't a fit night for man or beast and it's been a-stormin' for a fortnit. Hello thar, hello thar, hello, hello—
[*Crosses to phone and takes it off the hook and speaks into it.*]
Hello!
[*Replaces the phone on the hook*]

65

INDIAN CHIEF: How, Mr. Snavely.

SNAVELY: How, Chief.

SECOND INDIAN: How!

SNAVELY: And how! Vamoose! Ewscray!

[*Indians move to door,* INDIAN CHIEF *exits. Wind blows and finally* SECOND INDIAN *is yanked off by the* CHIEF. SNAVELY *crosses to the door and closes it.*]

It ain't a fit night out for man or beast.

[*He looks about the room furtively, then pulls the chain on one of the electric lights. The light on the other side of the window lights up. He goes to the lighted lamp, pulls the cord and the opposite light flashes on.*]

MRS. SNAVELY: [*Offstage*] Who's thar?

SNAVELY: 'S'me, Ma.

MRS. SNAVELY: [*Entering*] Did you find any gold down in the gulch?

SNAVELY: I found a nugget. Thar it be on the table.

MRS. SNAVELY: [*Seeing the nugget, she effusively exclaims.*] A nugget, a golden nugget. [*Picks it up with great care and deliberation*] A golden nugget—just what you have combed them thar hills for, for nigh onto thirty years. It must be worth almost a hundred dollars.

SNAVELY: That will help to pay off the mortgage on the old shack. [*Picks up a paper from the table*] Has that pill from Medicine Hat been here again?

MRS. SNAVELY: Yes, and he wants more money.

SNAVELY: Drat his hide.

MRS. SNAVELY: He says if he don't get it, he'll take our malamutes.

SNAVELY: He won't take old Balto, my lead dog!

MRS. SNAVELY: Why not, Pa?

SNAVELY: Because I 'et him. He was mighty good with mustard. We was a-mushin' all last night over Blind Nag Rim and I got pretty hungry.

MRS. SNAVELY: You'd better take off your mucklucks, Pa. Captain Pipitone of the Canadian Mounted smuggled a police dog across the border for you.

[*During this she has been taking off his mucklucks.*]

SNAVELY: He's got a police dog for me?

MRS. SNAVELY: Yes, he says for you to keep it under your hat.

SNAVELY: How big is it?

MRS. SNAVELY: [*Indicating about two feet high*] About that high.

SNAVELY: He's crazy.

MRS. SNAVELY: Come on, Pa, have your vittles. [*They start supper.*] Pa, do you know it's three years ago today since they put our dear son in jail for stealing them thar bonds and I know he never stole them.

SNAVELY: Certainly he didn't, Ma. Our Chester never stole nothing from nobody never.

[*He gets up and puts his arm on* MRS. SNAVELY's *shoulder.*]

MRS. SNAVELY: Do you think he'll come a-headin' for home, Pa, when they turn him loose from that plagued jail?

SNAVELY: I reckon, guess and calculate he will, Ma.

[*There is a knock at the door.* SNAVELY *turns and looks at the door, as does* MRS. SNAVELY.]

Who's thar?

[*Door opens—wind is howling—more snow is thrown into the room.* CHESTER *enters.*]

MRS. SNAVELY: [*Going to* CHESTER] Chester, my dear, my darling boy!

[*She takes* CHESTER *in her arms and weeps aloud.*]

SNAVELY: [*Closing door*] T'ain't a fit night out for man or beast. There, Ma, don't cry, we got our son back agin' now. Welcome home, Chester. [*He goes to table and stands with his hand on the back of the chair.*] But I don't suppose we'll have him with us long. Once the big city gits into a boy's system, he loses his hankerin' for the country.

CHESTER: [*Coming down to back of table*] No, Dad, I ain't ever a-goin' to leave the old farm agin'. I've come back here to stay with you and Mother. I ain't ever goin' to leave agin'.

[MRS. SNAVELY *has brought another chair to the table and placed it for* CHESTER. *She hands him a plate of soup from the table.* SNAVELY *reaches for it.*]

SNAVELY: 'S'my soup, Ma.

[MRS. SNAVELY *gets* CHESTER *another plate.*]

CHESTER: Dad, it's so good to see you both. I'm so glad to be home agin' to see you and Mother—I can't talk.

I'd like to go to my little room and lay on the bed and cry like I was a baby agin'.

[*Puts his head on his arms and cries.* SNAVELY *breaks down, rises and crosses to left.*]

SNAVELY: It ain't a fit night out for man or beast.

MRS. SNAVELY: [*Leading* CHESTER *to bedroom*] Go in your room, dear, and have a good cry. I know how you feel.

CHESTER: [*Still crying*] Good night, Dad, dear.

SNAVELY: Good night, Ches.

CHESTER: Good night, Ma, dear.

MRS. SNAVELY: Good night, Chester.

[CHESTER *exits into the bedroom and slowly begins disrobing.* MRS. SNAVELY *gazes after him admiringly.* SNAVELY *removes lantern from the wall and proceeds to light it. Then he puts on his hat.*]

SNAVELY: Ain't it good to have him back agin'? I think I'll go out and lock up the cow. [*He opens the door— more wind and snow.*] It ain't a fit night out for man or beast.

[*He exits and passes window.* MRS. SNAVELY *goes to* CHESTER's *door.*]

MRS. SNAVELY: Chester?

CHESTER: [*Offstage*] Yes, Mother, dear?

MRS. SNAVELY: Can I see you for just a moment before you go to sleep?

CHESTER: [*Coming into room*] Yes, Ma.

MRS. SNAVELY: [*Leading him to a chair, pathetically asks*] Chester, did you steal them bonds?

CHESTER: Yes, Ma! [*She sinks into the chair. He kneels beside her.*] I stole the bonds. I was a bank messenger at the time. They caught me fair and square. I wasn't framed.

MRS. SNAVELY: I thought you stole 'em, Chester, but I never would admit it to your father. If he thought you stole 'em it would break his old heart. He thinks you're innocent. Never tell him any different. Good night, Chester.

[*She kisses him and rises from the chair.*]

CHESTER: [*Rises*] Good night, Ma, and God bless you.

[*He exits into bedroom.* SNAVELY *is seen crossing window. He enters. More wind and snow, as before.*]

SNAVELY: It ain't a fit night out for man or beast. [*Takes his hat and scarf off*] Has Chester gone to bed yet, Ma?

MRS. SNAVELY: [*Moving chair away from table*] I don't think so, Pa.
[*She exits left.*]

SNAVELY: [*Crosses to* CHESTER's *room. Whispers*] Chester!
[*Crosses to door through which* MRS. SNAVELY *has just exited and starts to close it. It squeaks. He crosses back to* CHESTER's *room and again calls.*]
Chester!

CHESTER: [*Offstage*] Yes, Dad?

SNAVELY: Come and sit down, Son. [CHESTER *enters.* SNAVELY *crosses to back of table.*]
Sit down.
[*Indicates chair—*CHESTER *sits.*]
Son, did you steal them bonds?
[CHESTER *hangs his head.* MRS. SNAVELY *appears in doorway.*]
I knowed you was guilty, Son, but I never admitted it to your mother. If she thought you stole them bonds, it would break her old heart. She thinks you are innocent. Never tell her any different.

CHESTER: [*Raises head*] Oh, it's good to be home, Dad. I'm going to stay now with you and Mother for all time.

SNAVELY: Have you any of the bonds with you, Son, or any of that money?

CHESTER: No, Dad, I haven't a cent of the tainted money and I took those bonds and I threw them away.

SNAVELY: And you came back here to Ma and me?

CHESTER: [*Turns head to* SNAVELY] Yes, Dad!

SNAVELY: [*Quickly picking up long loaf of bread*] To sponge on us for the rest of your life!
[*Smashes* CHESTER *with loaf.* CHESTER *falls.* MRS. SNAVELY *screams and comes to table.*]

MRS. SNAVELY: My God! Do you want to kill him?

SNAVELY: Yes, I do!

MRS. SNAVELY: [*Handing him the nugget*] Then hit him with this!

BLACKOUT

THE WILL

by Billy K. Wells

It is, unfortunately, impossible to determine which show "The Will" was performed in. It was, however, copyrighted in 1929, hence its inclusion in this slot.

Characters

NEPHEW
UNCLE
SECRETARY

SCENE: UNCLE's *apartment. There is a table with chairs on each side. Plates of cake are on the table. At rise,* UNCLE *is discovered seated in one of the chairs attired in a bathrobe and skull cap, a forlorn expression on his face.* NEPHEW *enters followed by* SECRETARY, *who carries a briefcase.*

NEPHEW: Hello, Uncle Peter.

UNCLE: Hello, Martin.

[*They shake hands.*]

NEPHEW: This is my secretary, Mr. Thompson. Thompson, this is my uncle, Mr. Green.

SECRETARY: [*Shakes hands*] Glad to meet you, Mr. Green.

UNCLE: Thank you. Sit down.

[SECRETARY *sits and places briefcase on table.*]

NEPHEW: [*Sitting down*] Mr. Thompson attends to all my business; no matter what has to be done, he does it.

UNCLE: That's fine, because you'll need help. Martin, I'm a sick man. Last week, my doctor told me I was getting along fine, but advised me to make my will.

NEPHEW: That was very encouraging.

UNCLE: Well, I made my will and I made you the executor. You must see that my wishes are carried out to the letter.

SECRETARY: I'll attend to that.

NEPHEW: He'll attend to that. He attends to everything.

UNCLE: I am leaving ten thousand dollars to charities. Be sure they get it.

SECRETARY: [*Rises*] I'll attend to that.
  [*Sits*]
NEPHEW: He'll attend to that.
UNCLE: To the city hospital I am leaving one hundred thousand dollars providing they change the name to the Peter Green Memorial.
SECRETARY: [*Rises*] I'll attend to that.
  [*Sits*]
NEPHEW: He'll attend to that.
UNCLE: To you I am leaving fifty thousand dollars and my business which must be kept going.
SECRETARY: [*Rises*] I'll attend to that.
  [*Sits*]
NEPHEW: He'll attend to that.
UNCLE: One thing more, Martin. You wife is a beautiful but high-living, extravagant woman. To her I am leaving $25,000 providing she settles down and one year from today becomes the mother of a child.
SECRETARY: [*Rising*] I—
NEPHEW: [*Rising and shoving* SECRETARY *back into his chair*] *I'll* attend to that!

BLACKOUT

[VITAL NOTE: *It is important that the entire play should be acted calmly and politely, in the manner of an English drawing-room comedy. No actor ever raises his voice; every line must be read as though it were an invitation to a cup of tea. If this direction is disregarded, the play has no point at all.*]

SCENE: *A hotel bedroom. Two windows rear; door to the hall at the right, chair right center. Bed between windows. Phone stand right, downstage end of bed. Dresser upper left corner. Another door at left. Small table and chairs downstage left center.*
ED *and* BOB *are on the stage.* ED *is getting into his overcoat as the curtain rises. Both are at right door.*

ED: Well, Bob, it's certainly been nice to see you again.
BOB: It was nice to see *you*.
ED: You come to town so seldom, I hardly ever get the chance to—
BOB: Well, you know how it is. A business trip is always more or less of a bore.
ED: Next time you've got to come out to the house.
BOB: I want to come out. I just had to stick around the hotel this trip.
ED: Oh, I understand. Well, give my best to Edith.
BOB: [*Remembering something*] Oh, I say, Ed. Wait a minute.
ED: What's the matter?
BOB: I knew I wanted to show you something.
[*Crosses to table. Gets roll of blueprints from drawer*] Did you know I'm going to build?

ED: [*Follows*] A house?

BOB: You bet it's a house! [*Knock on door*] Come in! [*Spreads plans*] I just got these yesterday.

ED: [*Sits*] Well, that's fine!

[*The knock is repeated—louder. Both men now give full attention to the door.*]

BOB: Come! Come in!

BELLBOY: [*Enters*] Mr. Barclay?

BOB: Well?

BELLBOY: I've a message from the clerk, sir. For Mr. Barclay personally.

BOB: [*Crosses to boy*] I'm Mr. Barclay. What is the message?

BELLBOY: The hotel is on fire, sir.

BOB: What's that?

BELLBOY: The hotel is on fire.

ED: This hotel?

BELLBOY: Yes, sir.

BOB: Well—is it bad?

BELLBOY: It looks pretty bad, sir.

ED: You mean it's going to burn down?

BELLBOY: We think so—yes, sir.

BOB: [*A low whistle of surprise*] Well! We'd better leave.

BELLBOY: Yes, sir.

BOB: Going to burn down, huh?

BELLBOY: Yes, sir. If you'll step to the window you'll see. [BOB *goes to window.*]

BOB: Yes, that is pretty bad. H'm. [*To* ED] I say, you really ought to see this—

ED: [*Crosses up to window—peering out*] It's reached the floor right underneath.

BELLBOY: Yes, sir. The lower part of the hotel is about gone, sir.

BOB: [*Still looking out—looks up*] Still all right up above, though. [*Turns to boy*] Have they notified the Fire Department?

BELLBOY: I wouldn't know, sir. I'm only the bellboy.

BOB: Well, that's the thing to do, obviously—[*Nods head to each one as if the previous line was a bright idea*] notify the Fire Department. Just call them up, give them the name of the hotel—

ED: Wait a minute. I can do better than that for you. [*To*

the boy] Ring through to the Chief, and tell him that Ed Jamison told you to telephone him. [*To* BOB] We went to school together, you know.

BOB: That's fine. [*To the boy*] Now, get that right. Tell the Chief that Mr. Jamison said to ring him.

ED: *Ed* Jamison.

BOB: Yes, *Ed* Jamison.

BELLBOY: Yes, sir.

[*Turns to go*]

BOB: Oh! Boy! [*Pulls out handful of change; picks out a coin*] Here you are.

BELLBOY: Thank you, sir.

[*Exit* BELLBOY. ED *sits, lights cigarette and throws match downstage, then steps on it. There is a moment's pause.*]

BOB: Well! [*Crosses and looks out window*] Say, we'll have to get out of here pretty soon.

ED: [*Going to window*] How is it—no better?

BOB: Worse, if anything. It'll be up here in a few moments.

ED: What floor *is* this?

BOB: Eleventh.

ED: Eleven. We couldn't jump, then.

BOB: Oh, no. You never could jump. [*Comes away from window to dresser*] Well, I've got to get my things together.

[*Pulls out suitcase*]

ED: [*Smoothing out the plans*] Who made these for you?

BOB: A fellow here—Rawlins. [*Turns a shirt in his hand*] I ought to call one of the other hotels for a room.

ED: Oh, you can get in.

BOB: They're pretty crowded. [*Feels something on the sole of his foot; inspects it*] Say, the floor's getting hot.

ED: I know it. It's getting stuffy in the room, too. Phew! [*He looks around, then goes to the phone.*] Hello—ice water in eleven-eighteen.

[*Crosses to table*]

BOB: [*At bed*] That's the stuff. [*Packs*] You know, if I move to another hotel I'll never get my mail. Everybody thinks I'm stopping here.

ED: [*Studying the plans*] Say, this isn't bad.

BOB: [*Eagerly*] Do you like it? [*Remembers his plight*]

Suppose I go to another hotel and there's a fire there, too!

ED: You've got to take *some* chance.

BOB: I know, but here I'm sure. [*Phone rings.*] Oh, answer that, will you, Ed?
[*To dresser and back*]

ED: [*Crosses to phone*] Sure. [*At phone*] Hello—oh, that's good. Fine. What?—Oh! Well, wait a minute. [*To* BOB] The firemen are downstairs and some of them want to come up to this room.

BOB: Tell them, of course.

ED: [*At phone*] All right. Come right up. [*Hangs up, crosses and sits at table*] Now we'll get some action.

BOB: [*Looks out of window*] Say, there's an awful crowd of people on the street.

ED: [*Absently, as he pores over the plans*] Maybe there's been some kind of accident.

BOB: [*Peering out, suitcase in hand*] No. More likely they heard about the fire. [*A knock at the door*] Come in.

BELLBOY: [*Enters*] I beg pardon, Mr. Barclay, the firemen have arrived.

BOB: Show them in.
[*The door opens. In the doorway appear two* FIREMEN *in full regalia. The* FIRST FIREMAN *carries a hose and rubber coat; the* SECOND *has a violin case.*]

FIRST FIREMAN: [*Enters. Very apologetically*] Mr. Barclay.

BOB: I'm Mr. Barclay.

FIRST FIREMAN: We're the firemen, Mr. Barclay.
[*They remove their hats.*]

BOB: How de do?

ED: How de do?

BOB: A great pleasure, I assure you. Really must apologize for the condition of this room, but—

FIRST FIREMAN: Oh, that's all right. I know how it is at home.

BOB: May I present a friend of mine, Mr. Ed Jamison—

FIRST FIREMAN: How are you?

ED: How are you, boys? [SECOND FIREMAN *nods.*] I know your Chief.

FIRST FIREMAN: Oh, is that so? He knows the Chief—dear old Chiefie.

[SECOND FIREMAN *giggles.*]

BOB: [*Embarrassed*] Well, I guess you boys want to get to work, don't you?

FIRST FIREMAN: Well, if you don't mind. We would like to spray around a little bit.

BOB: May I help you?

FIRST FIREMAN: Yes, if you please.

[BOB *helps him into his rubber coat. At the same time the* SECOND FIREMAN, *without a word, lays the violin case on the bed, opens it, takes out the violin, and begins tuning it.*]

BOB: [*Watching him*] I don't think I understand.

FIRST FIREMAN: Well, you see, Sid doesn't get much chance to practice at home. Sometimes, at a fire, while we're waiting for a wall to fall or something, why, a fireman doesn't really have anything to do, and personally I like to see him improve himself symphonically. I hope you don't resent it. You're not anti-symphonic?

BOB: Of course not—

[BOB *and* ED *nod understandingly; the* SECOND FIREMAN *is now waxing the bow.*]

FIRST FIREMAN: Well, if you'll excuse me—

[*Turns with decision toward the window. You feel that he is about to get down to business.*]

BOB: [*Crosses*] Charming personalities.

ED: [*Follows over to the window*] How *is* the fire?

FIRST FIREMAN: [*Feels the wall*] It's pretty bad right now. This wall will go pretty soon now, but it'll fall out that way, so it's all right. [*Peers out*] That next room is the place to fight it from.

[*Crosses to door.* BOB *shows ties as* ED *crosses.*]

ED: [*Sees ties*] Oh! Aren't those gorgeous!

FIRST FIREMAN: [*To* BOB] Have you the key for this room?

BOB: Why, no. I've nothing to do with that room. I've just got this one.

[*Folding a shirt as he talks*]

ED: Oh, it's very comfortable.

FIRST FIREMAN: That's too bad. I had something up my sleeve. If I could have gotten in there. Oh, well, may I use your phone?

BOB: Please do. [*To* ED] Do you think you might hold this?

[*Indicates the hose*]

ED: How?

FIRST FIREMAN: Just crawl under it. [*As he does that*] Thanks. [*At phone*] Hello. Let me have the clerk, please. [*To* SECOND FIREMAN] Give us that little thing you played the night the Equitable Building burned down. [*Back to phone*] Are you there? This is one of the firemen. Oh, *you* know. I'm in room—ah—

[*Looks at* BOB]

BOB: Eleven-eighteen.

FIRST FIREMAN: Eleven-eighteen, and I want to get into the next room—Oh, goody. Will you send someone up with the key? There's no one in there? Oh, super-goody! Right away.

[*Hangs up*]

BOB: That's fine. [*To* FIREMEN] Won't you sit down?

FIRST FIREMAN: Thanks.

ED: Have a cigar?

FIRST FIREMAN: [*Takes it*] Much obliged.

BOB: A light?

FIRST FIREMAN: If you please.

ED: [*Failing to find a match*] Bob, have you a match?

BOB: [*Crosses*] I thought there were some here.

[*Hands in pockets.*]

FIRST FIREMAN: Oh, never mind.

[*He goes to window, leans out, and emerges with cigar lighted.* BOB *crosses to dresser; slams drawer. The* SECOND FIREMAN *taps violin with bow.*]

FIRST FIREMAN: Mr. Barclay, I think he's ready now.

BOB: [*Takes chair from table and sits*] Pardon me.

[*Lights dim to red on closing eight bars.*

[*They all sit. The* SECOND FIREMAN *takes Center of stage, with all the manner of a concert violinist. He goes into* "Keep the Home Fires Burning." BOB, ED *and* FIRST FIREMAN *wipe brow as curtain falls slowly.*]

THE AGE IN WHICH WE LIVE!

by Jack McGowan

First produced in *Murray Anderson's Almanac,* at the Erlanger Theater, on August 14, 1929, with the following cast:

HE Roy Atwell
SHE Eleanor Terry
HIM George Christie

SCENE: *A bedroom. It is rather late. Of course—being a bedroom, there must be a bed in it and as most of the action takes place there—nothing else matters. The room is in darkness and for a second or so there is extreme silence.*

SHE: [*Cooing*] It seems—it seems, I have known you— ALWAYS.

HE: Does it?

SHE: Yes. [*A pause*] Don't you feel that?

HE: [*Sparring for words*] Well—yes, we *have* gotten on.

SHE: It's the age in which we live.

HE: No doubt.

[*A sound as if* HE *were getting out of bed*]

SHE: Where are you going?

HE: Well, really—I must get dressed—

SHE: Another kiss?

HE: [*Hesitatingly*] Well—

SHE: Please.

[*There is the sound of a kiss.* HE *starts to dress.*]

SHE: Shall I turn on the lights?

HE: [*As he continues*] I'm sure it won't be necessary.

SHE: [*After a pause*] An hour ago we were strangers—

HE: [*Surprised*] An HOUR ago?

SHE: An HOUR ago.

HE: How time flies!

SHE: [*Thoughtfully*] Yes—it's the age in which we live.

HE: Hmmm.

SHE: The world is progressing. The element of time is no longer a factor. Fifty years ago a thing like this was unheard of—an impossible happening.

85

HE: Hmmm.

SHE: [*Purring*] It's the age—the age in which we live. [*Her tone is seductive—stretches lazily.*] Hmmmm.

HE: You may turn the light on now.

[SHE *switches on light and is discovered sitting up in bed.* HE *is fully dressed standing upstage of bed looking at her. The bed is at right—with the head of the bed against right wall.*]

SHE: [*Smiling guiltily*] Do you think I'm awful?

HE: Of course not.

SHE: Under the circumstances—I—er—I—hate questions.

HE: So do I.

SHE: But—I would like to know your name.

HE: I was wondering if you were going to ask.

SHE: Wouldn't you like to know mine?

HE: I don't know. [HE *gazes at her.*] My curiosity has been satisfied.

SHE: I wasn't going to ask you your name.

HE: I'm sorry you did. I had no intention of asking you either. You see—the extraordinary way that we met— the instant understanding and the very noticeable lack of the usual conversation which leads to such—such— er—er—

SHE: [*Softly*] I know—

HE: Well—I—had intended to let this be different. Familiarity very often results disastrously. If I could—I wanted to keep out anything common. Also—the idea of never knowing each other's name seems to me to be more or less a protection.

SHE: Protection?

HE: Yes. You don't know who I am. I don't know you—I won't try to find out. What we've been to each other— after I leave—will be a sort of dream. Either—good— or otherwise. Personally—it will be good.

SHE: I agree with you, but, really, I feel that you are much too nice to say good-bye to without knowing your name—at least. We need never meet again. I'm certain we couldn't. [HE *looks doubtfully at her.*] Oh, no, we couldn't.

HE: You're married.

SHE: Yes.

HE: I thought as much.

SHE: And you?

HE: No.

SHE: I thought as much.

HE: Why?

SHE: Your utter lack of eagerness with me. [*Pause*] My name is Thomas. Helen Thomas.

HE: [*Bows gallantly*] How do you do, Mrs. Thomas.

SHE: And how have I the pleasure of meeting?

HE: [*Correcting her*] Had the pleasure.

SHE: Pardon me.

HE: I'm Doctor Conrad.

SHE: Doctor? Doctor?

HE: Yes.

SHE: I told you the truth.

HE: [*Produces card which HE keeps in his hand*] So did I.

SHE: [*Looks at card*] I apologize.

HE: [*Offers his hand—SHE takes it.*] After all—what's in a name?

SHE: I know no more now—than I did.

[*They continue to hold hands.*]

HE: Nor I. Nor shall I try to know more.

[*Their hands tighten in understanding.*]

SHE: It's been a pleasure.

HE: [*Completely satisfied*] Hasn't it?!

SHE: A strange beginning—a stranger ending.

[*The slamming of a door in the outer room—a startled look from her—an alert expression from him*]

HE: [*Thoughtfully*] I wonder.

SHE: [*Frantically*] HIM! Oh, Doctor!

[*SHE starts to get out of bed.*]

HE: [*Quietly and authoritatively*] Stay where you are! Do as I say! [*Takes towel from chair*] Answer him. Weakly—you're ill!

HIM: [*Offstage*] Helen! Helen! Where are you, dear?

SHE: [*Weakly, as HE puts towel around her head*] Yes, dear!

HE: [*Taking thermometer from pocket*] Louder.

SHE: [*Much louder*] In here, dear!

HE: [*Puts thermometer in her mouth while it is open. Takes out watch and times her pulse—sits at bed side.*

With a professional air] I hardly think there's much to worry about.

[*Enter* HIM, *and is taken aback at the picture of physician at her bedside*]

You say you have severe pains in your back?

[*With the thermometer in her mouth* SHE *nods yes.*]

Perfectly natural—perfectly natural!

HIM: Helen, my dear, what has happened?

HE: [*Rising to* HIM] You are Mr. Thomas?

HIM: Yes.

HE: I am Dr. Conrad.

HIM: [*Nervously*] Is there—has there—

HE: Everything is all right. Your wife needed a little attention and called me in.

HIM: [*Goes to her*] Nothing serious, I hope. [*To her*] Tell me. How do you feel?

SHE: Better now.

HIM: [*To the Doctor*] What does it look like?

HE: It wouldn't surprise me if you became a father.

HIM: [*Reverently*] After all these years.

HE: Of course I may be wrong.

HIM: [*Kneeling to her*] Then we could take a place in the country. We'd have to! [*Rises*] For the child's sake. No child of mine will ever be raised in the city.

HE: [*Takes prescription pad from pocket*] That's the way I'd feel about any child of mine.

[HE *writes out a prescription.*]

HIM: [*To her*] And to think I never knew. That I never realized.

HE: [*Hands prescription to* HIM] Get that filled. I've written the directions. Follow them closely and I'm sure Mrs. Thomas will be herself again. [*Takes his hat—to her*] Good-bye, Mrs. Thomas. I doubt if you'll need me again.

SHE: Good-bye, Doctor, and thank you ever so much.

HE: Don't mention it. [*To* HIM] Good-bye, sir. [*Extends hand*]

HIM: Good night, Doc. But wait—haven't you forgotten something?

HE: [*Puzzled*] Why, nooo—I—

HIM: Your fee?

HE: [*Professionally*] Oh, dear me—so I have.

HIM: [*Takes bills out*] What is it?
HE: Ten dollars, please.
HIM: [*Gives bill*] Well, that's—
SHE: Very reasonable.
HE: It's the age—the age in which we live!
  [HE *starts for exit.*]

BLACKOUT

STOCKS

by Billy K. Wells

First produced in the tenth edition of *George White's Scandals*, at the Apollo Theatre, on September 23, 1929, with the following cast:

ANNOUNCERS Scott Sisters
THE BROKER Jack White
THE BUTLER Harry Morrissey
THE GIRL Frances Williams
FIRST DETECTIVE Willie Howard
SECOND DETECTIVE Eugene Howard
MESSENGER BOY Frank Mitchell

ANNOUNCER: For the benefit of those who play the stock market, we will now give you today's closing prices without interrupting the show.

SCENE: *A living room—table and chair right. On the table is a tobacco jar, pipe, decanter and glasses. At the left is a settee and a radio. At rise,* BROKER *is discovered sitting at the table reading the* Financial News.

BROKER: Kresge 37¼!
  [BUTLER *enters.*]
BUTLER: Yes, Mr. Kennecott 58⅜!
BROKER: Turn off that Columbia Graphophone 64⅞ and bring me a bottle of Canada Dry 108½.
BUTLER: Sorry, sir, all that Reeves Brothers 14¾ delivered was Coca Cola 168⅛.
BROKER: Then American Telephone 155⅜ to Park and Tilford 45½ for some at once.
BUTLER: Yes, sir.
BROKER: What have you to drink?
BUTLER: In the Kelvinator 13⅛ I have some American Ice 3¾, National Tea 107⅛—
BROKER: No!
BUTLER: How about a cup of Postum 74⅜?
BROKER: Don't bother. [*Picks up pipe; looks at empty tobacco jar*] Bring me some American Tobacco 179⅞!
BUTLER: Yes, sir.
  [*He starts to exit.*]
BROKER: Just a moment. Turn on the Radio 77¼!
BUTLER: Sorry, sir, but the Electric Storage Battery 87½ of the Zenith 44⅝ has run down.

93

BROKER: Then take the Nash 86⅜ and go over to the General Electric 349¼ and get a new one.

BUTLER: Yes, sir!

[*He starts to exit. Bell rings. He admits* MESSENGER BOY, *takes and signs for telegrams, crosses and hands them to* BROKER.]

Western Union 226¾!

BROKER: [*Takes telegrams*] Give the boy a tip!

BUTLER: [*Crosses to* MESSENGER BOY] Buy Sinclair Oil 36⅛!

MESSENGER BOY: Thank you! [*Exits*]

[BUTLER *exits.*]

BROKER: [*Reads telegram; picks up phone*] Pennsylvania 97⅜—Hello! Hello! Give me Phillip Morris 14⅛—Not in? When he returns, please tell him to call up Wabash 73½!

[*Hangs up receiver*]

BUTLER: [*Entering*] Miss Conda, sir!

BROKER: Anaconda 110¾?

BUTLER: Yes, sir, she arrived in a Checker Cab 71⅜!

BROKER: Great Northern 120⅜! She shouldn't be seen here!

BUTLER: I tried to Warner 61¼, but she insisted!

[GIRL *enters and brushes past* BUTLER.]

GIRL: Earl!

BROKER: Ana! I told you to stay in Richfield 41⅞!

GIRL: I couldn't Standard Oil 38⅝. I had to come. Montgomery Ward 129¾ found the American Bank Note 148⅝ we forged in his National Cash Register 126½!

BROKER: Great Atlantic & Pacific 395⅛! Who put 'em wise?

GIRL: Arnold Constable 19⅞!

BROKER: The Fox 91½! We must make a getaway before every bank of the United States 206½ gets after us! Take the Studebaker 75⅞ to the B. & O. 133¼, buy a ticket for Texas Gulf 73½ by way of Southern Pacific 146¾! If you are followed, go to the Paramount 68⅛ and watch the Motion Pictures 55¾ until the coast is clear!

GIRL: And *you?*

BROKER: I'll drive the Packard Motor 131⅛ to Erie 81¾,

cross and catch a Canadian Pacific 246½ for Minneapolis & St. Louis 2⅝!

GIRL: I hate to leave you!

BROKER: You must, Sugar 83½! Swift 128⅞! Go!

[*As* BROKER *leads* GIRL *to door,* FIRST *and* SECOND DETECTIVES *enter.*]

FIRST DETECTIVE: Stop!

SECOND DETECTIVE: Orders!

BROKER: Who are you?

FIRST *and* SECOND DETECTIVES: Abraham and Strauss 129⅞! Detectives for the Irving Trust 76¼, Chase National 208½ and Chelsea 99¾!

FIRST DETECTIVE: When people in the United States Steel 202⅜, we always get 'em!

SECOND DETECTIVE: Come! This means twenty years for you in the American Can 164⅞!

BROKER: [*Crossing to table and pouring drinks*] Let's talk this over!

FIRST DETECTIVE: [*Rubbing his hands together*] Ah! American Beverage 14⅞!

[*The* DETECTIVES *drink.*]

FIRST DETECTIVE: [*Sputters*] CHR—RYS—LER! 76⅛!

BLACKOUT

IN MARBLED HALLS

by William Miles and Donald Blackwell

First produced in *Three's a Crowd*, at the Selwyn Theatre, on October 15, 1930, with the following cast:

HE, a fairly decent young man   Clifton Webb
SHE, a nice enough young woman   Tamara Geva

SCENE: *The action of this piece takes place, we regret to say, in a bathroom of a New York hotel. The bathroom contains a tub to the right of a door in the center of the back wall. On the left is a window and downstage from the window is a wash-basin. That is all. The time is the present. As the curtain rises* HE *is discovered in the tub washing himself and singing in the confident way people do in the tub.*

HE: I'm singin' in the bathtub,
　　Happy once again,
　　Watchin' all my troubles
　　Go swingin' down the drain.
　　[*The soap slips from his hand.*]
　　Oh, damn!
　　[*As* HE *leans out to get the soap, the door opens and* SHE *enters.* SHE *closes the door after her.* HE *looks up just as* SHE *discovers the bathroom to be occupied.*]

SHE: Ohhh!

HE: Pardon me for not rising, Madame.

SHE: How dare you?
　　[SHE *fiddles with the door knob—the knob falls off.*]

HE: Now you've done it.

SHE: [*At door*] It won't open.

HE: Perhaps you're waiting for me to open the door for you?
　　[*Starts to get out of the tub*]

SHE: No! Stay where you are! [SHE *tries to open the door.*]
　　Ohhhhhhhhhh!

HE: Cheer up, cheer up. Don't let a little thing like that upset you.

SHE: [*Pacing*] What's going to happen? If anyone finds me here I shall be compromised.

HE: How about me? I'm just as much here as you are. I didn't ask you to come in.

SHE: You *left* the *door* unlocked.

HE: I was singing, wasn't I?

SHE: I *shouldn't* say so.

HE: I'll bet you wanted to come in here.

SHE: Of course I did—oh, dear!
[*Starts to cry*]

HE: There, there! Don't cry! I know just how you must feel.

SHE: [*More pacing*] Oh, what's to become of me. I mean how am I to get out? Where does that window lead to?

HE: Lexington Avenue. But look out for the first step. We're on the eighth floor.

SHE: What are we going to do?

HE: If you don't mind, I think I'll finish my bath. Will you please hand me the soap?

SHE: How dare you?

HE: Oh, all right, I'll get it myself.
[HE *starts to get out of the tub.*]

SHE: No, no! Stop! I'll get it.
[SHE *covers her eyes as she goes to pick up the soap.*] Where is it?

HE: A little to the right—now a little to the left—now a little behind. Yes, a little behind. [SHE *hands him the soap.*] Thanks! You're awfully good to me!

SHE: I suppose you say that to *every girl* that comes in here.

HE: Do you think I make a habit of this sort of thing?

SHE: You're unbearable!

HE: Won't you sit down?

SHE: Uh.

HE: You might as well sit down. It's going to be a long wait.
[SHE *sits on the wash-basin with her legs crossed in such a way that a great expanse of silk stocking is visible.*]
Pardon me, I hate to seem critical, but you're showing things.

SHE: *You* should talk! If you were a gentleman, you'd make a lot of lather.

HE: Lather! No one will ever say that I'm not a gentleman. [*Starts to make lather industriously. Suddenly*] My God!

SHE: Now what?

HE: Oh, my God!

SHE: What's the matter?

HE: It's terrible!

SHE: What's happened?

HE: Do something! Do something!

SHE: What is it?

HE: The plug!

SHE: The plug?

HE: I've lost it!

SHE: [*Gets off wash-basin*] Oh, my God!

HE: Get me something! All the water's running out of the tub! And all the lather is going down too!

SHE: Here! Use this!

[SHE *comes toward the tub with the doorknob retrieved from the floor.*]

HE: Too late! Too late! Don't look!

[SHE *has involuntarily looked over the edge of the tub.*]

SHE: Well, if it isn't Harry Smith! Fancy meeting you here!

BLACKOUT

FOR GOOD OLD NECTAR

by George S. Kaufman and Howard Dietz

First produced in *The Band Wagon*, at the New Amsterdam Theatre, on June 3, 1931. The playbills for the show do not list "who played what" in this sketch, but rather, simply listed the players, and they were:

Adele Astaire, Roberta Robinson, Frank Morgan, Jay Wilson, Philip Loeb, Francis Pierlot, Fred Astaire, and John Barker.

Characters

CHEERLEADER	BILL
USHER	MIKE
1ST SPECTATOR	PROFESSOR
2ND SPECTATOR	PARKINSON
BOY	FETCHBOTTOM
MAN IN THE STANDS	WIMPFHEIMER
JERRY	QUINCHLEY
HAZEL	TROWBRIDGE
VENDOR	3RD SPECTATOR
FLO	

ANNOUNCER: It's our idea, of course, to take up practically everything in this show, before the evening is over. It may take a while, but we figure that your time isn't important, or you wouldn't be here. So the next sketch is about college life. It's called "For Good Old Nectar." As you know, there has been quite a hue lately about college athletics. In the old days there would have been a hue and cry, but they had to take a cut. Anyhow, it's claimed that too much attention is being paid to football in the colleges and that more stress should be put on the scholastic end. So this shows what will happen when the emphasis is put on studying, instead of football.

SCENE: *A combination of classroom and stadium. There is the Professor's rostrum at right, with five students' desks facing it, but at the rear is a grandstand. This has an opening right and left, through which come the spectators.* PROFESSOR *and* STUDENTS *enter right and left, respectively. "Nectar" pennants are on the walls. At rise, the stands are nearly full. There is band music offstage and the crowd on the stands is just finishing a song.*

CROWD: So we sit all night
　　And we burn electric light
　　Till the hens and roosters crow.
　　Oh, it's cram, cram, cram
　　Till you pass that old exam,
　　For Good Old Nectar's sake.
CHEERLEADER: [*To* CROWD] Now then—
ALL: Nectar! Nectar! Nectar! N—E—C—T—A—R. Nectar!

[ALL *cheer.*]

CHEERLEADER: That's the stuff!

USHER: Get your programs. You can't tell students without a program!

1ST SPECTATOR: How're you bettin', Woods?

2ND SPECTATOR: Say, it's a cinch!

[*There are scraps of conversation among the spectators. A* BOY *passes through the students.*]

BOY: [*Calls*] Programs! You can't tell the students without a program! Programs!

MAN IN THE STANDS: Here you are, boy!

[*He makes a purchase. Two Old Grads, each accompanied by a girl, loom up in the entrance. The girls are decked out in fur coats and orchids, and carry pennants and balloons. The men are named* BILL *and* JERRY, *the girls are* FLO *and* HAZEL.]

JERRY: [*In a voice that booms through the general noise*] Here we are, in plenty of time! Where are these seats, boy?

USHER: [*Taking coupons*] Right this way, sir.

BILL: [*Proffering coupons*] Where are my seats, boy?

USHER: Right next to those.

[*He shows one couple to two seats right of the entrance, front row, and the other to the corresponding seats at left.*]

HAZEL: How soon do they start?

[*A* VENDOR *comes through the stands.*]

VENDOR: Popcorn and crackerjack! Get your popcorn here!

FLO: Oh, I want some!

BILL: Here, boy! [*Buys some; turns to* JERRY] Well, this is fine—close enough to talk, anyway. [*Recognizing friend in rear seat*] Hi, Mike!

MIKE: Hi, Bill!

JERRY: I thought maybe I'd run into you, Bill.

BILL: Say, I haven't missed a history examination since I left college. It's a great sight!

[FLO *twirls one of those little wooden clickers.*]

JERRY: I've been to all except one or two. I was sorry I missed last year.

BILL: Say! Greatest examination you ever saw! Carpenter,

you remember him, told the whole history of Ireland in five minutes.

JERRY: I'll bet the crowd went crazy.

VENDOR: Hot roasted peanuts, sandwiches!

FLO: Oh, I want some!

BILL: Here y'are, boy!

JERRY: [*To* BOY *in rear*] Hello, Jim!

BOY [JIM]: Hello, you big bum!

JERRY: [*To* BILL] They say this boy we're going to see today is awful good. Trowbridge!

BILL: Yeah, they say he's great. We got him from Colgate, didn't we?

JERRY: Yeah . . . Hazel here's never been to an examination before.

BILL: Neither has Flo. [FLO *stands up, and makes noise with ratchet.*] Did you see her show? The *Vanities?*

JERRY: Oh, yes.

FLO: Did you notice me in that dance with the two fans?

BILL: Yeah, who were they?

JERRY: Yeah! They were great.

VENDOR: Get your programs! You can't tell the students without a program!

BILL: Here y'are, boy!

VENDOR: Get your line-up for today's examinations!

JERRY: How'd you come up, Bill? Motor?

BILL: Yeah. Never saw the roads so crowded. They say there's eighty thousand people up here for today's examinations. I tried to get tickets for the law exams, but there wasn't a thing. By the way, you know what I heard? They say Trowbridge may not be allowed to take the examination.

JERRY: You don't say? What's the trouble?

BILL: Behind in his football.

[*There is a cheer offstage—cries of "Here they come!" "Here come the students!"* FOUR BOYS *enter—they are numbered on their backs. They are greeted with a cheer from the stands.*]

CHEERLEADER: Come on now, everybody—Nectar! Nectar! Nectar! N—E—C—T—A—R! Team! Team! Team! [*The students take their places.*]

BILL: They're lighter than last year's team.

FLO: [*Standing*] Oh, I want them!

MIKE: Sit down!

SPECTATOR: Down in front!

MIKE: Your old man wasn't a glazier!

[*Another cheer offstage. Cries of "Here comes Trow-bridge!" "Trowbridge!"*]

CHEERLEADER: Three cheers for Trowbridge!

ALL: Trowbridge! Trowbridge! Trowbridge! Hooray!

[TROWBRIDGE *enters to a great applause and cheers. He is followed by a trainer. Cries of "How's the boy?" "Hello, Trowby!"* TROWBRIDGE *goes over to the stands and greets several friends; he then takes his place at his desk.*]

BILL: Look at that forehead!

FLO: Oh, I like him! He's handsome!

[*The sound of a gong offstage indicates the* PROFESSOR's *entrance.*]

HAZEL: Are they going to start now?

JERRY: Sssh!

[*The crowd grows quiet and expectant. The* PROFESSOR *enters at right. The students rise and stand quietly as the* PROFESSOR *goes to his desk.*]

FLO: Oh boy, oh boy, oh boy!

[*The* PROFESSOR *blows a whistle and the students take their seats.*]

PROFESSOR: Let us start the examination!

[*The students rush into a momentary huddle. They come out of it and the* PROFESSOR *gives one long toot on his whistle.*]

BILL: [*In a whisper to* FLO] Here they go!

PROFESSOR: You will answer these questions in succession. [*There is a buzz of talk from the crowd.*] Who introduced tobacco into England?

PARKINSON: Sir Walter Raleigh.

PROFESSOR: When was the Battle of Hastings?

FETCHBOTTOM: Ten sixty-six.

[*One photographer dashes out and takes a picture.*]

PROFESSOR: Treaty of Verdun?

WIMPFHEIMER: Eight hundred.

PROFESSOR: What English poet wrote most of his work while blind?

QUINCHLEY: John Milton.

PROFESSOR: Mr. Trowbridge . . .

[*There is a buzz of excitement as* TROWBRIDGE *answers.*]

TROWBRIDGE: Yes, sir?

PROFESSOR: Mr. Trowbridge, what is the capital of North Dakota?

TROWBRIDGE: The capital of North Dakota: Bismarck. Population, 1930: 9,876. Principal exports: grains and furs.

[*Applause and cheers from the stands*]

CHEERLEADER: Three cheers for Trowbridge!

[*Another* SPECTATOR *enters.*]

3RD SPECTATOR: How do things stand? Am I late?

[*Takes his seat*]

MIKE: Where the hell have you been?

3RD SPECTATOR: I couldn't help it. I got tied up.

MIKE: Who was she?

BILL: Come on now, everybody stretch.

[ALL *rise.*]

MIKE: Come on now, show us something!

[PROFESSOR *toots his whistle.* ALL *become quiet.*]

PROFESSOR: Mr. Parkinson.

PARKINSON: [*Rises*] Yes, sir?

PROFESSOR: Mr. Parkinson, in every military conflict there have been certain battles which, while not always of a pivotal nature at the time, take on, in the estimate of history, the element of decisiveness.

VENDOR: White-Rock and Ginger-Ale. Get your cold drinks here.

PROFESSOR: There were, for example, ten outstanding battles during the World War.

FLO: [*To* BILL] What war?

BILL: Oh, for . . .

PROFESSOR: Will you kindly name them?

MIKE: Come on, Parky!

PARKINSON: There was the Battle of Marne . . . First Battle of Ypres . . . Second Battle of Ypres . . . Third Battle of Ypres . . . Battle of the Somme . . .

FLO: [*Inquiringly, to* BILL] Second Battle of the Somme?

PARKINSON: Battle of Cambrai . . .

BILL: He's groggy.

PARKINSON: [*Has been growing weak. He hesitates;*

slowly sinks into his chair.] I'm afraid I don't know any more.

[*Sympathetic sounds from the stand.* PROFESSOR *toots whistle.*]

PROFESSOR: Mr. Fetchbottom.

[FETCHBOTTOM *rises.*]

BILL: [*Turning program, speaks to* FLO] Number 7. Lawrence Fetchbottom. Head size 7¾.

FLO: I like him.

PROFESSOR: Will you answer the question, please?

MIKE: Tell it to him, Mr. Fetchbottom!

FETCHBOTTOM: Why, the First Battle of Ypres . . . Second Battle of Ypres . . . Third Battle of Ypres . . .

FLO: Fourth Battle of Ypres.

FETCHBOTTOM: Battle of the Somme . . . [*Gives up*] . . . no, sir.

BILL: Take him out!

[FETCHBOTTOM *sits, to the accompaniment of strained silence in the stands.*]

PROFESSOR: Mr. Wimpfheimer.

WIMPFHEIMER: Sir?

PROFESSOR: Will you answer the question, please?

WIMPFHEIMER: [*Stalling*] What was the question, sir?

BILL: He's gone.

MIKE: Good-bye, Wimpfy!

[PROFESSOR *toots whistle.*]

BILL: His father was wonderful! Old man Wimpfheimer. Remember?

PROFESSOR: Mr. Quinchley, can you answer the question?

QUINCHLEY: I don't . . . think so, sir.

MIKE: To the Clubhouse!

[*A murmur runs around the stands. "It goes to Trowbridge!" "Here's Trowbridge!"*]

PROFESSOR: Mr. Trowbridge!

TROWBRIDGE: [*Rising*] Yes, sir?

BILL: Look at the way he stands.

PROFESSOR: Mr. Trowbridge, can you name the ten decisive battles of the World War?

BILL: Eight to five he makes it!

JERRY: I'll take that!

BILL: Come on, Trowby!

TROWBRIDGE: Battle of the Marne, First, Second and Third Battles of Ypres, Battle of the Somme... [*He is getting a little weak.*] ... Battle of Cambrai ...

[PROFESSOR *nods;* TROWBRIDGE *growing very weak*]

JERRY: He's slowing up.

TROWBRIDGE: ... Second Battle of the Somme ... Battle of the Aisne ...

MIKE: Attaboy, Trowby! Right in there with the old cerebellum!

TROWBRIDGE: [*Puffing hard*] Battle of St. Mihiel ...

PROFESSOR: One more, Trowbridge!

MIKE: Come on there!

[TROWBRIDGE *tries hard, but falls back in a faint.*]

BILL: [*Standing up*] He's down!

[*Cries from the stand: "Is he out?" "What did I tell you?" An* ATTENDANT *rushes out with sponge and lily cups. Cries of "Give him a chance!"* TROWBRIDGE *takes a drink; makes a supreme effort.*]

BILL: He's up!

TROWBRIDGE: Battle of the Argonne.

PROFESSOR: Correct, Mr. Trowbridge!

[*The stands go wild! Yelling the college yell, they all stream down into the classroom and gather up the hero. Putting him on their shoulders, they weave in and out among the desks, yelling and cheering.*]

BLACKOUT

THE GREAT WARBURTON MYSTERY

by George S. Kaufman and Howard Dietz

First produced in *The Band Wagon*, at the New Amsterdam Theatre, on June 3, 1931, with the following cast:

IVY MEREDITH Adele Astaire
INSPECTOR CARTWRIGHT Frank Morgan
MRS. BOULE Helen Carrington
MR. BOULE Ed Jerome
MISS HUTTON Roberta Robinson
MR. DODD Peter Chambers
MR. WALLACE John Barker
WALKER Philip Loeb
FIRST POLICEMAN Jay Wilson
SECOND POLICEMAN Leon Alton
THE MURDERED MAN Francis Pierlot

SCENE: *The library in the home of Hugh Warburton.* MR.
WARBURTON, *who has been killed before the curtain
rises, is found slumped in a chair. On the table beside
him is a wineglass, almost empty, together with the re-
volver with which he has obviously been shot. On the
other side of the table is another chair—an easy chair,
and so turned that it seems likely that the murderer had
been sitting in this chair just before, or perhaps when,
he fired the fatal shot. Several men and women, all in
evening clothes, stand around in various attitudes of
shock and discomfort. In the main they are clustered
together at the right side of the stage, as though they
had entered the room together and remained almost in
a frozen group. Standing near the group, but a bit apart
from them, is a butler, named* WALKER. *Also present are
two* POLICEMEN—*one of whom stands near the body of
the dead man and seems to be in general charge. The
other is on guard at the left door.*

MRS. BOULE: I tell you I can't stand it!
MISS HUTTON: And neither can I!
MR. BOULE: [*To the* POLICEMEN] Surely something can
   be done about this. My wife is very nervous. Can't the
   women go into the other room?
DODD: Yes!
FIRST POLICEMAN: Sorry, sir. No one is allowed to leave
   until the Inspector comes.
DODD: But when's he going to get here?
FIRST POLICEMAN: He'll be here any minute, sir.
WALLACE: Any minute . . .

MR. BOULE: It's an outrage!

MISS HUTTON: Good heavens.

IVY: [*Detaching herself from the group*] Well, while we're waiting, who wants to shoot a little crap?

MR. BOULE: Ivy!

IVY: Sorry.

[*The door bell rings.*]

MR. BOULE: Here he is!

DODD: At last!

MRS. BOULE: Do you think we can go home now?

MR. BOULE: The Inspector will tell us.

MISS HUTTON: The whole thing is an outrage!

SECOND POLICEMAN: Right in here, sir.

MR. BOULE: Here he is now!

WALLACE: This is our man.

MRS. BOULE: And about time.

[*Enter* INSPECTOR CARTWRIGHT. *A quick look around, his gaze lands on* WALKER, *who is standing just inside the door*]

CARTWRIGHT: Is this the dead man?

FIRST POLICEMAN: No, here, sir.

CARTWRIGHT: Oh. [*He crosses and examines body.*] When did this happen?

FIRST POLICEMAN: About eight o'clock, sir.

CARTWRIGHT: How long have you been here?

FIRST POLICEMAN: [*Looking at watch*] Twenty minutes, sir.

CARTWRIGHT: Nothing has been touched?

FIRST POLICEMAN: No, sir.

CARTWRIGHT: [*A brisk nod; another look around; faces the group*] Good evening. [*There is a scattered response.*] My name is Cartwright. Inspector, First District.

[*Responses from guests*]

IVY: [*Approaching brightly*] I'm Ivy Meredith. We've had a little trouble here—

CARTWRIGHT: [*Shutting her up*] Good evening.

IVY: [*Taken aback*] Oh, the hell with you.

CARTWRIGHT: Now then, tell me what happened.

MR. BOULE: We were sitting in the D.R.

MRS. BOULE: There's been a man murdered.

WALLACE: I don't know anything about it.

[*Several guests start to reply.*]

CARTWRIGHT: If you please—I would like to hear from the officer.

FIRST POLICEMAN: Well, sir, the late gentleman here was giving a dinner. The dining room is in there. And, after it was over, the men were sitting in there drinking. The women had gone upstairs.

IVY: If you please!

FIRST POLICEMAN: Mr. Warburton said he wanted to get something and came in here.

MR. BOULE: That's right.

FIRST POLICEMAN: He brought the wineglass with him.

CARTWRIGHT: I see.

FIRST POLICEMAN: A minute later there was a shot, and they found him here.

CARTWRIGHT: Who found him here?

FIRST POLICEMAN: All of them, sir.

MR. BOULE: All of us.

FIRST POLICEMAN: The men came in from the dining room, and the women came downstairs.

CARTWRIGHT: But one of them *might* have come down before that?

FIRST POLICEMAN: Yes, sir.

CARTWRIGHT: And gone up again?

FIRST POLICEMAN: Yes, sir.

CARTWRIGHT: Or one of the men might have left the dining room?

FIRST POLICEMAN: Yes, sir.

IVY: I wouldn't have a mind like that—

CARTWRIGHT: Whose gun is it?

FIRST POLICEMAN: His own, sir. It was on the wall.

CARTWRIGHT: His own, eh? So it might have been—anyone.

FIRST POLICEMAN: Yes, sir. Anyone.

IVY: Maybe we'd better send for the police.

[CARTWRIGHT *stands beside chair; reaches toward gun; pretends to point it at dead man's head. Tries same thing from other side*]

FIRST POLICEMAN: Sir?

CARTWRIGHT: It can't be done from either side of the

chair. The gun was fired from this angle.
[*He draws an imaginary line that cuts squarely across the chair.*]

FIRST POLICEMAN: That's right, sir.

CARTWRIGHT: He might have stood back of the chair. But he never would have put the gun over there, because he couldn't reach it.

WALLACE: That's what he couldn't.

DODD: No.

MR. BOULE: He's right.

FIRST POLICEMAN: Maybe he sat in the chair, sir.

CARTWRIGHT: Exactly.

MR. BOULE: That's it.

WALLACE: He sat in the chair.

DODD: That's what he did.

CARTWRIGHT: [*Tries it, but does not actually sit*] He sat in the chair. Perfect for the gun. [*Illustrating*] Perfect for the bullet hole.

IVY: Marvelous for the bullet hole.

CARTWRIGHT: [*Straights up; looks at chair*] He sat in the chair. [*The phrase runs through the crowd, in little hushed whispers.*] No one has left this house since the murder was committed?

FIRST POLICEMAN: No, sir.

CARTWRIGHT: You're positive?

FIRST POLICEMAN: Yes, sir.

CARTWRIGHT: [*A second's thought*] You can take the body out. Have this officer stand guard until further notice. [*The* POLICEMEN *pick it up; there are expressions of relief from several of the women.*] I shall ask the ladies to step to this side of the room. If any of you are faint, you may sit down. [IVY *moves to sit in the fatal chair.*] Not there, please. [*The* POLICEMEN, *having removed the body, return as soon as possible.*] Ladies and gentlemen, no one has left this house since the murder was committed. I regret very much to inform you that the guilty person is in this room.

MRS. BOULE: Good heavens!

MISS HUTTON: What?

MR. BOULE: Do you mean to insinuate—

CARTWRIGHT: Not at all, sir. I am simply announcing a fact. Someone in this room had a motive for killing

H. W. Perhaps a business quarrel. Possibly—who can tell—[*Turning to the women*] some woman he had wronged. [*All four women drop their bags.*] Ladies and gentlemen, there can be no guesswork in modern crime detection. It is a matter of cold science. The man or woman who killed Hugh Warburton sat in this chair. No two people in the world, upon sitting in a chair, leave exactly the same impression.

[IVY *looks at cushion.*]

DODD: What did he say?

WALLACE: What's he trying to get at?

MR. BOULE: Search me.

CARTWRIGHT: Ladies and gentlemen, the murderer of Hugh Warburton has left his calling card on that cushion, just as plainly as if he had written his name.

DODD: Oh, come now.

WALLACE: What?

MR. BOULE: Absurd!

CARTWRIGHT: On the contrary, a scientific fact. Find the person who fits that cushion, and you will have the murderer of Hugh Warburton.

MISS HUTTON: Good heavens!

MR. BOULE: I don't believe it!

DODD: What an idea!

WALLACE: It's not true!

CARTWRIGHT: But it is true! There are no two exactly alike in the world.

MR. BOULE: Now, really!

IVY: [*After a moment's pause*] I don't know—it's kind of a comfort.

MR. BOULE: What!

IVY: You wouldn't want to have one just like somebody else's.

CARTWRIGHT: And now with your kind permission, ladies and gentlemen, we will proceed with the examination.

IVY: You will do what?

CARTWRIGHT: I will ask you all to take your places in line, please. Officer!

FIRST POLICEMAN: All right—line up, please! Line right up!

MR. BOULE: This is an outrage!

IVY: It certainly is.

CARTWRIGHT: I regret very much that I must ask you to do this—

IVY: You don't regret it at all, you probably get a great kick out of it.

CARTWRIGHT: Are we ready?

DODD: Well, I suppose if we must we must.

[CARTWRIGHT *takes out a tape measure; unrolls it with a little zipping sound. He looks at the line, which is facing the audience. He measures the print in the chair, then looks up again. He considers—shall he ask the line to turn around or not? Finally decides to take a trip around the back; goes accompanied by the two* POLICEMEN. *He conducts his inspection; each person tries to act unconcerned as he or she is reached.*]

IVY: [*As* CARTWRIGHT *comes to her, she sings a bit of song to show her unconcern.*] Are you looking for something?

CARTWRIGHT: [*In a low voice, to a* POLICEMAN] Sixty-two.

IVY: You mean across?

CARTWRIGHT: Never mind, madam. [*Clears his throat; comes in front of the line again*] Ladies and gentlemen, there is only one which—interests me—[*To* IVY] I'm sorry to inform you, madam, that—it belongs to you.

IVY: Me?

CARTWRIGHT: That is right.

IVY: What do you want to do now—make a bust of it?

CARTWRIGHT: Officer, will you bring down that chair please.

IVY: You mean you're going to take an impression?

CARTWRIGHT: [*Bowing*] That's the size of it.

IVY: What's the size of it?

CARTWRIGHT: [*Moves to a spot beside the fatal chair*] Won't you—sit down? [*She hesitates.*] If the shoe does not fit—I beg your pardon—then I shall have to admit my mistake.

[*With great dignity* IVY *advances to the cushion. Somewhat timidly, she sits. Bounces immediately up again.* CARTWRIGHT *peers quickly; the others strain to see.*]

MR. BOULE: Well?

CARTWRIGHT: [*A tense moment*] No. [*A general sigh*] I

seem to have been wrong. There's nobody else in the house?

FIRST POLICEMAN: Only a cook, sir. The kitchen's in the cellar—she couldn't possibly get up.

CARTWRIGHT: [*A long sigh. Takes handkerchief in hand and picks up the gun. Shakes his head; puts it down. Takes up the wineglass; regards it*] You men who were in the dining room with him—do you remember if this glass was full when he left the room?

DODD: I think it was.

MR. BOULE: I'd just filled it.

CARTWRIGHT: It would have taken him at least a minute to drink it.

WALKER: Not quite that long, sir.

CARTWRIGHT: What?

WALKER: The glass doesn't hold very much, sir. It has a false bottom.

CARTWRIGHT: Ah! A false bottom.

WALKER: Yes, sir.

CARTWRIGHT: A false bottom. [*Something about the way that he says it makes* WALKER *suspicious. He makes a bolt for it.*] Catch him, you men! [*The* POLICEMEN *grab him.* CARTWRIGHT *strides over and pulls a pillow out of the rear of his trousers.*] I thought so. Aha! Put him down there! [*The* POLICEMEN *put him on the cushion; pull him up.* CARTWRIGHT *quickly compares the print.*] Exactly! There is your man, Officer! Arrest him!

WALKER: I'm glad I did it! He wronged my sister!

IVY: [*Looking at the print*] Good heavens! [*Cries from the guests—"What is it?" "What's the trouble?" etc.*] He's my father! [*To* WALKER] Daddy!

BLACKOUT

THE PRIDE OF THE CLAGHORNES

by George S. Kaufman and Howard Dietz

First produced in *The Band Wagon*, at the New Amsterdam Theatre, on June 3, 1931, with the following cast:

JASPER, a negro servant   Philip Loeb
COLONEL JEFFERSON CLAGHORNE   Frank Morgan
SARAH, his wife   Helen Broderick
BREEZE, their daughter   Adele Astaire
SIMPSON CARTER   Fred Astaire
ELY CARTER   Francis Pierlot
MARTIN CARTER   Jay Wilson

SCENE: *The living room in the home of* COLONEL JEF-
FERSON CLAGHORNE, *down in ole Virginny. So Southern.
When the curtain rises, an ancient negro servant, aged
about 106, is putting a drink on the table. The drink, of
course, is a mint julep. And the negro's name, of course,
is* JASPER. *He puts the drink down and totters feebly to
the staircase. He has been humming a snatch of an old
Southern song, which unexpectedly goes into "Cheerful
Little Earful" at the finish.*

JASPER: I got your mint julep now, Colonel. You want it
up there? [*There is no answer.*] I got your mint julep,
Colonel.
[COLONEL JEFFERSON CLAGHORNE *comes down the
stairs. The flower of the old Southland*]
COLONEL: Ah, thank you, Jasper. Thank you. The sweet-
ness of the honeysuckle and the perfume of the jas-
mine! Is the julep ready, Jasper?
JASPER: Yes, suh. On the table, suh.
COLONEL: Ah! Golden fragrance! Sweet forgetfulness in
iridescent bubbles! Gad, sir, this is a drink!
[*He starts to pick up the lamp.*]
JASPER: No, that ain't it, Colonel. That's it over there.
COLONEL: Ah, yes! [*He raises the glass.*] To the South
that was, Jasper! To the finest of all lands in the finest
of all liquids! It's too bad you're not drinking.
JASPER: Yes, suh.
COLONEL: [*Sadly, as he puts his drink down*] The South
that was. Ah, memories, memories! Forgive an old man,
Jasper. I am sad tonight.
JASPER: I understand, suh.

125

[*There is singing in the distance*—"Ole Black Joe," *and pretty bad.*]

COLONEL: The darkies are a-singin' in the cornfield.

JASPER: I hears 'em, suh.

COLONEL: Yes, Jasper, I'm sad tonight. My little girl is being taken away from me, Jasper. My little Breeze. She ain't a-gwine to be a Claghorne anymore.

JASPER: Yes, suh. I know, suh.

COLONEL: Jasper, how long you-all been in the family?

JASPER: Since before the war, suh.

COLONEL: Befo' the wo'. You've seen the Claghornes come and go, Jasper. Come and go.

JASPER: Yes, suh. I'se seen them all.

COLONEL: Seen them all. You've seen them in times of stress and turmoil, Jasper. Never wincing in the face of life. Never yielding. Never surrendering.

JASPER: Yes, suh. You certainly is a ornery lot.

COLONEL: Jasper, you black rascal, you! [JASPER *laughs, a bit nervously, and the situation is saved.*] We're a proud family, the Claghornes. A proud family.

[*He stands very erect—so erect that he almost topples over.* JASPER *just saves him.* SARAH CLAGHORNE, *the* COLONEL's *wife, descends the stairs.*]

SARAH: Good evening, Jefferson!

COLONEL: [*With a deep bow*] Good evenin', my dear!

SARAH: Good evening to you-all, Jasper.

JASPER: Evenin', Mis' Sarah.

COLONEL: More juleps, Jasper. Juleps for your mistress, and Miss Breeze, and her young man.

JASPER: Yes, suh.

[*He goes.*]

COLONEL: Our little girl is a-gwine to leave us, Sarah. Our little Breeze is being wafted away.

SARAH: [*Pulling out the biggest piece of knitting in the history of the world. Probably a carpet for the new Waldorf-Astoria*] It's the way of life, Jefferson.

COLONEL: It seems like yesterday, Sarah, when our little girl came to us, and says, "Pappy and Mammy, I'm going to be married." Yes, suh, it seems like yesterday.

SARAH: It *was* yesterday, Jefferson.

COLONEL: So it was. We've done our best by her, Sarah—

we've raised her in the true tradition of the South. And
I'm proud of her. She's a true Claghorne.

SARAH: [*Not too rapidly*] Yes, Jefferson.

COLONEL: I don't like the way you-all said that. She *is* a
Claghorne, Sarah?

SARAH: Oh, yes, Jefferson.

COLONEL: [*Watching her narrowly*] Yes. And now—to
think of our little Breeze getting married.

SARAH: Jefferson.

COLONEL: Yes?

SARAH: Have you noticed anything peculiar about Breeze
lately?

COLONEL: What do you-all mean?

SARAH: Only the other day I found her a-sitting in a chair,
a-crying.

COLONEL: You found her a-sitting and a-crying. Where
was she a-sitting?

SARAH: In the a-sitting room. She's awful sad about something, I cain't quite make out what it is.

COLONEL: Sarah! You don't think—

[*There is a gay laugh outside the door—one of those
rippling ones. Too rippling*]

SARAH: Sssh!

[BREEZE CLAGHORNE *and* SIMPSON CARTER *come in.*
BREEZE *is in a white dress and is swinging a bonnet.*
SIMPSON *is an open-mouthed country boy who is just
about able to speak two words in succession.*]

BREEZE: Hello, Pappy and Mammy! I brought Simpson
along, Pappy and Mammy.

COLONEL: Ah, good evening, my boy!

SIMPSON: Hullo, thar!

COLONEL: And my little Breeze! Come to your pappy!

BREEZE: [*Running to him, and bumping right into him*]
Howdy, Pappy.

COLONEL: Look at me, daughter. [*She does so.*] There
ain't nothing the matter with you-all?

BREEZE: Me-all? Why, no, Pappy. Simpson and I have
been down by the sycamore tree. A-sitting.

SARAH: Just a-sitting?

BREEZE: We've been watching the river as it goes around
the bend. It's fun watching the river, with Simpson.

SIMPSON: [*Magnanimously*] It's a mighty fine body of water.

SARAH: You-all were down there for about five hours. Were you a-watching the river all that time?

BREEZE: Why, what do you-all mean, Mammy?

[JASPER *returns with a tray of juleps.*]

JASPER: Yes, suh. Yes, suh.

[*Meaning nothing, of course*]

COLONEL: Ah, just in time, Jasper! Pass them around! Let us drink to the happy couple! Here you are, young man! You're a-getting a fine man, girl—a real, upstanding American youth!

SARAH: [*Who knows different*] She's getting a river-watcher.

COLONEL: Drink!

SIMPSON: What's in it?

COLONEL: In it, suh? It's a mint julep, suh, and the finest mint julep in all the South.

SIMPSON: I wonder if I could have a Coca-Cola?

BREEZE: Simpson!

COLONEL: Raise your glass, suh, and drink! Drink to the South, suh, and to her women—the finest women God ever made! Drink, suh! [*Just as they raise their glasses there comes a terrific pounding on the door.*] What's that? Jasper!

JASPER: [*Hurrying to the door*] Yes, suh! Yes, suh!

[*He opens the door. Enter* ELY CARTER *and* MARTIN CARTER, *two stern and bearded Southerners. They are carrying shotguns.*]

SIMPSON: Daddy!

ELY: Come here, son! Come away from there!

SIMPSON: What?

COLONEL: What's the meaning of this, Ely Carter?

ELY: You hear me, son? Come here!

SIMPSON: Yes, Daddy.

COLONEL: What is this, suh? How dare you come in here in this way, suh?

ELY: I've come here to get my son, Jefferson Claghorne! Because I don't want him under this roof!

MARTIN: No!

COLONEL: What do you mean, suh?

ELY: That's all I've got to say, Jefferson Claghorne! Come on, Simpson!

COLONEL: Hold on, suh! [*The* CARTERS *stop.*] You've got to say more than that, Ely Carter. What's going on here? [*He turns slowly to look at his womenfolk.*] What's going on here?
[*And the* DARKIES *start singing in the cornfield again.* "Swanee River," *this time*]

ELY: [*Hesitates*] There's—talk in the village.

MARTIN: Yah!

COLONEL: What sort of talk?

ELY: [*A pregnant pause, as you might say*] I can't tell you, Jefferson. I can't tell you without the womenfolk leave the room.

SARAH: Just when it's gettin' good?

COLONEL: [*To the* WOMEN] You stay right where you are. [*To* ELY] Come, suh! Out with it!

BREEZE: [*Almost in tears*] Oh, Mammy!

ELY: It's—they're talking about your little girl.

COLONEL: [*Taking a pistol from his pocket*] I'll kill them!

BREEZE: [*Staying his arm*] No, no, Pappy!

COLONEL: [*Conquering himself*] Go on, suh!

ELY: I've always looked forward to the day when my boy would marry a true Southern girl—a girl from a proud Southern family.

COLONEL: We're a proud Southern family, Ely Carter. [*Again he straightens, and whenever he straightens, he totters, and whenever he totters,* JASPER *props him up.*]

ELY: Then—you might as well know it. They're saying in the village that—your girl Breeze—is a virgin.

COLONEL: A virgin! [*A deadly pause.* BREEZE *is softly crying.*] Who—says—that?

ELY: They're all a-saying it, Jefferson.

COLONEL: It's a lie! [MARTIN *lowers his gun.*] Breeze! [*He is not looking at her; one hears only the sound of her soft crying.*] Breeze!

BREEZE: Yes, Pappy.

COLONEL: Come here. [BREEZE *slowly comes to him.*] Look at me. I want you to look me in the eye and tell me what they're saying ain't true. [*A pause*] I'm—waiting. [BREEZE *is unable to speak; bursts into fresh crying.*] Oh, my God! [*Raising his hand*] You—

SARAH: Don't you dare strike our little girl! [*To* ELY] Well, if it's true, it's your boy's fault. That's all I can say.

COLONEL: My daughter! A Claghorne! The proudest family in all the countryside! And now—this!

SARAH: She didn't know, Jefferson. She didn't know what she was doing. Did you, Daughter? Tell him you didn't know!

BREEZE: I didn't know, Pappy. I went out with the boys, the way other girls did. But I guess I'm just different, Pappy—that's all. I'm different. Oh, my God! [*She breaks down.*]

SARAH: [*Scornfully looking at* SIMPSON] You river-watcher!

ELY: Come, Martin. I'm sorry it had to be me that told you, Jefferson. Come on, Simpson.

SIMPSON: Well, I'll see you under the sycamore tree, Breeze. What is she, Papa?
[*The* CARTERS *go; the* CLAGHORNES *are left alone. The* COLONEL *turns slowly toward his daughter. Determination is written in his face.*]

SARAH: No, no, Jefferson! What are you going to do? What are you going to do?

JASPER: [*Falling on his knees, like* AL JOLSON] Don't do anything to her, Master! I've knowed her ever since she was a little baby! I've dangled her on my knee!

COLONEL: [*To* JASPER *sternly*] Get up! [JASPER *gets up.*] Get out! [JASPER *gets out—and quickly. The* COLONEL *turns to* BREEZE.] Well, Daughter, you've made your choice!

BREEZE: But if I could have another chance, Pappy! Can't I have another chance?

COLONEL: From this day forth I have no daughter.

SARAH: Jefferson! You mean she's got to—*go*?

JEFFERSON: She's got—to go.

BREEZE: All right, I'll go. I'll go. But someday gals like me will be able to stand up before the world unashamed. Good-bye, Pappy.

COLONEL: Good-bye, Daughter–that–was. It ain't for me to censure you, but what has to be has to be.

BREEZE: Good-bye, Mammy.

SARAH: My poor little girl! Go forth, my daughter. Go forth and wander upon the face of the earth.

BREEZE: Good-bye, Pappy and Mammy!

SARAH: Good-bye, Daughter. You've made a great mistake, and you've got to go out into the world and rectify it.

BREEZE: I'll make good, Mammy. You watch! I'll make good!

[*Choked with emotion, she goes. You hear those* DARKIES *singing.*]

SARAH: [*Slowly*] Well, Jefferson, she's a-gone.

COLONEL: Yes, Sarah. Yes, she's a-gone.

SARAH: [*Settling in her chair*] She'll come back to us, Jefferson—I know she will. She'll come back when she's seen the error of her ways.

[*She picks up the elephantine knitting.*]

COLONEL: Our little Breeze. Who'd ever have thought it, Sarah? Who'd ever have thought it?

SARAH: She was always a peculiar child, Jefferson. Right from the start.

COLONEL: No, Sarah, no. It's the younger generation, that's what it is. The younger generation. They ain't got no use for old-fashioned ways.

[*He shakes his head sadly.*]

BLACKOUT

LOST IN A CROWD

by Howard Dietz and Charles Sherman

First produced in *Flying Colors*, at the Imperial Theatre, on September 15, 1932, with Charles Butterworth in the role of JONES.

CHARACTERS

JONES	3RD WOMAN
MAN	ITALIAN
ANOTHER MAN	POLICEMAN
1ST WOMAN	FOURTH WOMAN
2ND WOMAN	DETECTIVE
THIRD MAN	WHOOPS SISTER
FOURTH MAN	MAN WITH CARNATION
FIFTH MAN	CROWD

SCENE: *A street corner. People passing in both directions throughout the scene.* MR. JONES *enters looking right and left in vague bewilderment. He is a stranger in the city and acts as if lost. He observes sign on the corner.*

JONES: Let me see now—let me see—[*Reads card in his hand*] 216 West Twenty-eighth Street. This is Thirty-fourth Street . . . Twenty-eighth Street should be south. Six blocks south. [MAN *passes by hurriedly.*] I beg your pardon, I'm a stranger in the city. Which way is south?

MAN: [*Gesturing in both directions*] That way.

JONES: But—[*The* MAN *has gone on and* ANOTHER MAN *walks past in opposite direction.*] Just a minute, sir, will you please help me . . . I . . .

ANOTHER MAN: Sorry, old man, I'm out of work myself. Try someone else!

[*Exits.* TWO WOMEN *go by.*]

1ST WOMAN: He looks perfectly able to work.

2ND WOMAN: Here, my good man.

[*She puts coin into* JONES' *hand.* JONES *follows after them when he has recovered.*]

JONES: But—lady—

2ND WOMAN: I'm sorry, but that's all I can afford. Don't spend it on beer.

[*They exit.* THIRD MAN *enters.*]

JONES: Can you beat it! All I wanted was an address, and . . .

THIRD MAN: You want an address?

JONES: That's all. If you could . . .

THIRD MAN: 38 West Fifty-eighth Street. Say "Jackson"

sent you.

[*Exits.* FOURTH MAN *enters.*]

JONES: Could you tell me where I could find a police-man?

FOURTH MAN: [*They walk.*] Walk along with me. What do you want with a policeman? I'll give you much better terms.

[*Exits.* FIFTH MAN *enters with a package.*]

JONES: Hey, you!

FIFTH MAN: [*Dropping package and running*] It's not mine! I didn't steal it!

[*Exits.* THIRD WOMAN *enters.*]

JONES: Could you tell me . . . [THIRD WOMAN *slaps* JONES *and exits.* ITALIAN *enters.*] Could you tell me . . . [ITALIAN *chatters in the Italian language and exits.*] A foreigner. [POLICEMAN *enters.*] Officer, I want to find a party.

POLICEMAN: This is Saturday night. Crash any place.

JONES: I mean an address.

POLICEMAN: Not so loud! [*Takes batch of cards from his pocket and hands one to* JONES] Here. Give 'em this card or I don't get my commission.

[POLICEMAN *hurries off.* FOURTH WOMAN *enters, wheeling baby carriage.* JONES *makes movement toward her.* FOURTH WOMAN *catches gesture, stops, primps, throws back encouraging glance.* JONES *lifts his hat.*]

JONES: How do you do?

FOURTH WOMAN: How do *you* do?

JONES: I'm looking for 216 West Twenty-eighth Street. Which direction is it?

FOURTH WOMAN: [*Laughing*] Skip the formalities. Let's keep walking.

JONES: No. No. You don't understand. I . . .

FOURTH WOMAN: I'll get rid of the baby carriage and meet you right here. Now wait!

[*Exits*]

JONES: But I just want to find Twenty-eighth Street.

[DETECTIVE *enters sleuthily—shows badge.*]

DETECTIVE: Hey, you! What are you doing here? You a vagrant?

JONES: I must be.

DETECTIVE: I'd better frisk you then. Stick 'em up!

[*He searches* JONES. *As he is examining* JONES, *the* PO-
LICEMAN *returns, sees* JONES *being held up, rushes to
arrest* DETECTIVE. POLICEMAN *drags* DETECTIVE *off.*]

POLICEMAN: Right in the crowded thoroughfare. What is
this city coming to?

DETECTIVE: But I'm a detective!

POLICEMAN: A likely story.

[*They exit.* JONES *feebly motions a protest offstage.
Meanwhile, a* WOMAN, *looking like one of the Whoops
Sisters, is examining the dazed* JONES *and comparing
him with a photograph. He comes to and sees her.*]

WHOOPS SISTER: Rodney! Darling Rodney!

JONES: Where does it say "Rodney?"

WHOOPS SISTER: Oh, Rodney, you look exactly like your
picture. But where's the carnation?

JONES: Lady, I don't know what your business is, but . . .

WHOOPS SISTER: Business! I've never been so insulted
in my life! I'll call a policeman! Officer!

POLICEMAN: [*Reenters*] Say, that *was* a detective! What's
going on here?

WHOOPS SISTER: Oh, you know him, do you? He has a
record, eh?

JONES: I haven't even got an address.

POLICEMAN: What's the trouble, lady?

WHOOPS SISTER: Trouble? If there was any justice in this
country, brutes like him would be behind bars.

[*A* MAN *comes on wearing a carnation.* WHOOPS *rushes
to him.*]

MAN WITH CARNATION: Emily!

WHOOPS SISTER: Rodney!

MAN WITH CARNATION: What's the excitement?

WHOOPS SISTER: He attacked me!

[CROWD *enters. Exclamations from the* CROWD *as they
enter.*]

DETECTIVE: What's the trouble here?

JONES: I attacked her.

CROWD: [*Heckling the* POLICEMAN *while the crushed*
JONES *looks on*] Do your duty, Officer! This man's been
insulting everyone on the street. He's a pickpocket.
I've seen him here for an hour!

POLICEMAN: [*To* JONES] Pick up your package and beat
it, and don't let me see you here again!

JONES: Package? It's not mine. I only wanted . . .

CROWD: [*Divides lines, as before*] If the package isn't his, then he's a thief. What's in it? Maybe it's burglar tools. Maybe it's a human torso.

JONES: All right—I'll take it.

POLICEMAN: If it's not yours and you take it, then you're surely a crook!

JONES: It's mine! It's mine!

CROWD: [*Divides lines, as before*] He's a bootlegger! I'm for Prohibition enforcement, and I'll prefer charges, Officer!

POLICEMAN: Come on, you! [*Puts handcuffs on* JONES]

JONES: Where are you going to take me, Officer?

POLICEMAN: To the Seventh Precinct on Twenty-eighth Street.

JONES: Twenty-eighth Street! Thank God!

BLACKOUT

ON THE AMERICAN PLAN

by George S. Kaufman and Howard Dietz

First produced in *Flying Colors*, at the Imperial Theatre, on September 15, 1932, with Clifton Webb in the role of MR. TILLEY and Patsy Kelley as MISS MCGONIGLE.

CHARACTERS

PAGE BOY
BELLHOP
FIRST GUEST
SECOND GUEST
MR. TILLEY
MISS MCGONIGLE

MAN
SECOND MAN
THIRD MAN
FOURTH MAN
FIFTH MAN

SCENE: *The lobby of the Remington Arms Hotel.* MR. TIL-
LEY, *a clerk, and* MISS MCGONIGLE, *a stenographer, are
behind the desk.* PAGE BOY *crosses.*

PAGE: Paging Mr. Grimes; Mr. Gormley; Mr. Johnson.
   Paging Mr. Grimes—
   [*Exits.* TWO GUESTS *cross, preceded by a* BELLHOP.]
FIRST GUEST: I had two million dollars in caster stock. If,
   instead of the stock, I had two million dollars worth of
   casters, think of all the casters I'd have had.
   [*Both exit.* PAGE *reenters.*]
PAGE: Paging Mr. Grimes; Mr. Gormley; Mr. Johnson . . .
   [*Exits*]
TILLEY: [*With a newspaper*] Yes, Miss McGonigle, it
   looks like another big day for the hotel.
MISS MCGONIGLE: That's good.
TILLEY: [*Indicating paper*] Stock market down another
   ten points. That means things will be booming here.
MISS MCGONIGLE: [*Looking at her board*] We're about
   three-quarters full already. They've been coming in
   steadily since the market closed.
TILLEY: [*Also looks at board*] What are most of them
   doing—jumping or shooting themselves?
MISS MCGONIGLE: They're mostly jumpers.
TILLEY: I like that. Clean cut. [*Phone rings*] Room clerk!
   . . . Yes, sir—right away. Front! [*The bell. Calls off
   stage*] Prussic acid in twelve-eighteen. [FIRST MAN *enters.*] Yes, sir—single room?

[*Offers register and pen. The* MAN *nods, signs the register.*]

MISS MCGONIGLE: Five-sixteen.

TILLEY: Oh, very nice. That's high enough for a jump and has a nice long mirror in case you prefer shooting. Or were you thinking of poison?

MAN: I think I'll shoot!

TILLEY: Right! Front!

[*Hands man gun.* MAN *exits.* MISS MCGONIGLE'S *phone rings.*]

MISS MCGONIGLE: Hello . . . just a minute . . . It's that guy in nine-twenty. He says he doesn't like the way that cyanide tastes.

TILLEY: Tell him to mix it with orange juice.

MISS MCGONIGLE: [*Into phone*] Mix it with orange juice. [*Other phone rings.*]

TILLEY: Room clerk! . . . I'm sorry, sir, but that's really the best suite in the hotel. Southern exposure. Wide windows and perfect landing space . . . Oh, yes, we keep the street clear. Cars not allowed to park. Very well, sir. [*Hangs up.* SECOND MAN *enters.*] Yes, sir?

SECOND MAN: [*As he signs*] Something high up.

TILLEY: [*Extending a key*] Thirty-first floor—you couldn't ask anything better.

SECOND MAN: Thanks.

TILLEY: Stationery?

SECOND MAN: Let me see . . .

TILLEY: [*Counting out note paper*] Two notes are customary—wife and sweetheart.

SECOND MAN: Thanks.

TILLEY: Happy landing! [SECOND MAN *exits. Phone rings.*] Yes? . . . Report from the nineteenth floor. [*Signals* MISS MCGONIGLE *to stand ready*] Yes, floor clerk? . . . 1902 clear. Gentleman just checked out . . . 1907 . . . on his way down . . . You don't say? [*To* MISS MCGONIGLE] He says it was a beautiful takeoff. Very well! [*Hangs up*]

MISS MCGONIGLE: I go mad trying to keep these records straight.

TILLEY: Yes, the turnover in this hotel is enormous.

[THIRD MAN *enters. Foreigner, with whiskers*]

THIRD MAN: [*Fiercely*] I do not understand your America!

TILLEY: How's that?

THIRD MAN: America! What *is* it?

TILLEY: Miss McGonigle, will you take care of little Russia?

MISS MCGONIGLE: Vacancy on the twenty-eighth floor.

TILLEY: Twenty-eighth floor. Twelve dollars a day.

THIRD MAN: But I have only five dollar. America!

TILLEY: Five dollars! I can give you a room on the second floor. Of course, it's not high enough for jumping, but that's the best I can do for five dollars. Second floor!

THIRD MAN: America!

TILLEY: I wish you'd stop saying "America." There must be some other country.

THIRD MAN: Give me the key! I try it! I jump hard! America!

[*Exits*]

MISS MCGONIGLE: He's the spittin' image of a friend of mine. [MISS MCGONIGLE's *phone rings.*] Hello ... Yes? ... Just a minute ... [*To* TILLEY] It's the housekeeper on the sixth floor. That man in 608 has been in the tub for two hours and isn't drowned yet.

TILLEY: Make a note that drowning is a dollar extra after this. It takes too long.

MISS MCGONIGLE: Yes, sir. [*Into phone*] All right—we'll look after it.

[FOURTH MAN *enters.*]

TILLEY: Yes, sir?

FOURTH MAN: I want a room. [*Registers*]

TILLEY: Front! [*Hands out key*] One-eleven!

MISS MCGONIGLE: [*At her board*] One-eleven occupied! [*A shot off stage*] One-eleven free.

[FOURTH MAN *exits.* THIRD MAN *returns.*]

THIRD MAN: You were right! It was not high enough! America!

[*Exits. Phone rings.*]

MISS MCGONIGLE: Hello! ... Got caught in an awning? We'll send right up.

[*Hangs up.* FIFTH MAN *enters.*]

FIFTH MAN: Good afternoon.

TILLEY: Yes, sir?

FIFTH MAN: I'm a theatrical producer—

TILLEY: [*As* TILLEY *and* MISS MCGONIGLE *hand him a gun*] Say no more!

[FIFTH MAN *exits. Phone rings.*]

BLACKOUT

THE SURGEON'S DEBUT

by Howard Dietz

First produced in *Flying Colors*, at the Imperial Theatre, on September 15, 1932, with the following cast:

DR. ERIC TREVELYAN Clifton Webb
HAROLD JASPER Charles Butterworth
MISS MARIS Imogene Coca
DR. KAUFMAN Philip Loeb
MRS. BALFOUR-CHATFIELD Helen Carrington
KATHERINE June Blossom
FANNY Jean Sargent

SCENE: *An operating room. At rise,* MISS MARIS, *a nurse, is arranging flowers in several tall vases that are on the floor. She is softly humming while she works.* DR. KAUFMAN, *an intern, is holding some telegrams.*

KAUFMAN: I'd make a better surgeon than this new doctor they've got.

MARIS: You mean Dr. Trevelyan? He's so attractive.

KAUFMAN: Attractive?

MARIS: He has such gentlemanly bearing, such a beautiful mouth. So continental.

KAUFMAN: You don't judge a surgeon by his looks. He's gotta have good aim.

MARIS: Are those telegrams for Dr. Trevelyan? Give them here!

KAUFMAN: Can you beat it? A guy is sick, and they send the *doctor* the flowers and the telegrams.

MARIS: That's because it's his first case and he has lots of friends.

[DR. ERIC TREVELYAN *enters.*]

ERIC: Good morning, Miss Maris.

MARIS: Good morning, Dr. Trevelyan!

ERIC: Good morning, Dr. Kaufman. My busy little staff. [*Calling offstage*] Oh, fellow! Bring the things right in. [INTERN *enters carrying tray containing cocktail shaker and glasses.*] Put them over there! [INTERN *sets tray on table and exits.*]

KAUFMAN: What are those?

ERIC: Those? Those are the goodies!

MARIS: [*Handing over the telegrams*] Here are some more wires. I never heard of anyone being so popular.

147

ERIC: Yes, they are all such devoted friends. The walls of my dressing room are just plastered with telegrams. [*Reads address*] It's from Genevieve—Genevieve Stuyvesant, you know—

KAUFMAN: We used to play shinny together.

ERIC: [*Reading*] "Best wishes on your first case. Am sure you'll pull through all right" . . . She's a dear. Keep these for me, Doctor.

KAUFMAN: Shall I make a scrapbook?

ERIC: Miss Maris, you lack a sense of color harmony. Please change the position of the roses.

MARIS: Y—yes, Doctor.

KAUFMAN: Don't you think it would be better if she looked after the patient?

ERIC: Dr. Kaufman, this is no time to trifle with my nerves. You might at least wait till the operation is over. Besides, what's wrong with the patient?

MARIS: He's got gallstones!

ERIC: Oh, those! Well, he's in good hands at least. Has anyone arrived yet?

KAUFMAN: There was a casket salesman.

MARIS: There have been hundreds of phone calls, Doctor. [*She pins a flower on his lapel.*]

ERIC: I'm sort of expecting some people—guests. They want to be present at my debut.

KAUFMAN: What is this, the *Follies*?

ERIC: I'm particularly expecting Mrs. Balfour-Chatfield. She was even present at my first guinea pig.

MARIS: I've seen her picture in the rotogravure—she's always on the beach.

KAUFMAN: A sand-louse.

ERIC: Tell me, Dr. Kaufman, do I look all right?

KAUFMAN: Say, that's as nice a surgical suit as I ever saw in my life. Who made it?

ERIC: A little tailor in Bond Street. You wouldn't know him. These are lightweight—for summer operations.

MARIS: [*To* ERIC] Don't you think you'd better start operating, Doctor? The patient is awful sick!

[INTERN *enters with white apron for* ERIC.]

ERIC: Don't flurry me. I wouldn't think of starting before my guests arrive. They said they were coming straight from Margaret Garfield's party. I was scheduled to go, but just couldn't make it with this on my mind. Better start mixing the cocktails, Doctor!

KAUFMAN: Now?

ERIC: Certainly. I wouldn't dream of inviting my friends here without giving them a little something. It wouldn't be hosty.

KAUFMAN: "Hosty"—that's one for the book!

ERIC: [*In revery*] If Dr. Liebschen, my teacher, could only see me now. A full-fledged surgeon, ready to take wings. There he was, calm and scientific, his face imperturbable.

KAUFMAN: He had a deadpan.

MARIS: A deadpan. That reminds me where I left the patient!

[*She exits.*]

ERIC: [*Continuing*] And now, I, his pupil, am about to don *his* mantle. I see it all, the whole rosy path before me. My own clinic, a shrine for the injured, and me— a god among men—the man who cures all broken bones, hardening of the arteries . . .

KAUFMAN: Softening of the brain . . . Here's the patient, Doctor!

[*The* PATIENT *is wheeled in by* MISS MARIS. *Simultaneously from the opposite entrance,* INTERN *delivers box of flowers.* ERIC *pays no attention to the patient, but gazes on the open box of lillies of the valley.*]

JASPER [*The* PATIENT]: Is everything gonna be all right, Doctor?

ERIC: Why, they're lillies of the valley. Just what the room needs. Put them over there!

[INTERN *puts flowers on table and exits.*]

JASPER: [*To* KAUFMAN] Ask him if everything's gonna be all right!

ERIC: [*Examining card in flower box*] Why—they're for you! [*To* JASPER] Were *you* expecting flowers?

JASPER: Oh, Doctor, I feel numb all over. Is that normal?

ERIC: Don't worry, my good man. I'll have you up and about in jig-time.

JASPER: Even waltz-time would be all right!

MARIS: You'd better work fast, Doctor!

ERIC: Don't flurry me. I can't possibly start till my guests arrive. What time is it?

[MRS. BALFOUR-CHATFIELD, KATHERINE and FANNY *enter, chatting gaily.* ERIC *rushes to greet them.*]

ERIC: Oh, here they are now! Chatfield! Katherine! Fanny! What a welcome surprise! I sent you the invitations but I had no idea you'd stay up till this ungodly hour!

KATHERINE: Eric, those were the cleverest invitations I ever saw in my life.

ERIC: My idea!

KATHERINE: "I want you to be present at my cutting-out party!" I tell you, I died!

[*They all laugh.*]

JASPER: Very amusing!

FANNY: Eric, we missed you at Margaret's party. But everyone understood.

MRS. CHATFIELD: We did nothing but talk about you. Bill Clawson and Dwight Sellers got into a drunken argument over you.

ERIC: Argument? Over me?

[*Laughs*]

MRS. CHATFIELD: [*Laughing*] Yes, it all started when Bill said you shouldn't be allowed to operate on anyone.

JASPER: Who won the argument?

MRS. CHATFIELD: I don't believe we've been introduced.

KATHERINE: [*Noticing* JASPER] No. Who is he?

ERIC: [*Crossing*] Oh, he. He's my patient! His name is Cowperthwait—or Mills or Buchanan—something like that. I've got it written on a card!

JASPER: My name's Harold Jasper.

ERIC: [*To* JASPER] Ssh! Be quiet!

MRS. CHATFIELD: [*Who has been peeking at* JASPER] Oh, he's the one we're going to watch you cut up!

ERIC: You put things so crudely.

JASPER: Doesn't she?

FANNY: Eric, I love the way you've done this room!

KATHERINE: Yes.

FANNY: It's so clinical!

ERIC: Now there'll be no speeches of any kind. All perfectly simple. Isn't that the best? Now before I start, let me get you people a drink. Dr. Kaufman, start the cocktails, will you? [*Under his breath*] Kaufman's my intern, you know. A very ordinary fellow.

MRS. CHATFIELD: They do say that all the surgeons are butchers. I had my appendix taken out and my stomach looks like Al Capone.

JASPER: They call her "Scar Belly."

FANNY: Are we allowed to watch, Eric?

ERIC: Of course, children, of course! That's what you're here for. Miss Maris! Some chairs, please!

MARIS: Yes, Doctor.

KATHERINE: Oh, Eric, can we see everything—the blood and all?

JASPER: The blood isn't enough—she has to have all.

ERIC: Now then, girls, group yourselves around the operating table so you can see how I work. After this is over, we'll have a rubber or two of bridge.

JASPER: I'm being operated on by Culbertson.

[*The cocktails are served.*]

KATHERINE: I love bridge!

JASPER: I like pinochle.

MRS. CHATFIELD: He's just that type.

FANNY: I think he's rather nice. Too bad, he's in such a hopeless condition.

JASPER: [*To* MISS MARIS] Has my mother been here?

MARIS: Yes, but of course they wouldn't allow her in here. [JASPER *moans.*] I told her to wait.

KAUFMAN: You should have told her to start digging.

MARIS: The anaesthetic is wearing off, Doctor!

ERIC: You see, ladies, I gave him a spinal anaesthetic so that he is enabled to see all that goes on instead of being dead to the world.

KAUFMAN: That'll come later.

[ERIC *is now busy adjusting bandages on his head and donning rubber gloves.* MISS MARIS *holds a mirror while he does this.*]

MRS. CHATFIELD: You know, I've never been to an operation before in my life.

KATHERINE: My first, too.

ERIC: My first, too. Ha, ha!

JASPER: Mine too!

ERIC: Now you make yourselves as comfortable as possible while I—return to my mutton, as it were.

JASPER: That's the best compliment I've had so far.

MARIS: I'm going to give him another jab with the needle. [*She jabs.*]

ERIC: Good idea!

JASPER: Oh!

ERIC: Hurt?

JASPER: No, I didn't feel it at all.

[ERIC *starts operating.* MISS MARIS *lifts the sheet.* KAUFMAN *holds the instrument tray.*]

MRS. CHATFIELD: He must have led a wild youth!

ERIC: Shall we begin? Goody. Dr. Kaufman, hold the tray here. Now, you see, ladies, I take this long, slender rapier sort of thing . . . well, I've never seen that before. Oh, no matter! And make a quick mark over the part of the body that I'm about to cut.

JASPER: Doctor, is this really your first operation?

ERIC: Yes, indeed. It's my premiere. But I'm not nervous.

JASPER: You're sure you're not trembling just a little bit?

ERIC: Oh, but that'll wear off as soon as we really get down to things.

JASPER: My phone number is Rhinelander 6—2—6—2.

ERIC: Now I take this beautiful curved implement— [*Notices card attached with blue ribbon*] Look—Aunt Harriet sent it to me. [*Reads card*] "From the one person who still believes in you." Now isn't that sweet? Isn't that sweet?

[*They all admire it.*]

JASPER: Oh, it's ducky!

ERIC: [*Continuing*] And with a graceful swoop—note the arc of the body, the position of the head—it is important to hit the precise spot. So.

[*They applaud.*]

MRS. CHATFIELD: It's amazing that Eric ever became a surgeon, he was always so clumsy with his hands.

FANNY: Used to drop things.

JASPER: Oh, a schlemiel!

MARIS: But, Doctor, hurry—!

ERIC: Don't flurry me. Now the next step in an operation is the actual probing. Dr. Kaufman, hold the tray just a little higher. Give me my probing knife. Here's where the real test of a surgeon comes in. The stance is very important. You take the instrument—one that might be called a niblick, if this were golf . . .

JASPER: Isn't it?

MRS. CHATFIELD: Eric's a great golfer—

FANNY: Ssh!

ERIC: Then—

KATHERINE: Oh, Eric. I can't see a thing!

ERIC: [*To* JASPER] Move back just a bit so Katherine can see.

JASPER: [*Moves*] Is that all right now?

KATHERINE: Thanks, that's fine!

ERIC: Then raising the niblick—so to speak—aloft—[*A knock on the door*] Oh, that may be the Harrimans. Wait a minute! Wait a minute!
[*Goes to door*]

JASPER: I don't want to meet anyone else!
[PHOTOGRAPHER *enters.*]

PHOTOGRAPHER: Doctor Trevelyan?

ERIC: I'm Dr. Trevelyan.

PHOTOGRAPHER: [*Extending card*] My card!

ERIC: Oh, how do you do? Pardon my glove. Oh, girls, he's the photographer . . . from the *Vanity Fair.* Wants to take a picture of me, operating.

KAUFMAN: I want a print of that one.

ERIC: Now, let me see . . . Where would the light be best?

JASPER: You'll tell me when to smile?

ERIC: [*Strikes pose*] How would this be? [*To* JASPER] Just move that way a little!

PHOTOGRAPHER: That's fine! Hold that! [*Snaps picture*] Thank you.
[*Starts to exit*]

ERIC: Don't mention it. Won't you stay for the operation? Is there another chair?

JASPER: You can take my place.

PHOTOGRAPHER: No, thank you, I'm all right.

ERIC: Now let me see, where was I?

JASPER: You were just teeing off.
[THREE MUSICIANS *enter and take positions in the room as* ERIC *resumes operation.*]

ERIC: Oh, yes. Then, holding the niblick aloft—

MARIS: Just a minute, Doctor. The band has arrived.

ERIC: Lord, I almost forgot. I ordered a little three-piece orchestra to help us along in case things lagged.

MRS. CHATFIELD: Eric is so thoughtful!

KATHERINE: [*Crosses toward band*] What a splendid idea! Does one of them croon?

JASPER: If he does, I don't care what happens!

ERIC: All right, boys!
   [*Band plays.*]

MRS. CHATFIELD: What are they playing, Eric?

ERIC: It's "Just One More Chance!"

JASPER: That's an exaggeration.

ERIC: [*To* MRS. CHATFIELD] Shall we dance?

KAUFMAN: [*To* KATHERINE] May I?
   [*They dance around.*]

ERIC: [*To* JASPER] Aren't you dancing?

JASPER: I think I'll sit this one out!

BLACKOUT

MOURNING BECOMES
IMPOSSIBLE

by Jack McGowan

First produced in the tenth edition of the *Earl Carroll Vanities,* at the Broadway Theatre, on September 27, 1932, with the following cast:

MORTIMER Milton Berle
MILLIE Lillian Shade
SIDNEY Will Fyffe
EMMA Helen Broderick
GIRL Euna Sinnott
GEORGE Lester Crawford
PENNANT MAN Jack Reese
SARA Beryl Wallace
CHUCK John Hale

Loosely based on the actual goings-on when Rudolph Valentino's body was lying in state after his funeral in 1926. The sketch, as printed here, is basically the version prepared by its author. When it was performed in the *Vanities,* it was slightly revised and abbreviated—the TICKET SPECULATOR entered after the GIRL with the roses faints for the second time and their scene played more or less as written. After the fight between GEORGE and SID, SID and EMMA went off and it was then that the exchange between MORTIMER and MILLIE occurred. The blackout came after MORTIMER's "Minsky's" line.

SCENE: *A street with a single line of people stretched across the stage from right to left. These people are waiting to view the body of a famous motion picture actor which is lying in state at the chapel of an undertaking establishment further up the street.*

They are a curious looking group and among them are MILLIE, SARA, EMMA, MORTIMER *and* SID—*who will speak for themselves.*

When we see them the line has been standing for two hours without moving any closer to its object. They are impatient but silent.

It is night and the characters are seen in the shadows—however the speaking parts are covered by a faint lighting from overhead.

After a slight pause—

MORTIMER: [*To* MILLIE *in a half-whisper*] Come on, sweetheart, let's go home. We've been standing in the same spot for two hours without movin' an inch.

MILLIE: No.

[*Line moves forward six steps.*]

MORTIMER: [*After a slight pause*] I can't understand why you wanna go and look at a dead movie actor, anyhow!

MILLIE: [*Indignantly*] Oh, you can't?

MORTIMER: No, I can't. He wasn't so hot when he was alive!

MILLIE: I owe it to him . . . a last tribute of respect.

MORTIMER: [*Sarcastically*] I think you're still stuck on that guy.

MILLIE: [*Pitifully*] Mortimer, please—

MORTIMER: [*Angrily*] You were always stuck on him! Every time he was in a movie it cost me a buck to sit and watch you lookin' at him like he was the guy that'd ruined you.

MILLIE: [*Accusingly*] Is that so! You *know* who did that!

MORTIMER: Well, then—what's all this respect you owe *him?*

MILLIE: You can't seem to understand that he was my favorite actor and the least I can do is to attend his last personal appearance.

MORTIMER: [*Quarreling*] Well . . . why drag me along?

MILLIE: I didn't ask you to come!

[STOOGE, *who is behind* MORTIMER, *taps him on shoulder.*]

MORTIMER: What do you want?

STOOGE: Can you spare two dollars and ten cents for a cup of coffee?

MORTIMER: Two dollars and ten cents for a cup of coffee? What are you, a phoney? All I got is ten cents. [*Gives him dime*] Get out of here.

[STOOGE *exits. There is a movement in the line of about ten paces. The crowd mumbles as they move forward. This brings* EMMA *and* SID *onstage at right. These people are of a lower class than* MORTIMER *and* MILLIE. GEORGE *is directly behind* SID. *He is a tough-looking individual. The line stops and there are grumblings from the crowd—silence.*]

SID: [*To* EMMA] Did you bring the Kodak?

EMMA: [*Exhibits camera-case which is slung over her shoulder*] Yeah, but I'm afraid we won't get much of a picture of him, though.

SID: Why not . . . there's no chance of him movin' now, is there?

EMMA: No . . . and you never heard of anybody gettin' Kleig eyes from candles, have you?

SID: Candles, huh! I'll bet he's lit up like an airport.

EMMA: And besides we gotta be careful we don't get caught snappin' him.

SID: Yeah, why?

EMMA: He's still under contract to the Warner Brothers.

SID: Yet ... even now, you mean?

EMMA: Certainly ... they've got a lot of dead ones.

SID: Maybe silent pictures is comin' back again, hey?

MORTIMER: [*To* MILLIE] Would you go to all this trouble if it was me? ... I ask you, would you?

MILLIE: [*Wearily*] Mortimer, please—

MORTIMER: You bet you wouldn't.

MILLIE: [*Sadly*] You've never understood me ... and now in this hour ... when I need you most—

MORTIMER: Aw, Millie, for the love of Ker—

MILLIE: [*Quickly*] Don't you dare swear.

   [MORTIMER *turns angrily away from her. A* MAN *enters with an armful of pennants with the name of "D'ERRICO" blocked on them in brilliant colors.*]

PENNANT MAN: Pennants ... pennants ... buy a pennant of the great actor D'errico while they last. [*To* MILLIE] Pennant, lady?

MILLIE: How much are they?

PENNANT MAN: Only a dollar.

MORTIMER: [*Sore*] We don't want any.

MILLIE: Well, I do.

MORTIMER: [*Almost crying with rage*] What the hell do you want with a pennant of a thing like this for?

MILLIE: [*Takes pennant from the man*] Give the man a dollar.

MORTIMER: Oh, my God! [*Hands the man a bill*]

MILLIE: [*Gives the pennant to* MORTIMER] Here, you carry it.

   [MORTIMER *shoulders the pennant in a rage.*]

PENNANT MAN: [*Moving along line*] Pennants! Pennants!

SID: Hey, mister ... how much are those pennants?

PENNANT MAN: A buck.

SID: You want one, Emma?

EMMA: Let's get two of 'em. We can send one down home to the folks.

SID: Yeah, that's a good idea. Give us two, fellow. [*The transaction is made.*]

PENNANT MAN: [*As he goes off right*] Pennants! Pennants!

SID: They're sure doin' this thing right, ain't they?

EMMA: Swell.

[STOOGE *enters and walks up to* MORTIMER.]

STOOGE: Hey, can you spare a dime?

MORTIMER: What is this, a racket? Didn't I just give you a dime?

STOOGE: Were you the guy?

MORTIMER: Yes.

STOOGE: Okay!

[*Marks a cross in chalk on* MORTIMER'S *coat, then exits*]

SID: [*Sees* SARA *coming in the distance*] Ain't that Sara Falkner comin' this way?

EMMA: [*Looking ahead off left*] Sure it is— Oh, Sara! Sara!

[SARA *enters left walking slowly with handkerchief to her eyes.*]

SARA: Hello, Emma. How are you, Sidney?

EMMA: Did you see him?

SARA: Yes, I saw him. I'm goin' back and get into line again.

EMMA: How does he look?

SARA: As natural as anything. They have him in a glass casket and only show him down as far as the waist.

[*Exits*]

SID: Why do they only show him down as far as the waist?

EMMA: Guess he hasn't any pants on.

SID: I'm starving.

EMMA: Did you bring the sandwiches, Sidney?

SID: Ha-ha, did I?

[*Holds up briefcase*]

EMMA: I'm hungry—let's eat.

[SID *opens briefcase and hands her a sandwich. They eat.*]

MORTIMER: Listen, Millie, I wanna go home.

MILLIE: Well, don't let me stop you.

MORTIMER: Do you insist upon going through with this?

MILLIE: [*Determinedly*] I see no reason why I shouldn't.

[*A pair of scissors drops to the ground from* MILLIE'S *coat.* MORTIMER *picks them up.*]

MORTIMER: What are these for?

MILLIE: None of your business.

MORTIMER: Millie—what are these scissors for?

MILLIE: If you must know . . . they're to get a lock of his hair with.

MORTIMER: What?

MILLIE: Give them to me.

MORTIMER: You mean to tell me now . . . you're stuck on that guy?

MILLIE: [*Weeping*] Of course I'm not!

MORTIMER: What's the idea of wantin' to give him a hair-cut, then?

MILLIE: I want those scissors.

MORTIMER: You won't get them.

MILLIE: If you don't give them back—I'll scream.

MORTIMER: You wouldn't dare.

MILLIE: Wouldn't I?

MORTIMER: No.

[*A* GIRL *standing center stage carrying a large bunch of roses screams at this cue and falls to the stage in a faint. All in the line become excited and gather around her with ad-lib chatter.* TWO MEN *stand the* GIRL *on her feet. As quickly as line broke it forms again.* SID *is left out of the line. He speaks to* GEORGE *who is now standing behind* EMMA.]

SID: Listen, brother, you're in my place.

GEORGE: [*Toughly*] Oh, am I? Well, try and get it back.

SID: I'll get it back . . . don't worry about that!

[SID *tries to edge back into line. There is a tussle but* SID *is unsuccessful.*]

EMMA: [*To* GEORGE] You're one of those wise guys, ain't you?

GEORGE: [*Just as toughly to* EMMA] Shut up!

SID: Don't you talk to my wife like that.

GEORGE: Pfui!

[*Pushes* SID *in the face with his open hand*]

EMMA: Don't pay attention to him, dear. Get in ahead of me. [*Makes room for* SID *and he gets into line. Then she gets out of line and* SID *makes room for her.*] We'll show that wise guy.

[*They are in their original places.*]

SID: [*Laughs sarcastically at* GEORGE] Ha-ha-ha—how do you like that?

GEORGE: Perfect. [*Pushes* SID *out of line again—*SID *struts before him.*]

SID: [*As he struts*] Ooooooh, you wanna be that way, do you?

EMMA: Now don't fight, Sidney.

SID: You keep outa this. Thinks he can pull that kind of stuff, does he. [*Up to* GEORGE] Say, listen, you— [GEORGE *pushes him in the face again.*] So that's the way you feel about it, hey? Ooooooh, I see, well— [*Makes a pass at* GEORGE *but* EMMA *gets it in the back of the neck and lets out a yell*]

EMMA: Sidney, please. [*Then to* GEORGE] Now you see here— [*Then* GEORGE *pushes* EMMA *out of the line.*]

SID: If you don't give us our places back—I'll call a policeman.

EMMA: You've gotta nerve—you have. [*The* GIRL *with the roses faints again and everybody gathers around her as before.* SID *and* EMMA *however go to their places and make a line of their own. Then the crowd gets the* GIRL *back on her feet again and they form their own line leaving* SID *and* EMMA *standing alone.*]

SID: Come on, Emma, we'll show this guy he can't do this and get away with it.

[*Exits.* EMMA *follows him off.*]

MORTIMER: [*To* MILLIE, *who is weeping*] Now what's the matter?

MILLIE: The more I think of it—the worse it seems.

MORTIMER: What?

MILLIE: That I'll never hear the silver tones of his voice again.

MORTIMER: [*Steps out of line*] Listen, Millie, I'm fed up—I'm through. [*Hands her the pennant*] Here's your goddamned souvenir. I'm goin' where I can see something.

[*He starts off.*]

MILLIE: Where are you going?

MORTIMER: Minsky's.

[*Exits.* EMMA *and* SID *enter at right.* SID *goes up to* GEORGE.]

SID: There'll be a copper here in a minute. Then we'll see.

[GEORGE *merely pushes* SID *in the face.*]

EMMA: If you don't stop pickin' on my husband . . . I'm gonna have you arrested.

[GEORGE *pushes* EMMA *in the face.*]

SID: I'd just like to see you do that again. [GEORGE *pushes* EMMA *in the face again.*] Well ... now I ask you, what're you gonna do with a guy like that?

EMMA: I don't know—but I'm gettin' pretty sick of him. [CHUCK *enters. He's a ticket speculator and a fast talking salesman he is too.*]

CHUCK: [*To* SID] How about a pair right down in front?

SID: [*Bewildered*] What's that?

CHUCK: Do you want to buy standin' room in the line— down near the front?

EMMA: How much?

CHUCK: Two dollars apiece.

SID: Geez, you ticket scalpers sure put the hooks in, don't you?

CHUCK: If you think you can do any better—it's okay with me.

EMMA: Is that the cheapest you got?

CHUCK: No ... I can give you a pair right about in here for fifty cents each.

EMMA: Ain't that a little high?

CHUCK: Do you realize, lady—that this is the biggest hit in town?

SID: Give us those fifty-centers.

[*Hands* CHUCK *a dollar bill*]

CHUCK: [*Speaking to* TWO BOYS *in the line just ahead of* GEORGE] All right, boys, fall out. [*To* SID, *as the* BOYS *leave the line*] There you are, sir. [EMMA *and* SID *get into their original places*—CHUCK *speaks to the* TWO BOYS.] Fall in below, boys.

[CHUCK *and the boys exit right.*]

SID: [*To* GEORGE] Ha-ha-ha—how do you like this?

GEORGE: Perfect.

[GEORGE *pushes* SID *out of line again.* SID *is about to argue when he looks out and over the heads of the audience.* EMMA *sees him and becomes curious. She leaves the line and looks up where* SID *is watching.*]

EMMA: What is it, Sidney?

SID: They'll never get that safe in such a small window.

EMMA: [*After she has watched a second or two*] Yes, they will. I've seen 'em get 'em in smaller windows than that.

[*Two or three of the line become interested in the safe being hauled up and join* SID *and* EMMA. *Of course the safe will never be hoisted successfully unless there is a crowd to watch. Anyhow it never has been done up to now.*]

SID: No, they won't—I'll bet they'll have to take the window all apart.

[*Nearly all of the line is now looking up where the safe is being held. They have forgotten about the moving picture actor—so let's leave the goddamned fools watching the safe. This same crowd will go from here to watch an excavation somewhere and so on and so on—but what the hell, let's black out on them while their mouths are open and their eyes are popping out of their heads at nothing.*]

THE END

SPEED

by David Freedman

First produced in *Strike Me Pink*, at the Majestic Theatre, on March 4, 1933, with the following cast:

ANNOUNCER Roy Atwell
MR. DUNCAN Jimmy Durante
MRS. DUNCAN Carolyn Nolte
THEIR SON Johnny Downs
HIS WIFE Dorothy Dare
A FRIEND Milton Watson
NURSE Wilma Cox
BUTLER Frank Conlan

ANNOUNCER: We're living in a fast age. Aeroplanes, radio, television. We can travel 500 miles an hour or send a message around the world in two seconds. We talk fast, eat fast, sleep fast, walk fast. Nothing but speed, speed, speed. If it keeps up, we can soon expect to see something like this:

SCENE: *Cut-out modernistic interior of living room. Doors center, right and left. Discovered are* MR. DUNCAN, *his* FRIEND, *and* MISS GREEN.

FRIEND: Mr. Duncan, meet Miss Green. Good-bye.
    [*Exits center*]
DUNCAN: How do you do? Will you marry me?
MISS GREEN [*Now* MRS. DUNCAN]: Yes. Don't be late for dinner, John.
DUNCAN: I won't, dear. If I'm detained in China, I'll call you.
    [*Exits*]
MRS. DUNCAN: These domestic scenes get on my nerves!
    [*Exits left*]
DUNCAN: [*Returns center*] Gosh! Those Chinese can talk!
NURSE: [*Enters left*] Mr. Duncan, it's a boy!
DUNCAN: Great! Can I see him?
NURSE: Surely.
    [*Opens door left. His* SON, *a college boy, enters with a pennant.*]
SON: Hello, Dad! Harvard won!
    [NURSE *exits left.*]
DUNCAN: Fine! I've made you my junior partner.
BUTLER: [*Enters right*] Dinner is ready.

DUNCAN: All right. I'll fetch Mrs. Duncan.
    [*Exits*]
SON: [*To* BUTLER] Gee, I haven't got the heart. Tell the
    old guy I'm eloping!
    [*He exits.*]
BUTLER: Yes, sir.
    [MR. *and* MRS. DUNCAN *enter, gray and old.*]
SON: [*Comes back with* WIFE *and baby*] Dad, Mother—
    my wife and baby.
DUNCAN: What a day!

BLACKOUT

A SMOKING CAR
by David Freedman

First produced in *Strike Me Pink*, at the Majestic Theatre, on March 4, 1933, with the following cast:

MAN Eddie Garr
WOMAN Lupe Velez
CONDUCTOR Milton Watson

SCENE: *A smoking car. At rise,* MAN *is discovered reading a newspaper. His grips are on the seat. A* WOMAN, *entering the car, is being stopped by the* CONDUCTOR.

CONDUCTOR: You can't go in there, lady, [*strongly*] that's the smoking car.

WOMAN: [*Backing in*] I paid for my ticket and I'm entitled to a seat.
[*The* WOMAN *carries an overnight grip and a dog. Not seeing the* MAN, *she puts the grip on him. He throws it off. They look at each other indignantly.*]

MAN: [*Aggressively*] This is the smoking car, lady.
[*She looks at him indignantly.*
He lights a cigar.
She sniffs the smoke, then throws his cigar out the window.
He looks at her. Throws her dog out the window.
She looks at him and throws away his hat.
He looks at her and throws her hat off.
He has his feet crossed at this time and is just rocking his knee.
She looks down at his shoe. Takes his shoe off and throws it out the window.
He looks at her and throws her shoe away.
She runs to him, pulls his coat off and throws it away.
He looks at her and pulls the skirt off her.
They fight and wrestle on the floor.

171

CONDUCTOR *enters and notices them on the floor.*
They continue to wrestle.]
CONDUCTOR: Hey, this is the *smoking* car!

BLACKOUT

FRANKLIN D. ROOSEVELT TO BE INAUGURATED TOMORROW

by Moss Hart

First produced in *As Thousands Cheer,* at the Music Box Theatre, on September 30, 1933, with the following cast:

MR. HOOVER Leslie Adams
MRS. HOOVER Helen Broderick
FRANK Hamtree Harrington

SCENE: *A room in the White House. It is littered with suitcases and boxes.*

MR. HOOVER: [*Offstage*] Lou! Oh Lou! Where do you want this, Lou?

MRS. HOOVER: [*Entering*] Bring it in here, Herbie.

MR. HOOVER: [*Entering with pedestal*] What do you want to lug that thing along for, Lou? It'll cost more than it's worth to ship it to California.

MRS. HOOVER: Never mind! I'm not going to leave anything for those Roosevelts, I can tell you that. Did you bring that electric toaster up from the kitchen, Herbie?

MR. HOOVER: No!

MRS. HOOVER: Well, go down and get it. I'd like to see myself leaving 'em a perfectly good electric toaster. Like fun.

MR. HOOVER: All right.

MRS. HOOVER: Oh, Herbie. Better take your fruit salts while you're downstairs, Herbie. You know what a long train ride does to you.

MR. HOOVER: All right.

FRANK: [*Entering, carrying a wrapped item*] In here, Mrs. Hoover?

MRS. HOOVER: Yes, Frank. Thank you.

MR. HOOVER: What's that? What's that piece of wire?

MRS. HOOVER: That's the aerial.

MR. HOOVER: Now for goodness sake, you're not going to take the aerial. Now, Lou, you go put that back.

MRS. HOOVER: Put it back? I nearly broke my neck taking it down. Thank you, Frank.

175

[FRANK *exits*.]

MR. HOOVER: What's that?

MRS. HOOVER: This is nothing, Herbie—nothing at all. Just a little souvenir for my room at home.

MR. HOOVER: Let me see it.

MRS. HOOVER: But it's nothing, Herbie.

MR. HOOVER: Then let me see it. [*He uncovers the package—it is a painting.*] Now, Lou, you go right down and put that back. You can't take that. It's very valuable. It's Government property. You want to be stopped at the train?

MRS. HOOVER: Herbie, they'll never miss it. This house is lousy with pictures of George Washington.

MR. HOOVER: I don't care. You go put that back. Why those democrats are liable to pick on a thing like that and cause a whole Senate investigation.

MRS. HOOVER: All right, I'll put it back. We'll just go back to Palo Alto with nothing at all to show for your having been President of the United States.

MR. HOOVER: Nobody else in the country has got anything to show for it either.

MRS. HOOVER: That's right. Wise cracking is going to help us a lot.

MR. HOOVER: Now, Lou, things might have been a lot worse. Suppose I'd been re-elected.

MRS. HOOVER: You know what Palo Alto is. It's going to be very nice, isn't it, for me to go to bridge parties and luncheons and have all my old girl friends saying, "Herbie get anything to do yet, Lou? Well, don't worry. Something'll turn up sooner or later." I can just hear 'em.

MR. HOOVER: I've still got my Civil Engineer's license, don't forget that.

MRS. HOOVER: Oh, sure! Now you remember it, after fiddling away a whole four years. I hate to say I told you so, Herbie—but you can't say I didn't warn you.

MR. HOOVER: But it seemed like such a good idea at the time—being President.

MRS. HOOVER: Not to me it didn't. We were doing so well too. Everything was going along beautiful for us. Then you had to go and become President. Herbie, there's a streak in you that makes you do the most simple-minded things sometimes. Had to become President. Couldn't leave well enough alone.

MR. HOOVER: Well all I can say is, when as smart a man as Ogden Mills comes to you and says that—

MRS. HOOVER: Ogden Mills! Don't talk to *me* about Ogden Mills! If Ogden Mills was so smart he'd have a job now instead of sitting around writing letters to the *Times* and signing himself "Friend of the American Indian."

MR. HOOVER: Well he is.

MRS. HOOVER: When you came home that night and told me the Republican Party wanted you, I told you what to tell 'em, didn't I?

MR. HOOVER: Oh, Lou, I couldn't tell 'em that.

MRS. HOOVER: And all those other Palo Alto boys have done so well for themselves—every one of them. They were all crazy about me too. You know the chances I had. Why even Eddie Harris—I laughed at him when he proposed—he owns the largest knit-goods factory in southern California now.

MR. HOOVER: He wouldn't have made any better President than I did.

MRS. HOOVER: I didn't say he would. All I say is, here we are going back to Palo Alto after all these years and what have we got to show for it? A medicine ball; a couple of dozen silver spoons. Yes, I took the spoons and I'd like to see the Army and the Navy make me put 'em back. A couple of dozen silver spoons and some campaign posters you can't hang up anyway. That's what we've got.

MR. HOOVER: Why can't you hang 'em up?

MRS. HOOVER: Do you want to look at Charlie Curtis?

MR. HOOVER: No.

MRS. HOOVER: That reminds me. [*Into telephone*] Get me Dolly Gann, please.

MR. HOOVER: What are you going to do?

MRS. HOOVER: This is something I've wanted to do for a long time. [*Into phone*] Hello, Dolly? This is Lou Hoover. For four years, Dolly, you've been upsetting my dinner parties and getting in everybody's hair. How would you like to take a running jump in the lake? [*Hangs up*] I may call up Andrew Mellon and Henry

Stimson later. I may go through the whole gang of 'em.
If you were half a man you'd call up Mellon and Stimson yourself and tell 'em what you think of them. God
knows, you've bellyached to me long enough about
'em.

MR. HOOVER: Oh, Lou, I couldn't do that.

MRS. HOOVER: What have you got to lose? You're never
coming back here.

MR. HOOVER: For two cents I'd do it.

MRS. HOOVER: I dare you. I doubly dare you.

MR. HOOVER: I will. [*Into phone*] Get me Mr. Mellon. [*To
LOU*] Oh boy, oh boy, oh boy.

MRS. HOOVER: Give it to him good.

MR. HOOVER: [*Into phone*] Hello. I want to talk to Mr.
Andrew Mellon. Mr. Hoover calling. Hoover. *Hoover!*
"H" as in Harry, "O" as in oboe. Yes—Hoover.

MRS. HOOVER: By the time we get to the coast we'll be
lucky if the servants and the dogs know us.

MR. HOOVER: Hello, Andy? This is Herbie. Greatest Secretary of the Treasury since Alexander Hamilton, eh?
Well, how would you like to meet me in Macy's window?

MRS. HOOVER: [*Grabbing phone*] And bring Ogden Mills
along.

MR. HOOVER: [*Into phone*] Ambassador to the Court of
St. James, eh? You know what you looked like in those
knee-breeches? Like an old ostrich!

MRS. HOOVER: [*Into phone*] Yeah—you old ostrich!

MR. HOOVER: Go back to Pittsburgh and wipe the soup
off your moustache!

[*Hangs up*]

MRS. HOOVER: Doesn't that make you feel good?

MR. HOOVER: Like a new man. What time do they dis-
connect the telephone, Lou?

MRS. HOOVER: In about half an hour.

MR. HOOVER: We gotta work fast. Who's next?

MRS. HOOVER: Henry Stimson.

MR. HOOVER: We'll both call him.

MRS. HOOVER: All right. I've got a few words I want to
say to his wife. [*Into phone*] Get me Henry Stimson,
please. Herbie—

[*Whispers to him*]

MR. HOOVER: You're an angel, Lou.

MRS. HOOVER: [*Into phone*] Hello, Henry? This is Mr.
and Mrs. Herbert Hoover. Is Mrs. Stimson there? No,
don't you go away. Put Mrs. Stimson on the extension.
We want to talk to both of you. Are you on, Mrs. Stimson? Just a moment. Are you there, Henry? That's fine.
[*To* MR. HOOVER] One, two, three.
[*The* HOOVERS *give a bronx cheer into the phone and
hang up.*]

MR. HOOVER: [*Singing*] Tony's wife, the boys are all wild
about you, Tony's wife—

MRS. HOOVER: [*Singing*] Fit as a fiddle and ready for love.
[*They both toss the medicine ball.*] Herbie!

MR. HOOVER: Yes, Lou?

MRS. HOOVER: The Roosevelts?
[*They both dash for the phone.*]

BLACKOUT

WORLD'S WEALTHIEST MAN CELEBRATES NINETY-FOURTH BIRTHDAY

by Moss Hart

First produced in *As Thousands Cheer*, at the Music Box Theatre, on September 30, 1933, with the following cast:

JOHN D. ROCKEFELLER, SR. Clifton Webb
JOHN D. ROCKEFELLER, JR. Leslie Adams
MRS. JOHN D. ROCKEFELLER, JR. Helen Broderick
JOHN D. ROCKEFELLER JR.'S CHILDREN Peggy Cornell, Jerome Cowan, Harold Murray, Thomas Hamilton
REPORTER and CAMERA MAN Hal Forde, Ward Tallmon

SCENE: *A room in the Rockefeller mansion. It is festively decorated.*

MRS. JOHN D. JR.: Now children, you'd better go into the dining room until we're ready for you. Your father and I have something to talk over with Grandpa. [*The children murmur a "Yes, Mother" and move toward the large double doors at the back.*] You sure you know what to do? When you hear your father shout "Surprise!" you all come in with the cake singing: "Happy Birthday, dear Grandpa, Happy Birthday to you!"
[*Another "Yes, Mother" from the children*]

JOHN D. JR.: Not until you hear me shout "Surprise!"

CHILDREN: Yes, Father, we understand.
[*They exit.*]

MRS. JOHN D. JR.: [*Prompting them as they exit*] "Happy Birthday to you . . ."

REPORTER: [*Offstage*] May we have just one more picture, Mr. Rockefeller? Turn your face a little more to the left. Thank you very much.

MRS. JOHN D. JR.: Now, John, you've *got* to tell him, so you might as well make up your mind and get it over with.

JOHN D. JR.: I know, my dear—but it isn't going to be easy.

MRS. JOHN D. JR.: Well, it's no use crying now. I don't know what you wanted to build the thing in the first place for.

REPORTER: [*Offstage*] Thank you, Mr. Rockefeller. Thank you very much.

183

JOHN D.: [*Entering*] That, gentlemen, is my recipe for a hearty old age.

A REPORTER: Mr. Rockefeller, have you a birthday message we can give to the public? Some *one* great thing you've learned from life?

JOHN D.: Well, sir, I'm ninety-four years old today, and a man learns a lot by the time he reaches that age. [*The* REPORTERS *laugh appreciatively.*] I think the one great thing I've learned in my life, gentlemen, is to hold on to your money. [*The* REPORTERS *write busily.*] I've been through a lot of depressions in my time and the only thing I've learned is to sit tight. Sit tight and no foolishness. That's all.

THE REPORTERS: Thank you, Mr. Rockefeller.

JOHN D.: Oh, just a minute, boys, Here's a little something for you to remember my birthday with.

[*He plunges his hand into his pocket, brings out a handful of silver and distributes a single piece to each* REPORTER.]

A REPORTER: Why, Mr. Rockefeller—these are nickels!

JOHN D.: Well, it's been a pretty tough year for all of us. [REPORTERS *exit.*] Well, my dears, they took some very nice pictures of me. Very nice pictures indeed.

MRS. JOHN D. JR.: I'm so glad. You always take a good picture, Father.

JOHN D.: It's been a very nice birthday, hasn't it?

MRS. JOHN D. JR.: Lovely. And it isn't over either. The day's young yet. I always say you never can tell *what* a birthday has in store for you until the very end.

JOHN D.: Yes, I always like birthdays. Junior! Don't you think that was a good birthday message I gave them? "Sit tight and hold on to your money."

JOHN D. JR.: Yes. Yes, indeed, Father.

JOHN D.: Pretty nice thing to be able to say on your 94th birthday the family fortune is still intact, eh, Junior? 'Tisn't everybody that can say so.

JOHN D. JR.: Yes. Yes, indeed.

JOHN D.: And the only way to do it is to put your money in the ground. *Oil!* I never held to any of these real estate speculations even when land was cheap. No sir!

MRS. JOHN D. JR.: Oh, I don't know Father—*some* real estate is good.

JOHN D.: *None* of it's any good. None of it. You take my advice. You let the other fellows put up the buildings— [*There is a slight pause during which* MRS. JOHN D. JR. *motions frantically to her husband and whispers huskily:* "Go on! Tell him! Go on!"]

JOHN D.: [*Catching the last of one of her frantic gestures and interpreting it in his own way*] Na! Na! Na! Ah!! Now, children—you haven't been going about and spending a lot of money on a birthday present for me, have you?

JOHN D. JR.: [*Choking*] Why—why—

JOHN D.: Lot of foolishness, I always said. Couple of handkerchiefs and a pair of socks is a good enough present for anybody.

MRS. JOHN D. JR.: [*Forcing the issue*] Oh, but not good enough for *you*, Father. John's got a *real* birthday present for you! Haven't you, John!

JOHN D. JR.: Yes.

JOHN D.: Well, that's very nice now, Junior. What is it?

JOHN D. JR.: Radio City.

JOHN D.: Well, I'm sure I appreciate it, Junior, but you take it back to the store and get your money. I never listen to 'em—and they're always getting out of order, anyway. Wouldn't have one in the house. Wouldn't have one on the premises.

MRS. JOHN D. JR.: [*As* JOHN D. JR. *stands helpless*] But, Father, this isn't a radio—it's *Radio City!*

JOHN D.: Radio City?

JOHN D. JR.: Yes.

JOHN D.: What's that?

JOHN D. JR.: Why—it's a *city*, Father!

JOHN D.: A city? Whose city?

JOHN D. JR.: It's *your* city. All yours! It's my birthday present to you!

[JOHN D. *stares at him unbelievably.*]

MRS. JOHN D. JR.: Tell Father about it, John.

JOHN D. JR.: Oh, it's a wonderful thing, Father! Got the largest theatre in the world in it! 6,500 seats! Wait till you see it!

MRS. JOHN D. JR.: Wait till he takes a peek at that stage, eh, John? With the hydraulic curtain and the rising orchestra! And the ushers in full dress!

JOHN D. JR.: And it's got another awful cute theatre in it too, Father. It's only got 3,000 seats. We call it "Dingbat" up at Radio City.

MRS. JOHN D. JR.: And the office building, John—

JOHN D. JR.: Eighty stories high, Father—and a sunken plaza with gardens and fountains.

MR. & MRS. JOHN D. JR.: Doesn't it sound wonderful?

[A pregnant pause, then]

JOHN D.: Junior, you sell it *right* back to whoever sold it to you! Somebody took you over!

JOHN D. JR.: But—I didn't buy it from anybody. I built it myself.

JOHN D.: You *what?*

MRS. JOHN D. JR.: He built it for *you*, Father—as a birthday present!

JOHN D.: Now—wait a minute. One minute, please. You mean to say this thing is all *built?*

MRS. JOHN D. JR.: Oh, yes. You really can't miss it if you walk past Fiftieth Street and Sixth Avenue. It's a lot of buildings and it says "Radio City." You can't miss it.

JOHN D.: What did it cost?

JOHN D. JR.: Well, we don't know yet, Father—they're still building. At first we figured about 50 million but as we got into it we—

MRS. JOHN D. JR.: They've really been very thrifty. They were going to build an opera house, too—but they just held themselves back!

JOHN D.: How many tenants in that eighty-story building?

JOHN D. JR.: Well, there's just ourselves and the ushers and a man named Arthur Vogel for the time being—

JOHN D.: Those theatres making money?

MRS. JOHN D. JR.: Well, you see, Father, it's kind of an out of the way place—Fiftieth Street and Sixth Avenue. And we've just had the Jewish holidays, too.

JOHN D.: Junior—that's no birthday present! That's a dirty trick!

JOHN D. JR.: Why, Father!

JOHN D.: Don't "Why, Father!" me. Giving me this Radio City for a birthday present! Why didn't you buy me Muscle Shoals, too? Eighty-story building—6,500 seats—how could you *do* such a thing! Answer me that!

How could you ever get into such a thing in the first place? [JOHN D. JR. *stands helpless.*] Poppycock!

MRS. JOHN D. JR.: Go ahead and tell him, John. Tell him the truth! It really wasn't his fault at all. He didn't know *what* they were building until the first theatre was all done, did you?

JOHN D. JR.: I thought it was something for the Red Cross for a whole year.

MRS. JOHN D. JR.: Go ahead and tell him the whole thing, John.

[*A pause*]

JOHN D.: 6,500 seats! Well?

JOHN D. JR.: Well, about two years ago it was raining. I was sitting in my office. Sometimes I think if it hadn't been raining that afternoon the whole thing wouldn't have happened. I was just about leave when my secretary said Roxy wanted to see me.

JOHN D.: What's that?

JOHN D. JR.: Well, it's—well, he's rather hard to explain, Father.

MRS. JOHN D. JR.: He's a man who goes around building big theatres for people.

JOHN D.: Ought to be put away, a man like that.

MRS. JOHN D. JR.: Oh, he isn't dangerous. Once he sees the cement being mixed he's as gentle as a child.

JOHN D. JR.: Anyway, he came in and said, "Wouldn't it be wonderful if New York City had the largest theatre in the world?" I said, "Yes, it certainly would"—and he went away. Just like that it happened. I didn't think much about it at the time—never even mentioned it at home that night, did I?

MRS. JOHN D. JR.: First thing *I* knew about Radio City was when John kept coming home with mud on his shoes.

JOHN D. JR.: Well, Father, the next thing I knew there I was standing in a big excavation on Fiftieth Street and Sixth Avenue. After that, the only thing left to do was to paint the elevated station aluminum.

MRS. JOHN D. JR.: He even tried to turn it over to the government for a war memorial, but they never even answered his letter.

JOHN D. JR.: That was when I got the idea of giving it to you as a birthday present, Father.

[*Utter silence.* JOHN D. *is trying to speak but seems to be having some difficulty in making sounds issue. When he does speak, his voice is pretty terrifying.*]

JOHN D.: But the buildings—letting the buildings go up—you must have known about that, didn't you?

JOHN D. JR.: Well, yes, Father, I did.

JOHN D.: Oh, you did, you did well. Why didn't you tell me about this months ago—months ago?

JOHN D. JR.: [*Tearfully*] I wanted it to be a surprise, Father—a surprise!

[*At the word "surprise," the double doors at the back are flung open and the* CHILDREN *appear bearing a huge birthday cake on the top of which is an enormous replica of Radio City—all lit up. They come blithely into the room singing:*

"*Happy Birthday to you,
Happy Birthday to you,
Happy Birthday, dear Grandpa,
Happy Birthday to you!*"

One of the children gives cake knife to JOHN D. *who rises and crosses towards* JOHN D. JR. *who flees in terror.*]

BLACKOUT

A DAY AT THE BROKERS'

by David Freedman

First produced in *Life Begins at 8:40,* at the Winter Garden Theatre, on August 27, 1934, with the following cast:

THE BROKER Brian Donlevy
BILL LEONARD Bert Lahr

SCENE: *A stockbroker's office.*

CLERK: A gentleman to see you.

BROKER: [*Yawning at ticker*] Send him in.

CLERK: This way, sir.

BROKER: [*Greeting customer*] Well, Bill, I see you got my message. Come on in. Come on in.

BILL: [*Hesitating*] I'm in far enough.

BROKER: Now listen, Bill. Wall Street is different now. We've had bull markets and bear markets.

BILL: But this is a skunk market. No one wants to get near it. I'm a very happy fellow. I'm working and I just played eighteen holes of golf.

BROKER: Doctor's orders, I suppose.

BILL: No, I love golf. It keeps me in shape and I feel swell.

BROKER: Well, I guess the sunburn covers it up.

BILL: Certainly—covers what up?

BROKER: Well you look kind of tired to me.

BILL: Tired? What do you mean? Say, playing five shows a day in these picture houses ain't no cinch.

BROKER: Wait a minute, your left eyelid just quivered.

BILL: Is it warm in here?

BROKER: No, it's cool. You probably have a fever.

BILL: It's a funny thing. You know, I feel hot all over. Is there a rash coming out or something?

BROKER: Why don't you sit down and rest. [*Pushes* BILL *into chair*] Do you want an aspirin?

BILL: I feel awful. Now that you mention it, I have a terrific headache.

191

BROKER: You're run down. One of these days you'll collapse on the eighth hole.

BILL: It's a funny thing. I was putting the other day and I got a terrific stitch right here.

[*Points to right side*]

BROKER: That's your heart.

BILL: Huh?

BROKER: Sure, that's a reflex pain.

BILL: I better see a doctor.

[*Gets up to go*]

BROKER: [*Makes him sit down*] Wait . . . don't waste your money on doctors. What you need is a rest. Now with a little wise investment, you can get yourself a nest egg and retire.

BILL: That sounds great, but all I got is five thousand dollars. What could I do with that?

BROKER: You just make out your check and I'll show you.

[*Hands him book and pen*]

BILL: [*Making out check*] Maybe this is my lucky day. That retiring business sounds good. I can play all the golf I want. Maybe I'll take up lacrosse.

BROKER: Sure—

[*Takes check and sits down*]

BILL: What should I buy?

BROKER: Don't breathe this to a soul. [*Confidentially*] Silver Mine. Silver Mine.

BILL: That's the real stuff. The inside.

BROKER: The best.

BILL: Okay, buy me a hundred shares of Silver Mine.

BROKER: [*Phoning*] Hello, pick me up a hundred shares of Silver Mine at the market, for the account of Bill Leonard.

BILL: You don't mind if I sit here and watch my nest egg hatch?

BROKER: No, go right ahead . . . [*Phone rings*] Yes—that's fine. [*Hangs up*] Bill, you got it at a great price . . . 29.

BILL: Okay—now I don't want to be greedy, but sell when it gets to 60.

BROKER: You'll get plenty of action with that stock.

[*Ticker starts.*]

BILL: Gee, there goes that ticker. [*Reads*] 110 . . . 112 . . . sell! Sell!

BROKER: [*Runs excitedly to ticker*] Wait a minute—that's A.T.&T.

BILL: Never mind about A.T.&T. What's Silver Mine?

BROKER: Great news, Bill. Congress passes a new bill to devaluate the dollar.

BILL: Gee, that ought to be great for Silver Mine.

BROKER: Sure.

BILL: What is it now?

BROKER: 28.

BILL: What happened?

BROKER: They always sell off on good news.

BILL: Yeah—

BROKER: Sure—it's 27 now.

BILL: I'm here two minutes, and I'm out two hundred bucks.

BROKER: Oh, boy, more good news.

BILL: I'll be ruined. What is it now?

BROKER: 25.

BILL: You better sell before the next good news.

BROKER: All you can get now is 24.

BILL: 24.

BROKER: 23.

BILL: 23.

BROKER: 21.

BILL: What happened to 22?

BROKER: Wait a minute, Bill, all you can get now is 20. Why don't you buy another hundred shares at 20 and even out?

BILL: I won't pay 20. I won't pay 20.

BROKER: It's up to 21.

BILL: Oh, am I sorry.

BROKER: It's down to 20 again.

BILL: Oh—am I glad . . . but I won't buy it.

BROKER: It jumped to 22.

BILL: Oh—am I sorry.

BROKER: It's back to 21.

BILL: Oh—am I glad.

BROKER: 22.

BILL: Am I sorry.

BROKER: 21.

BILL: Am I glad.

BROKER: 23.

BILL: Am I sorry.

BROKER: The market broke. It's down to 19.

BILL: Am I glad. [*Suddenly realizing*] 19, and I got it at 29. I'm out a thousand dollars. Can I have another aspirin?

BROKER: [*Still reading ticker*] Sure—[BILL *goes to desk and takes aspirin.*] Wait a minute, Bill. There's a drought in the middle west. Thousands of acres of wheat are burning up for lack of rain.

BILL: Oh—that's my finish. It'll go down to nothing. What is it now?

BROKER: It jumped to 22.

BILL: 22, that's great. It was just 19. Why did it go up?

BROKER: On account of the drought. All the farmers will be ruined.

BILL: Oh—those poor farmers! Ha—ha—ha!

BROKER: Look—another hundred shares of Silver Mine just sold at 23. Another hundred shares at 23½.

BILL: Oh boy—the boom is starting.

BROKER: The drought is spreading.

BILL: You mean there'll be no more wheat? The cattle are dying—the homes are burning?

BROKER: Sure—

BILL: Gee—that's wonderful—if that drought spreads over the whole country, I'll be even in no time. What is it now?

BROKER: 19.

BILL: Why did it go down?

BROKER: On account of the drought.

BILL: I thought you told me the drought was good.

BROKER: I know, but the drought spread so far all the wheat got burned. Now the farmers won't have any money. It's down to 16.

BILL: Down to 16. What am I losing now?

BROKER: Only thirteen hundred dollars.

BILL: Only thirteen hundred dollars.

BROKER: I just thought of a maneuver. Why don't you sell it and buy it back cheaper. It'll go down to 5.

BILL: It'll go down to 5. Alright, maneuver. Sell it, and when it goes down to 5 buy me two hundred shares. Will you maneuver?

BROKER: Okay— [*Phoning*] Sell a hundred shares of Silver Mine at the market . . . No, sell it—sell it.

BILL: Do you mind if I take off my coat?
[*Puts coat on back of chair*]

BROKER: No, go ahead. [*Answers phone*] Well, Bill, you sold your hundred shares at 16.

BILL: Thank heavens I'm out of it. I never want to hear of that stock again as long as I live. What is it now?

BROKER: 19.

BILL: [*Gets up from chair*] Why did it go up?

BROKER: Why, the government just promised the farmers relief.

BILL: [*Shouting*] What's the government butting in for? Gee, I ought to buy it back.

BROKER: There you go—there you go. That's how you lose your money. Wait—study opinions first. [*Reaches for pamphlet*] Here, listen to the advice of Professor Babson Fisher. [*Reads*] "Expert opinion leans towards the upside, providing of course, the market does not get out of hand and lean towards the downside."

BILL: Upside—downside. There's one side they left out and that's where I'm getting it.

BROKER: [*Starts to read again*] "Here are—"

BILL: Never mind. Never mind. What's Silver Mine? What's Silver Mine?

BROKER: [*Goes to ticker*] 22.

BILL: Take your time—study opinions. It went up six points and I haven't got it.

BROKER: Well, you wanted to sell, didn't you?

BILL: [*Screams*] Who wanted to sell it? You told me I could buy it back at 5.

BROKER: You'll never see it at 5 now. They just decided to print new money with silver as a basis. It's 25.

BILL: I demand you buy it back.

BROKER: 26.

BILL: Get it.

BROKER: 27.

BILL: Get it—get it—get it—get it—get it—get it—

BROKER: Okay. [*Phoning*] Get me another hundred shares of Silver Mine and call me back.

BILL: Have you got another aspirin? I got a terrific congestion up here.

[*Points to head*]

BROKER: Bill, I'll bet it's the strain from that acting.

BILL: Oh, my heavens. I'll be late for the matinee. [BROKER *holds him to chair.*] They'll dock my salary.

BROKER: Oh, forget that salary. I'll show you how to make a hundred and fifty thousand dollars, with only two dollars and a half.

BILL: Are you kidding?

BROKER: No—here—I'll sell you a ticket on the Irish Sweepstakes.

BILL: You sell lottery tickets too?

BROKER: Oh—it's just a hobby.

BILL: Okay—you know, my janitor won one of these once.

BROKER: [*Answering phone*] Hello—okay. Well, Bill, you got your hundred shares of Silver Mine at 29.

BILL: That's the second time I got it at 29.

BROKER: Don't you worry. Wait until that stock starts moving.

BILL: Yeah—what is it now?

BROKER: 27½.

BILL: Just a temporary reaction.

BROKER: Sure—the market strengthens its technical position that way. It's down to 24.

BILL: 24? Boy is that market strong. Strong, but it's muscle-bound. It's a fish market.

BROKER: Why, that's marvelous. 24 is its resistance level. It'll never break through 24. Here, read this opinion from our own statistician.

[*Hands him pamphlet*]

BILL: [*Reads*] "In 1896 Silver Mine stayed around 24 until 1902. Then in 1910, only eight years later, it jumped to 24½." Say, that's a pretty good resistance point at that. Wait a minute, I want to maneuver—buy me another hundred shares at 24.

BROKER: 25.

BILL: Get it.

BROKER: 25½.

BILL: Get it.

BROKER: 26. [*Goes to phone*] Hello—

BILL: If it goes to 29 I'll be making three points. [BROKER *nods*] Get it—get it—get it—get it.

BROKER: [*Still phoning*] Get me another hundred shares of Silver Mine at the market and call me back.

BILL: Boy, that's maneuvering—

BROKER: Yeah, you're becoming quite a trader. Say, Bill, while we're waiting for the answer from the floor—how would you like to put a fiver on Black Crow?

BILL: What is that, a stock?

BROKER: No, no, that's a horse.

BILL: Oh—you're a bookie, too . . . say, do you buy up old tin foil?

BROKER: Well, stocks are all right for a long pull, but with a horse you get a quicker turnover. Now Black Crow is a six to one shot. He's bound to come in.

BILL: Well, whom am I to doubt you? Alright, put this on the nose. Can you imagine if all three come in—Silver Mine— [*Eats aspirin*] Sweepstakes—and Black Crow. [*Eats aspirin*] Boy, these aspirins are good.

BROKER: [*Answering phone*] Hello—okay. [*Gets up*] Put it there, Bill. [*Takes* BILL's *hand and walks him downstage*] You certainly put it over that time. You got your hundred shares of Silver Mine at a great price —29.

BILL: [*Goes out of his mind*] 29—29—29—29—29—29— 29—29— [*After* BROKER *calms him*] Why do I always get it at 29? What's the high for all time?

BROKER: 29.

BROKER and BILL: But it will go higher.

BROKER: [*Goes to ticker*] Oh boy, big news. Secretary Morganthau declares embargo on silver. Fifty percent tax on all those who have it.

BILL: Is that good?

BROKER: That's bad.

BILL: Well, what is it now? Don't tell me.

BROKER: A thousand shares just sold at 27. Another two thousand at 24. Boy, this is the biggest bear raid since 1929. The bottom is dropping out of everything. Can you imagine what they'll do to Silver Mine—oh boy! Ha—ha.

BILL: Ha—ha—ha—ha. Some fun, eh, kid?

BROKER: Silver Mine is down to 16. It's dropping four points at a time. It's down to 12. It's down to 8. [BILL,

all this time, is going crazy.] It's down to 5. Now we'll
put—

[*He grabs* BILL *and tries to brace him up.*]

BILL: Pencils—pencils—pencils—apples—and spear-
mint.

BROKER: What's the matter, Bill. What's the matter?

BILL: I'm all wiped out.

BROKER: You mean, you haven't any more money?

BILL: All I got left is a nickel car-fare home.

BROKER: What? You still have a nickel? [*Reaches to desk
and gets punchboard*] Here, take a chance on this
punchcard. With a nickel chance you're liable to win
a ten dollar gold piece. It may be the start of a new
fortune.

BILL: My last nickel.

BROKER: That's alright. You've got a fifty-fifty chance. All
the even numbers win. [BILL *reluctantly drops nickel
in* BROKER'S *hand, takes a stub from board and slowly
looks at number, then groans.*] What's the matter?

BILL: TWENTY-NINE!

BLACKOUT

CHIN UP

by Alan Baxter

First produced in *Life Begins at 8:40,* at the Winter Garden Theatre, on August 27, 1934, with the following cast:

RICHARD Bert Lahr
THE BUTLER Charles Fowler
THE FATHER James MacColl
AGATHA Luella Gear
THE MOTHER Winifred Harris

The title of this sketch during the show's tryout run was "Today We Die."

SCENE: *A drawing room. Well furnished. At rise,* BUTLER *enters, places card on table, and exits.*

RICHARD: [*Puts down newspaper, reads card*] Dinner with the Duchess. Six o'clock. [*Puts down card, looks at watch*] Must dress. [*There is a knock at the door.*] Come. [PATER *enters.*] Hello, Pater.
PATER: Hello, my boy.
  [*A moment of silence*]
RICHARD: Not well?
PATER: Not well.
RICHARD: What is it?
PATER: Gambling debt.
RICHARD: Gambling debt?
PATER: Can't pay it. Broke.
RICHARD: Borrow?
PATER: Can't borrow. No credit.
RICHARD: Well?
PATER: One thing to do.
RICHARD: Poison.
PATER: Right. Honor of family.
RICHARD: Other way out?
PATER: Not sporting.
RICHARD: Right. Stout fellow.
PATER: Have you a bit here?
RICHARD: Poison?
PATER: Right.
  [BUTLER *enters—glass on tray.*]
RICHARD: Here you are.

PATER: Thanks. [BUTLER *exits*—PATER *raises glass*.] Give you the Duchess.

RICHARD: How jolly. [PATER *drinks poison*.] Does it hurt?

PATER: Rather.

RICHARD: Well, chin up.

PATER: Chin up.

RICHARD: Stiff upper lip.

PATER: Stiff upper lip.

RICHARD: Honor of family.

PATER: Honor of family. [*Falls to chair*] Cheerio, my boy.

RICHARD: Cheerio, Pater. [*Glances at watch*] Must dress. [*Starts to walk left—knock at door*] Come. [AGATHA *enters*.] Hello, Agatha.

AGATHA: Hello, Dick.

RICHARD: Chin up, Agatha, the Pater.

AGATHA: Passed out?

RICHARD: Passed *away*. Gambling debt.

AGATHA: Too bad.

RICHARD: Right.

[*Starts to go left*]

AGATHA: Dick.

RICHARD: Yes, Agatha?

AGATHA: Our wedding anniversary.

RICHARD: Right.

AGATHA: Something to tell you.

RICHARD: Right.

AGATHA: Other man.

RICHARD: [*Walks over to her*] You?

AGATHA: Right.

RICHARD: Not faithful?

AGATHA: Not faithful.

RICHARD: Rotten business.

AGATHA: Putrid.

RICHARD: One thing to do.

AGATHA: Poison?

[BUTLER *enters*.]

RICHARD: Right.

AGATHA: Got any?

[BUTLER *is at her elbow, poison on tray*.]

RICHARD: Here you are.

AGATHA: Thanks. [*Takes glass*—BUTLER *exits—raises glass*] To the Duchess.

[*Drinks*]

RICHARD: How jolly. Does it hurt?

AGATHA: Rather.

RICHARD: Too bad ... well, chin up.

AGATHA: Chin up.

RICHARD: Stiff upper lip. Honor of family.

AGATHA: Honor of family. Cheerio, Dick.
  [*She falls to floor.*]

RICHARD: Cheerio, Agatha. [*Looks at watch*] Must dress.
  [*Starts to walk left. Knock on door*] Come.
  [MATER *enters.*]

MATER: Richard, my boy.

RICHARD: Mater—

MATER: Yes?

RICHARD: The Pater. Dead.

MATER: Right—and Agatha?

RICHARD: And Agatha.

MATER: Beastly.

RICHARD: Right.

MATER: Chin up.

RICHARD: Chin up. Stiff upper lip.

MATER: Right. [RICHARD *starts to leave.*] Richard.

RICHARD: Not well?

MATER: Perfectly well. Something to tell you.

RICHARD: Right. [*Pause*] Difficult?

MATER: Terribly difficult.

RICHARD: Right.

MATER: You—

RICHARD: Yes?

MATER: Not legitimate.

RICHARD: Not legitimate?

MATER: Not legitimate.

RICHARD: Bastard?

MATER: Quite.

RICHARD: [*Reeling*] Chin up.

MATER: Chin up.

RICHARD: [*Blubbering*] Stiff upper lip. Honor of family.

MATER: Honor of family.

RICHARD: [*Stands erect*] And you?
  [BUTLER *enters.*]

MATER: One thing to do.

RICHARD: Right.

MATER: [*Sees* BUTLER *at her elbow*] This it?
RICHARD: Rather.
MATER: Thanks. [*Raises tumbler*] To the—
RICHARD: Duchess.
MATER: Duchess.
　[BUTLER *exits*.]
RICHARD: Jolly. [MATER *drinks poison*.] Does it hurt?
MATER: Hurt.
RICHARD: Badly?
MATER: Terribly.
RICHARD: [*Starts to go*] Cheerio.
MATER: Not yet. [RICHARD *stops and turns*.] Got an engagement?
RICHARD: Right. Dinner with the Duchess.
MATER: Sorry, didn't know.
RICHARD: Quite all right.
MATER: Must be on time. Honor of family. Cheerio, Dick.
　[*Falls dead*]
RICHARD: Cheerio, Mater. [*Glances at watch*] Must dress.
　[*Starts to go, turns when door behind him opens.* BUTLER *enters with tray*.] For me?
BUTLER: Right.
RICHARD: Late for dinner?
BUTLER: Right.
RICHARD: [*Takes tumbler.* BUTLER *exits*.] To the Duchess. [*Drinks—falls to floor—gasps*] Needn't dress.

BLACKOUT

THE DEAD COW

by Alan Baxter and Harold Johnsrud

First produced in *Parade*, at the Guild Theatre, on May 20, 1935, with the following cast:

PAW Charles D. Brown
MAW Eve Arden
JOHNNY Leon Janney
MARY Lois Leng
THE OFFICIAL J. Elliot Leonard

SCENE: *A simple home, unfurnished except for a gnawed plain table and an ungnawed antique whatnot.* FATHER, MOTHER *and the* CHILDREN *are clad only in copies of the N.Y. Journal. One copy of the* Journal *is in the hands of the* FATHER. MOTHER *has wooden knitting needles and is making a dress out of rough twine. On the table is a box of kitchen matches. Otherwise there is absolutely nothing but the three walls, a door and a window. At rise,* MOTHER *is chewing the table top,* FATHER *is reading,* MARY *and* JOHNNY *are standing up center.*

FATHER: [*Jovially*] Hey now, Mother, just you save some of that table top for me. You know I ain't et yet.

MOTHER: You gotta fine right to complain. I'm savin' a whole leg for you, ain't even been touched.

FATHER: Yes, but you know durn well the top's the best part. Them legs is maple. You lived with me long enough to know I'm partial to white pine.

MOTHER: All rightie! There's still a nice piece left around the nail. You know, Henry, sometimes I sorta wish we had somethin' else to eat outside of the papers and this here table. Not that I'm complainin'. You sure are a good provider, Henry. I don't know what we'd do without that there subscription to the *Noo York Journal*. It was a right smart thing to do with yer savin's. With the *Journal* comin' in ev'ry day for three years, we ain't got a thing to worry about. We c'n burn 'em to keep warm, wear 'em for clothes, an' them comics and pitcher sections makes right flavorsome eatin'.

FATHER: Eatin'? Maw, you're gettin' sensual. [*To* JOHNNY,

who has come down and is about to sit on the table]
Johnny, get off my dinner. I guess we're all glad we're
livin' in the good old U.S.A. Fer instance, looka these
here pitchers in the *Noo York Journal*—looka this
one—a Rooshian family. Looka them starvin' Rooshian
kids standin' around by that there dead pig. My gosh,
ain't that terrible?

JOHNNY and MARY: Shure is, Paw.

MOTHER: Yes sir, Henry, it sure is awful. But I can't help
wishin' we had a pig like that.

FATHER: What fer, Maw?

MOTHER: Fer eatin', Henry, fer eatin'.

FATHER: Durned if you ain't right. Ya can eat 'em,
cantcha? I plumb forgot.

MOTHER: They taste right good if they're cooked.

FATHER: Well now, I dunno!! My self, I'm partial to jest
plain white pine. 'Tain't fancy, but it's right solid eatin'.
Say!!!!

JOHNNY and MARY: What, Paw??

FATHER: I almost forgot. Today's the day the Government
Relief Man promised to send us a butchered cow.

MOTHER: Oh, Henry, honest???

FATHER: Sure, I spoke to him last year about this time,
an' he said he'd send one this year on April Fool's Day
and that's today.

MOTHER: Why that's wonderful, Henry! It almost makes
me wish we had that old stove we hocked.

FATHER: What fer, Maw? Yer can't eat that. Come on,
Johnny, get out of my place. You know I always stand
there. Well, this what I call solid comfort. Gosh, these
here are swell pitchers of Rooshia. I wonder how they
got 'em. It must be awful dangerous, takin' pitchers in
Rooshia. Mr. Hearst is sure got a lotta guts to live over
there and be takin' snapshots.

MARY: Paw, I'm cold.

FATHER: Cold! Well, of all the nerve! There y'be, covered
with a perfickly good sports section of the *Journal*, an'
yer whinin' about bein' cold. If it wouldn't break yer
Maw's heart I'd have you deported. Un-American! Un-
American!

[MARY *takes box of matches and is about to light*
FATHER'*s clothes.*]

JOHNNY: Hey, Maw! Looka Mary!!!

MOTHER: [*Pulling* MARY *away from* FATHER] Mary, what on earth are you a'doin' with them matches?

MARY: Well, gee, Maw, I'm cold.

MOTHER: Well, that ain't no reason to set fire to yer Paw.

FATHER: What, settin' fire to me, was she?? That's the last straw. Fetch me that table, Maw. I'm gonna have my dinner. Gimme that match-stick, Mary. That'll make a good dessert. [*Turns and sees* JOHNNY *gnawing on the whatnot*] Hey, Johnny—what in tucket are ya at? Durn ya, how many times I gotta tell ya to stop chewin' on that there whatnot?

JOHNNY: Aw, Paw. It tastes good.

FATHER: I don't care how it tastes. Ya don't want to break yer Maw's heart, do ya? That there whatnot belongs to yer Maw's Grandpaw what fit in the Civil War.

JOHNNY: [*Laughing*] But, Paw. I'm hungry.

FATHER: Well hold yer horses—wait'll that Government Relief Man gets here with that butchered cow. I won't have yer eatin' yer Maw's Grandpaw's whatnot.

MOTHER: [*Rushing in from door*] Henry, the relief man air here. He jes' driv' up in a big truck with a butchered cow—jes' like he said.

FATHER: [*To Kids*] There y'are. What'd I tell ya?

[YOUNG MAN *enters with newspaper camera.*]

YOUNG MAN: All right, men, just bring it in here. [*To family*] How do you do? Gather around, please. For the *New York Journal.*

[FATHER, MOTHER, MARY *and* JOHNNY *gather around a cow which* TWO MEN *have carried in and thrown on the floor. The three men who have just entered are dressed in overcoats, hats and gloves. The* YOUNG MAN *snaps a picture of the family around the dead cow.*]

YOUNG MAN: All right, men. Take it away. [*They do so.*]

FATHER: Wait, mister! I thought you was gonna leave that cow for us to eat.

YOUNG MAN: Oh, did you? We just want a picture of a starving family for the *New York Journal.*

BLACKOUT

HOME OF THE BRAVE

by Frank Gabrielson and David Lesan

First produced in *Parade,* at the Guild Theatre, on May 20, 1935, with the following cast:

THE ANNOUNCER Earl Oxford
MR. JOHN SMITH Charles D. Brown
MRS. JOHN SMITH Eve Arden
JOE Jimmy Savo
THE INSPECTOR Ralph Riggs

[*In front of the curtain—in a Brooklyn accent*] And what's Adolph Hitler done? He's Goimanized Goimany, that's what he's done. He said to his people, "We gotta purify our stock. We gotta be pure Goimans, an' there's only one way we can do it. We gotta retoin to them heroic days of our ancestors, when ev'rybody was heroes! Now!!" What we need in *this* country is an American Hitler—a guy who'll stand up and say, "What we gotta have is America for Americans," a guy who'll make this country retoin to the days when all us Americans was real Americans.

SCENE: *The living room of a New York City apartment of the future. No tables, chairs, etc; but all manner of Indian weapons and paraphernalia. At right is a small teepee, in front of which is a small rug, a wood fire, a book that has been singed, a bowl and pestle and a bow drill. Up center is a rock upon which is a French phone. Down center is another rock against which rests a papoose. Several skins are hung on the walls and up left is a totem pole with the topmost head showing a likeness to Hitler, with hair parted and low on the brow and a small clipped mustache. Up center is a small radio on a tree stump.* JOHN SMITH *is dressed in a business suit with an Indian blanket over it, moccasins and a red headband with a feather in it. His* WIFE *is dressed in an Indian skirt, high moccasins, modern shirtwaist and a headband with a feather. She has long blonde braids, hanging down almost to her waist.* JOE *is dressed in trousers and shoes, red sweater, Indian blanket, derby hat with band*

213

of small bells and a single feather. He has a small tom-
ahawk and a bundle of cigars. The INSPECTOR *and*
SCALPING SQUADRON *are dressed in policemen's uni-*
forms, but moccasins instead of shoes, strings of beads
around their necks, red headbands with a single feather
in each. The INSPECTOR *wears an Indian chief's head-*
dress. At rise, JOHN SMITH *sits on rug before teepee*
grinding corn in a bowl with pestle. The radio is playing
"Sky-blue Water." WIFE *enters with bundle of twigs on*
her back which she drops upstage of the rock.

WIFE: For God's sake, John, stand up! It's the national
anthem. Suppose the neighbors should see you.

SMITH: Then turn the damn thing off. None of it's any
good since they beheaded Amos 'n Andy.

WIFE: [*Turns radio off*] John, why can't you be like other
men? You're the worst brave in the building. You can't
build a birch-bark canoe; you won't ride a pony to
work; we never even have fresh meat.

SMITH: I'd like to see you take that bow and arrow and
hit one of those damn little rabbits.

WIFE: You might try.

SMITH: Yes, and hit a policeman's horse like I did last
Saturday. If I didn't know the Judge, I'd be in a Nordic
concentration camp.

WIFE: And this disloyal passion for foreign foods—
spaghetti, sauerkraut and sardines.

SMITH: Don't speak of them.

WIFE: Thoroughly un-Indian.

SMITH: What are we going to have for dinner?

WIFE: Corn bread.

SMITH: What, again?

WIFE: The maid's out.

SMITH: Where is she?

WIFE: She's having a baby.

SMITH: My God, another?

WIFE: Don't fret, dear. She'll be back tomorrow. You
know how sturdy we native women are.

SMITH: Well, I'm sick of corn bread. You go down to the
corner and get some jerked horse-meat. I'll take care of
the rest of the dinner.

WIFE: I won't go. It's dangerous.

SMITH: Go, squaw!

WIFE: John, I refuse.

SMITH: I have spoken. [*Folds his arms, à la Indian.* WIFE *looks at him—seeing a new person—and goes center.*] Say, there's something in this. Here, take some change. [*Hands* WIFE *a string of beads—wampum—which he pulls from pocket—about eight feet of it.*] It won't be more than a quarter. [WIFE *exits.* SMITH *kneels on rug, puts a long pipe in his mouth and tries to light it with bow drill, without success. Throws drill and pipe down and goes to phone.*] Susquehanna 1492. Hello, Joe? This is John Smith—Teepee 8A in the Wigwam Arms. Listen, Joe. I want six Irish potatoes and I want them quick. And, Joe—none of those Idahoes. I want real Irish potatoes with knobs on them.
[*Hangs up*]

WIFE: [*Reentering*] John, the inspector's downstairs. For God's sake get that French phone out of sight. [*Hides phone back of rock. Picks up book*] Where did this forbidden book come from? "The Courtship of Miles Standish."

SMITH: Oh that. I was poking around in the ashes the day of the last book-burning.

WIFE: John, you're hopeless. Don't you know these books tell nothing but lies? The white man never really overcame the Indians. That's just vicious Pilgrim propaganda.

SMITH: Don't you go maligning the Pilgrims. My ancestors were Pilgrims. Why, the day the Mayflower sailed into—

WIFE: [*Puts her hand over* SMITH'S *mouth*] My God, John, don't boast of it. You promised you'd never tell. You'd better keep quiet or we'll have a pogrom down on our heads.

SMITH: Pogrom be damned! [*There's a terrific scream from offstage.*] My God, what's that?

WIFE: [*Rushes to window—looks—recoils at sight*] It's the Scalping Squadron. It's terrible. They've got the family downstairs.
[*More screams from offstage*]

SMITH: What for?

WIFE: Wait a minute—I'll find out. [*Calls out window*] Yoo-hoo, Mrs. Palemoon, what did they find?

VOICE: [*Offstage*] Irish potatoes.

SMITH: What did she say?

WIFE: Irish potatoes.

SMITH: [*Grabs phone*] Susquehanna 1492. It's life and death. [*Another scream from offstage*] Hello, is that you, Joe? What's that? You say Joe's on his way up *here?* [*Hangs up*] Oh, my God! Oh, Great Spirit! Oh, Great Spirit!!

[*A loud "Whoopee" is heard offstage.*]

WIFE: John, the inspector's coming. I'll get things ready. [*Exits*]

SMITH: [*Kneels in front of totem pole and salutes*] How! How! How!

[JOE *enters with blanket over his head, turning and spinning about, shouting "Whoopee." He comes upstage of* SMITH *and opens blanket.*]

JOE: How!

SMITH: [*Relieved that it's not the* INSPECTOR] Oh, it's you, Joe.

JOE: Here's the package of potatoes. Hurry up and pay me. I got to beat it.

SMITH: Listen, Joe, I've decided I don't want those potatoes.

JOE: I don't neither. Not after what I saw downstairs.

SMITH: What happened?

JOE: A complete sterilization—two men and a boy—just like that. [*Snaps his fingers three times.* SMITH *lights cigarette with lighter.*] And they caught one guy with a cigarette lighter.

SMITH: What did they do to him, Joe?

JOE: They slipped him the poige. He's up to his ears in castor oil.

SMITH: Not for one teeny little cigarette lighter?

JOE: Yeah, it ain't Indian. And have they got it in for them Pilgrims. I'm glad I'm a genuine Indian. Whoopee! [*Dances around*]

SMITH: [*Stopping him*] Joe, I can't take those potatoes.

JOE: What do you mean, you can't take? You ordered them, didn't you?

SMITH: Yes, but please, Joe.

JOE: [*Arms folded*] I have spoken.

[*From outside is heard the war cry and tom-tom.* SMITH *puts potatoes in pocket at back of papoose.* SCALPING SQUADRON *enters, one of them beating a tom-tom; all of them doing the Indian war cry with their hands to their mouths. They take a diagonal line and are followed by the* INSPECTOR. SMITH *and* WIFE *take up kneeling postures in front of totem pole.*]

INSPECTOR: [*Salutes totem*] How!

SMITH and WIFE: [*Salute totem*] How!!

SQUADRON: [*Salute totem*] How!!!

INSPECTOR: [*With Irish brogue*] You Brave Strongheart Smith?

SMITH: Yes, sir! [WIFE *nudges him with elbow.*] Ugh!!

INSPECTOR: Ugh. Your squaw, Grim Dawn?

SMITH and WIFE: Ugh!!

INSPECTOR: [*Seeing* JOE] Who him?

JOE: Me a friend. I just came up to spend Shabbos. [SQUADRON *make threatening gestures with toma- hawks.*] Me Indian!! [*He does war whoop and takes a tomahawk from his belt, bundle of cigars from pocket and poses, à la wooden Indian.*]

INSPECTOR: [*To* SMITH, *indicating papoose*] Your man- child? [*Pats papoose—discovers potatoes—pulls one out*] Irish potatoes!! [*To* SQUADRON] Braves, catchum prisoner! [SMITH *runs up center, but is caught by* SQUADRON *and brought down center.* INSPECTOR *sits on rock and holds up potato.*] Him! Him guilty! Him catchum purge with castor oil.

SMITH: [*Shuddering*] Ugh.

INSPECTOR: Him also catchum sterilization.

WIFE: [*Stamps foot and turns*] Oh!!

[JOE *does war whoop to attract her attention and mo- tions that she can have him.* SMITH *tries to get at* JOE *but is held by* SQUADRON.]

INSPECTOR: Scalpum!!

[SQUADRON *catch hold of* SMITH *and raise tomahawks.*]

SMITH: [*On knees*] Wait, boys, wait!!! Me no Pilgrim—me Injun!!

INSPECTOR: You no Injun. You name Smith.

SMITH: Sure, my name Smith, but me got royal Injun

blood in veins. Great-great-great-grandfather, he Captain John Smith. He hold heap big pow-wow with little Injun girl named Pocahontas. [*Faces front*] Then have plenty damn big affair.

INSPECTOR and MEN: [*All raise their hands in salute to* SMITH—*the* INSPECTOR *standing and the* SQUADRON *kneeling.*] How! How!! How!!!

SMITH: [*Arms folded*] How the hell do you suppose?

BLACKOUT

THE GIGOLO BUSINESS

by Howard Dietz

First produced in *At Home Abroad*, at the Winter Garden Theatre, on September 19, 1935, with the following cast:

OTIS Herb Williams
HENRIETTA Vera Allen
RENE Reginald Gardiner
FLO-FLO Julie Jenner

SCENE: *A hotel room in Nice. There are doors right and left, a sofa right, a chair left, and a phone on a table above the sofa.* HENRIETTA *and a* BELLBOY *are discovered.*

HENRIETTA: [*A cable in her hand*] Just a minute, boy. I want to be sure you get this cable off at once. "To Josephine Wilson, Towers, New York." You see, I promised to send her a cable from every port regardless of the expense. Next week I'll send one from England. I love England. It's so British. I don't suppose you've understood a word I've said. Were you born in Paris?

BELLBOY: I was born in Astoria, Long Island.

[*Exits*]

HENRIETTA: [*Crossing to door*] Can't I ever find a Frenchman—not even in France? [*Phone rings.*] Otis, answer that.

[*She exits as* OTIS *enters in a towel with his face all covered with lather.*]

OTIS: Every night you have to put on the soup and fish, stay up till all hours. For what? I wish we'd get the hell out of Europe. [*Answers phone*] Hullo. Keska? Keska what? Clerque? No, Madame didn't order any garçons. This is Mr. Hatrick's flat. Yes, we're Americans. What's it to you? [*Hangs up*] Europe.

HENRIETTA: [*Entering*] Who was that?

OTIS: Some frog trying to give me some keska-ing. Why don't they learn to talk like people.

HENRIETTA: I wish you'd learn to be more European, Otis. It keeps you young.

221

[*Doorbell rings.*]

OTIS: I don't want to be young.

HENRIETTA: Shhh. Come in. [*Door opens.* RENE *enters.*] Ah, Rene.

RENE: Ah, Madame. Vous êtes très jolie.
[*Crosses to her; kisses her all the way up her arm.* OTIS *circles around them.*]

OTIS: Europe.

HENRIETTA: Rene, vous êtes très charmant.

RENE: It always takes two, Madame.

HENRIETTA: Call me 'enriette.

RENE: I will call you "mon ange."
[*He kisses her other arm.*]

OTIS: Are you looking for something?

HENRIETTA: Otis! [*She crosses to center.*] Otis, this is Rene. He's my escort for the evening. Rene, I want you to meet Mr. Hatrick. He's my husband.

RENE: Your husband.
[*All laugh.*]

OTIS: A distant relative. Pleased to meet you, young man—in a sense.

HENRIETTA: Rene is taking me to dinner at the Negresco.

OTIS: I thought you and I were going out together.

HENRIETTA: Don't be silly, darling. This is the Riviera. Husbands and wives don't go out together. It's passé. It isn't done. Now you two chat for a while. I'll finish dressing.
[*During latter part of this speech, she pats* RENE's *head, he blows a kiss to her, she goes to door at right and exits.*]

OTIS: Europe.

RENE: Won't you sit down, Monsieur.

OTIS: [*Putting on his pants*] No thanks.

RENE: You like Europe, n'est-ce pas?

OTIS: Love it. They ought to give it back to the Indians. [*Sees cigarette case in* RENE's *hand*] That's a nice case you got there.

RENE: It was given to me by Madame Tuttle of New Rochelle. That's in New York.

OTIS: Uptown or downtown? Say, what is your racket?

RENE: Comment?

OTIS: How do you make your living?

RENE: I'm a gigolo.

OTIS: A gigolo?

RENE: What you call a "ladies'-man." I make love for a living.

OTIS: Nice work if you can get it.

RENE: You ought to see some of the women I meet. Big, fat American wives. They come to the Riviera. Rich, fat, grand American wives.

[*They both laugh.* OTIS *stops.*]

OTIS: What the hell are you laughing at?

RENE: Pardon, Monsieur. I was thinking.

OTIS: That's what I thought. Do you make a lot of money?

RENE: That generally depends on the husband. The wife gets it from the husband; sometimes a little, sometimes a lot. Presents, diamond bracelets, diamond rings, tiaras . . .

OTIS: Did anyone ever give you a brassiere? How do you spend your day?

RENE: I get up at five o'clock.

OTIS: In the morning?

RENE: In the afternoon. Then I arrange my toilette.

OTIS: Your toilet? Do you have to arrange that?

RENE: Oui, Monsieur. It takes hours. Then I call for Madame. I take her to dinner. Then we go to the theatre. Maybe we go dancing. Sometimes we go home.

OTIS: I get it. Just what do you do when you get her home?

RENE: Madame usually changes into something comfortable.

OTIS: Do you change into something comfortable too?

RENE: That depends on Madame—on her mood.

OTIS: What about your mood?

RENE: I am always ready. I am like your American Minutemen.

OTIS: That's pretty good time. Now as I understand it, you get her home and you get her into something comfortable. Then what happens?

RENE: [*Rises*] No matter what happens, at six o'clock I quit.

OTIS: You quit?

RENE: Oui, Monsieur. I will not work later. At six o'clock I stop whatever I am doing.

OTIS: Does a whistle blow? I never knew this was a regular business, this gigolo thing.

RENE: Oui, Monsieur. We have a union.

OTIS: Organized labor?

RENE: Skilled labor. It takes skill to handle women of fifty, sixty, seventy, eighty, ninety.

OTIS: Did you ever break a hundred? Do you have gigolettes as well as gigolos?

RENE: Oui, Monsieur. And they have the same union rules. Last year we went on strike.

OTIS: What for?

RENE: A minimum age. Then you sympathize with our, what you call it, racket.

OTIS: Sympathize? I'm going to muscle in on it.
[*Doorbell rings.* OTIS *sings* "Gigolo." FLO-FLO *enters.*]

RENE: Ah, bon soir, Flo-Flo.

FLO-FLO: Bon soir, Rene. [*Crosses to* OTIS] Vous êtes très jolie. Vous êtes très charmant. C'est magnifique. Mon petit bon-bon. Mon petit chou-chou. Je t'adore. [*Sits on his lap*] You are maintenant my daddee, yes-no?

OTIS: Europe. What are you doing here?

RENE: Monsieur, I took the liberty.

OTIS: A happy thought, Rene. I was wondering how to kill the evening.

RENE: I thought the best was to let the evening kill you.
[HENRIETTA *enters.*]

HENRIETTA: All ready now, Rene. What have you two been up to? [*Sees* OTIS *and* FLO-FLO] Otis.

OTIS: Hello, Hattie. [*Tusseling with* FLO-FLO, *trying to get her off his lap*] Just a minute, this is Henrietta, my wife. Just a minute.

HENRIETTA: What are you trying to do?

OTIS: I'm a Minuteman.

HENRIETTA: Well, maybe we'd better go out together.

OTIS: Henrietta, don't be passé. Be modern. You're abroad. I'm abroad. And she's a cute little trick.

RENE: It is very late, Madame.

HENRIETTA: Well, if I'm in the way here. Good night, Otis. Good night, Miss ... I don't even know your name.

OTIS: Oh, I'm sorry. Henrietta, I want you to meet Room
Service.

BLACKOUT

THE AUDIENCE WAITS

by Howard Dietz

First produced in *At Home Abroad,* at the Winter Garden Theatre, on September 19, 1935, with the following cast:

SONIA Beatrice Lillie
BABUSHKA Vera Allen
DOUBLECHEK Reginald Gardiner
PILNIK Eddie Foy, Jr.
OTISIVITCH Herb Williams
KAMEROFF James MacColl

SCENE: *A dressing room of the Imperial Ballet. There is a sofa, a table, a chair, and a door.* SONIA *is discovered doing toe exercises.* BABUSHKA *enters.*

SONIA: Any word yet, Babushka?

BUBUSHKA: No, Madame, I have received no word.

SONIA: But if he does not come what will happen to Polanariskaya? I could not face all those people. I would not have the heart. Oh, Babushka, tell Polanariskaya he will come.

BABUSHKA: He will come, Madame.

SONIA: What would I do without you, Babushka?

BABUSHKA: Frankly, Madame, I do not know. You are my baby, my babishka.

SONIA: Your babishka, Babushka.

BABUSHKA: Your Babushka, babishka.

SONIA: You have always been with me, Babushka. From the time I was two-and-a-half years old when I first entered the Imperial Ballet. I had to walk four miles through the snow to get to rehearsals because I could not afford a droshki. I walked all the way on my toes to make my toes tough. [*She sits.*] I have tough toes, haven't I, Babushka?

BABUSHKA: You have the toughest toes in the whole ballet.

SONIA: You were with me when I danced the mazurka for the Czarevitch Alexis and when I did the "Dying Drake" for the Little Father himself. Then came the revolution, remember? But I could not dance for the mujiks. I could not face the mujik. So what did they do? What did they do? One night they dragged me out

of bed. Out of bed, mind you. And I had to hurry home,
gather my few possessions, and flee. [*She walks.
Pauses*] I trekked from St. Petersburg to Moscow. From
Moscow to Omsk. From Omsk to Pinsk.

BABUSHKA: I know.

SONIA: Just a second. Finally I trekked all the way across
the border where we artists met and again formed the
Imperial Ballet. But I am tired now, Babushka, and I
cannot trek anymore. [*She sits.*] I became a great star,
[*She rises.*] the greatest star that has ever lived. Is that
not right, Babushka?

BABUSHKA: That is not right, babishka.

SONIA: The Czarevitch was gone. The Little Father was
gone. The mujiks were gone. But you were not gone.
Never gone, Babushka. Oh no, not you. [*Indicates the
door*] And now Otisivitch, my lover, has not come yet.
When will he come? When? When?

[DOUBLECHEK *enters.*]

DOUBLECHEK: What a night. Glittering. Gala. Almost regal. And 20,000 francs in the house. Monte Carlo has
turned out en masse. They are hanging on the rafters.
Think of it, Sonia. This will be the greatest night in the
history of the ballet. 20,000 francs. [SONIA *bends over.*]
Like a pink petunia, the flower of the dance. And when
you stand on your toes ... [*She does*] Gut. Gut, they
will cheer. And Anton Doublechek will cheer with
them. [SONIA *crosses to* BABUSHKA.] Come, you are
about to go on to another great Polanariskaya triumph.

SONIA: It is no use, Doublechek, I cannot perform tonight.

DOUBLECHEK: Cannot perform? What in hell's the matter
with you?

SONIA: I am unhappy.

DOUBLECHEK: Unhappy? What has that got to do with it?
There are 20,000 francs in the house.

SONIA: That does not make me happy. I would be unhappy if there were 50,000 francs.

DOUBLECHEK: Supposing there were 100,000 francs.
Would you still be unhappy?

SONIA: I would ... 100,000 francs?

[PILNIK *enters.*]

PILNIK: Ready for the "Dying Drake." Everybody on
stage. [SONIA *pouts.*] Still fits, eh?

[PILNIK *exits as* KAMEROFF *enters.*]

KAMEROFF: Out of my way, Pilnik. What is the meaning of this? I stand waiting with my baton raised for the cue. But there is no cue. I hear in whispers: "Polanariskaya will not go on."

DOUBLECHECK: 20,000 francs.

SONIA: All you care about is money. What about my heart?

DOUBLECHECK: [*Kneels beside her. Takes out gift from his pocket*] Look, Sonia, it is a bauble. I picked it up in Paris. It is for you.

SONIA: [*Taking it*] What do I care about baubles. He has not come yet.

KAMEROFF: Who has not come yet? Who is this "he"?

BABUSHKA: It's Otisivitch.

DOUBLECHECK: [*Rising*] Otisivitch?

SONIA: Otisivitch.

BABUSHKA: She cannot go on until she knows that he loves her. She has to have love.

[PILNIK *enters.*]

PILNIK: Can I be of any help? I give.

DOUBLECHECK: We must find him. Pilnik, run to the Casino. Look everywhere, but get Otisivitch. [PILNIK *exits.*] The ballet must go on. Sonia, darling, the audience waits. [*He and* KAMEROFF *pace.*] 20,000 francs. They are waiting for you. 20,000 francs. How are you? They want to see you dance.

SONIA: I will never dance again.

DOUBLECHECK: You won't dance?

SONIA: Don't ask me.

KAMEROFF: Then I will never play again.

DOUBLECHECK: And I will never produce again.

SONIA: And I will have to trek again.

[PILNIK *enters.*]

PILNIK: I found Otisivitch.

ALL: At last.

PILNIK: [*Announcing from the door*] Otisivitch, her lover. [OTISIVITCH *enters.* PILNIK *exits.*]

OTISIVITCH: I am a Minuteman. Tell the taxi to wait.

DOUBLECHECK: Hurry up. Make love. Save the Imperial Ballet.

OTISIVITCH: [*Crossing to* SONIA] What is wrong, my little tough toes?

SONIA: Where have you been? I have waited.

[SONIA *and* OTISIVITCH *assume three ludicrous and grotesque lovemaking poses.*]

DOUBLECHEK: I cannot stand it any longer. I will send on the understudy.

SONIA: [*Rises*] The understudy? There is no understudy for Polanariskaya. I will go on.

ALL: The Imperial Ballet is saved!

[BABUSHKA, DOUBLECHEK *and* KAMEROFF *exit.*]

SONIA: [*Getting her cape, goes to the door*] I'm sorry, Otie, but my art, you know. What can I do for you while I am gone?

OTISIVITCH: [*On the sofa*] Send in the understudy.

BLACKOUT

SWEEPSTAKES TICKET

by David Freedman

First produced in the *Ziegfeld Follies of 1936*, at the Winter Garden Theatre, on January 30, 1936, with the following cast:

NORMA SHAEFFER Fannie Brice*
MESSENGER BOY Duke McHale
MONTY SHAEFFER Hugh O'Connell
MR. MARTIN John Hoysradt

"Sweepstakes Ticket" was used in the MGM film *Ziegfeld Follies of 1946*. It was performed by Fannie Brice, in her original role; the HUSBAND was played by Hume Cronyn and MR. MARTIN was played by William Frawley.

*In the playbills for the shows in which she appeared, Miss Brice's name was spelled either "Fannie" or "Fanny"—often both spellings appeared in the same program. For the sake of consistency, I have opted for the spelling used more frequently.

SCENE: *A small apartment uptown. At rise,* NORMA *is on the telephone.*

NORMA: Hello, operator? I want a number. What? No outgoing calls? I mailed you a check yesterday. You'll positively receive it by tomorrow. You'll leave the phone open? Thank you. Now please get the number. Who is this, the butcher? This is Mrs. Schaeffer. I got to have two pound lamb chops right away for dinner. No meat? I mailed you a check yesterday. You'll positively receive it by tomorrow. Oh, I'll get the lamb chops tomorrow. [*She hangs the phone up then crosses and gets tureen. The doorbell rings. She picks up the phone.*] I mailed you a check . . . Oh, it's the door. Come in.

[*A* MESSENGER BOY *enters.*]

MESSENGER BOY: Mrs. Schaeffer?

NORMA: Yes.

MESSENGER BOY: A cablegram.

NORMA: A cablegram?

MESSENGER BOY: Yeah, from Ireland. I think you won the sweepstakes.

NORMA: [*Reading*] "Congratulations. Your ticket 44678 has been drawn in the Irish Sweepstakes." Heh. [*To the* MESSENGER BOY, *giving him an apple*] Here, I got no change.

MESSENGER BOY: [*As he exits*] Thanks.

NORMA: You're welcome. [*She crosses, still carrying the tureen. She suddenly realizes what she's read, and drops the tureen.*] Oh my God, I won! I won! [*Runs around*] I won! Where's somebody? I won! [*Picks up phone*] Hello, I won! [*Starts to pick up pieces of tureen*] Aw, hell with it. [MONTY *enters*.] Monty, Monty, I love you. [*Embraces him*]

MONTY: [*Pushing her away*] What's the matter? You been untrue to me?

NORMA: You bad boy, we won the sweepstakes.

MONTY: We won the sweepstakes?

NORMA: Yes. All our troubles are over. We're rich! Dance. Do something!

MONTY: I'm not in the mood. A terrible thing has happened.

[*He sits.*]

NORMA: What could be terrible when we won the sweepstakes?

MONTY: I met the landlord in the hall and had to pay the rent—$45.

NORMA: What's that? We'll buy the house. [*Goes to get the silver*]

MONTY: You don't understand. All I had was $42.50 so I made up the other $2.50 by giving the landlord the sweepstakes ticket.

NORMA: So what? [*Drops silver; freezes*] What did you say?

MONTY: I gave the landlord the sweepstakes ticket.

NORMA: Monty, dear, you should drop dead.

MONTY: I'd like to throw myself out of the window.

NORMA: Who stops you?

MONTY: [*Rises*] Something has got to be done. I'll take gas.

NORMA: I'll mail 'em a check. But first we must get back that ticket by hook or crook.

MONTY: But if the landlord knows the ticket won he won't give it back.

NORMA: But if he don't know, we'll get it.

[*Shoves him towards the door*]

MONTY: [*Resisting*] Oh, but that wouldn't be honest.

NORMA: [*Shoving*] Is this a time to be honest? Quick, get him.

MONTY: He's right out in the hall. [*Calls*] Mr. Martin! Oh, Mr. Martin!

[MR. MARTIN *enters. General ad lib to get him in*]

MR. MARTIN: What is it?

NORMA: [*Finally*] Sit down. You look so pretty.
[MR. MARTIN *nods.*]

MONTY: Look, Mr. Martin, remember I don't have the full month's rent so I gave you a ticket?

MR. MARTIN: What do you expect me to do? Give you the ticket back?

MONTY: Mr. Martin, my wife has a superstition about that ticket. If you let us have it back I'll give you the $2.50 tomorrow.

MR. MARTIN: [*Rises*] If that's what you called me in for, I'm going. I've got that ticket right in the wallet of my coat and that's where it stays. Good-bye.

NORMA: [*Shoving him back*] No ... no ... please, Mr. Martin. Sit down, make yourself comfortable. Have a glass of tea.

MR. MARTIN: Don't mind if I do.

NORMA: Make yourself comfortable. Take off your coat. It's so wrinkled, I'll press it for you. [*He takes it off, but puts wallet in his pants.*] Oh, your pants is wrinkled too. You know I could press your whole suit in a jiffy.

MR. MARTIN: [*Showing the ticket*] Nonsense. You know, I just have a funny feeling this ticket might win.

NORMA: Pardon me, I don't feel so good. [*She and* MONTY *go into the kitchen.*]

MONTY: What'll we do?

NORMA: I'll call up my cousin, Hildegarde, maybe she has $2.50.

MONTY: Okay.

NORMA: [*Into phone*] Hello, Cousin Hildegarde?

MONTY: First dial the number.

NORMA: Oy, I'm so excited. Watch him he shouldn't escape. [*She dials wildly.* MONTY *goes into the other room and waves at* MR. MARTIN.] Hello, Hildegarde? This is Norma. I wanted to ask you ... I'm all right, how are you? Which doctor? What sanitarium? You don't say? [MONTY *taps her.*] I had to ask her how she was.

MR. MARTIN: [*Rises*] Well, I'll be going.

NORMA: Wait a minute. Good-bye.

MR. MARTIN: Good-bye.

NORMA: Not you, Mr. Martin. [*Into phone*] Good-bye. [*Hangs up and rushes into the other room*] Don't go. Look, I'm in the middle of pressing your suit. It'll look beautiful. [MR. MARTIN *sits down again. Bell rings.*]

MONTY: Come in.

[MESSENGER BOY *enters.*]

MESSENGER BOY: Cablegram, Mrs. Schaeffer, congratulations.

NORMA: Thank you. Beat it.

[MESSENGER BOY *exits. She reads.*]

MR. MARTIN: Why did he offer you congratulations?

NORMA: A relative died.

[*She and* MONTY *go into the other room.*]

MONTY: What happened now?

NORMA: A London syndicate is offering us $25,000 for the ticket. What'll we do?

MONTY: Honesty is the best policy; tell him the truth— maybe he'll give us half.

NORMA: Poison he'll give us. [*Very agitated*] You know what the trouble with you is? You're too excited. You're too excited. I got an idea. We'll go in there and act as if nothing happened. Nonchalant. Here, take a cigarette and don't forget—nonchalant—so he shouldn't suspect. [*She and* MONTY *enter the living room with much forced laughter.*]

MONTY: You know, Mr. Martin, we are so in love with that ticket . . .

NORMA: Not that it means anything, just a whim.

MONTY: Imagine if it won, what would you do?

MR. MARTIN: What would I do? I'd go right to Ireland and collect the money.

[*Bell rings.*]

NORMA: Come in.

[MESSENGER BOY *enters.*]

MESSENGER BOY: Cablegram, Mrs. Schaeffer, congratulations.

NORMA: Yeah.

[*She pushes him out.*]

MR. MARTIN: What happened now?

NORMA: Another relative died.

MR. MARTIN: Too bad.

NORMA: Yeah, it's terrible. [*She and* MONTY *go into the kitchen.*] Monty, they're offering us $50,000 for the ticket. What'll we do?

MONTY: Honesty is the best policy. Tell him the truth.

NORMA: There's one thing you shouldn't mention in this house—and that's the truth.

MONTY: George Washington told the truth.

NORMA: Did he win a sweepstakes? Besides, this man is holding back our property. [*Picks up vase*] Here, take this vase.

MONTY: What for?

NORMA: Just a light tap—not hard—just a little tap on his head.

MONTY: Why should I hit him?

NORMA: Say he attacked me.

MONTY: [*Laughing*] Who would believe it?

NORMA: Is that so? I'll show you. [*Ties a shawl around her waist*] I'll captivate him. [*Strikes a pose*] Captivating?

MONTY: I never noticed it before. Don't go too far.

NORMA: [*Going into the living room*] No, just far enough to get the ticket. [*Starts vamping*] You know, Mr. Martin, I find life just too dull for words, ain't you?

MR. MARTIN: What?

NORMA: All my life I've been languishing away in this terrible flat.

MR. MARTIN: Why? Is there something wrong with the plumbing?

NORMA: No, it's not that. It's my husband. He don't understand me.

MR. MARTIN: Is that so? You know, Mrs. Schaeffer, you're looking very attractive.

NORMA: You think so? [*Chucking his chin*] Ichel, bichel. Would you like to loll away the time? [*He nods.*] I'll turn on the radio. We'll dance. [*She turns on the radio. They dance, but he stops her from getting his wallet out of his pocket.*] Let's change the dance. Could you do the Westchester?

MR. MARTIN: I'll take a chance.

[*They dance more slowly, but still his arm interferes*

with her purpose. Finally she puts her hand right on his rear pocket. Misunderstood, he does the same to her. Again, he knocks her hand away.]

NORMA: Let's change the dance. [*She goes to the radio and turns the knob.*] Ah, Spanish, Señor Martin. Now I'll turn around, then you'll turn around. Now back up. [MONTY *finally steals out of the other room and puts his hand in* MR. MARTIN'S *pocket. His hand gets stuck, but he pulls it out with the wallet in it.* MR. MARTIN *feels it and snatches the wallet from* MONTY.]

MR. MARTIN: So that's what's been going on here, eh? The old badger game. Well, you won't get away with it. [*Turns radio off*] I'll have the police after you.

NORMA: Please, Mr. Martin, don't do that. I may as well tell you the truth. The ticket you got won the Sweepstakes and they're offering $50,000 for it.

MR. MARTIN: [*Takes out the ticket*] This ticket won?

NORMA: It won. [MR. MARTIN *faints.* NORMA *takes the ticket out of his hand and turns to* MONTY.] Monty, you was right all the time. Honesty is the best policy.

BLACKOUT

BABY SNOOKS GOES HOLLYWOOD

by David Freedman

First produced in the *Ziegfeld Follies of 1936*, at the Winter Garden Theatre, on January 30, 1936, with the following cast:

MRS. HIGGINS Eve Arden
DIRECTOR Bob Hope
BABY SNOOKS Fannie Brice
CAMERAMAN George Church
CLARK GABLE Rodney McLennan
JOAN CRAWFORD Jane Moxon
PHOTOGRAPHER Roger Davis
OFFICIAL John Hoysradt

SCENE: *A stage in a Hollywood studio. Lights, camera,
etc. Studio chairs around the set.*

DIRECTOR: [*Enters*] All right. All right. We're ready to
shoot. Mrs. Higgins, where in heaven's name is your
daughter? Where is Baby Snooks?

MRS. HIGGINS: Baby Snooks will not come on the lot until
you get her the proper supporting cast.

DIRECTOR: Why, what's the matter now?

MRS. HIGGINS: In her next picture, Shirley Temple will
be assisted by John Barrymore, W.C. Fields and George
Arliss and unless Baby Snooks has as good a supporting
cast, I won't let her appear.

DIRECTOR: But, my dear Mrs. Higgins, how can you com-
pare Baby Snooks to Shirley Temple?

MRS. HIGGINS: What? Why, Baby Snooks is only a little
child of five and look what the critics said about her
last picture. [*Takes clipping out of her handbag*] "If
Katharine Cornell were her age, she'd be another Baby
Snooks."

DIRECTOR: Well, we've arranged for Clark Gable and
Joan Crawford to play her father and mother and we're
getting Greta Garbo to be her nursemaid.

MRS. HIGGINS: Well, that's certainly a break for them.

DIRECTOR: Now can we get Baby Snooks to go on with
the picture?

MRS. HIGGINS: Yes. [*Calls offstage*] Baby Snooks! Snooksy,
darling!

SNOOKS: [*Offstage*] Awight.

MRS. HIGGINS: Come to mother, sweetums.

SNOOKS: [*Entering*] Here I is, Mummy.

MRS. HIGGINS: You can go ahead, darling. Everything is fixed.

SNOOKS: Yeah? And will Clark Gable make love to me?

MRS. HIGGINS: No, child. Clark Gable is your father.

SNOOKS: Oooh, does Daddy know?

MRS. HIGGINS: Go ahead, dear. Mr. Bullfinch will explain the story of the picture to you. Good-bye, dear. [*Quietly*] Stand up for your rights.
   [*Exits*]

SNOOKS: Good-bye.

DIRECTOR: Now, Snooks, in this picture there's a quarrel between Clark Gable and Joan Crawford who are your father and mother. And you love your mother.

SNOOKS: No, I don't.

DIRECTOR: Why not?

SNOOKS: Because I love Clark Gable.

DIRECTOR: But he's a cruel father to you. He's not nice to little girls.

SNOOKS: Yes he is.

DIRECTOR: Now your poor mother is heartbroken at your father's indifference and becomes very sick and is taken to the hospital.

SNOOKS: Waaaa.

DIRECTOR: But she gets well.

SNOOKS: Ha-ha.

DIRECTOR: But the very next day your mother goes out and is hit by an automobile.

SNOOKS: Waaaa.

DIRECTOR: But it's only a scratch and your mother collects a lot of money.

SNOOKS: Ha-ha.

DIRECTOR: Then one day . . .

SNOOKS: Waaaa.

DIRECTOR: Your father . . .

SNOOKS: Ha-ha.

DIRECTOR: And your mother . . .

SNOOKS: Waaaa.

DIRECTOR: [*Stepping back*] Why do you keep laughing and crying?

SNOOKS: Because you keep stepping on my foot.
   [GABLE *and* CRAWFORD *enter.*]

GABLE: Mr. Bullfinch, we're ready to do that scene. [*They get set.*]

DIRECTOR: All right, Gable. Now, Snooks, this is the big reconciliation scene. Watch me closely. First you take your father by the hand, like this, and lead him over to your mother, like this, and join their hands. And then you say: "Daddy, dear, why don't you forgive Mummy?" Now let's hear you say the line.

SNOOKS: I do that?

DIRECTOR: That's right.

SNOOKS: "Daddy, dear, why don't you forgive Daddy?"

DIRECTOR: No, no, no.

SNOOKS: I thought yeah.

DIRECTOR: Nooo. He can't forgive himself. He has to forgive your mother.

SNOOKS: Why?

DIRECTOR: Because you're bringing them together. Now remember, your daddy is forgiving your mother.

SNOOKS: Awight. "Daddy, dear, why don't you forgive your mother?"

DIRECTOR: [*Upset*] Now wait a minute. Can you remember the two words, "Daddy, dear?"

SNOOKS: Uh-huh.

DIRECTOR: Well do that.

SNOOKS: [*To* CRAWFORD] "Daddy, dear. . ."

DIRECTOR: No, no, no. Look, you're getting five thousand a week. Five thousand and you can't remember a simple sentence.

SNOOKS: Yes I can.

DIRECTOR: Well say it.

SNOOKS: What?

DIRECTOR: "Daddy, dear, please forgive Mummy?"

SNOOKS: Awight. "Daddy, dear, please forgive . . ." Waaaa . . .

DIRECTOR: What are you crying about?

SNOOKS: Shirley Temple gets six thousand a week.

DIRECTOR: Ohhhhh. Well, what do you want to get this line right?

SNOOKS: Half interest in the picture.

DIRECTOR: Awright. Awright. Camera!

CAMERAMAN: Lights!

[*Lights go on*]

SNOOKS: "Daddy, dear, why don't you forgive Mummy?"

GABLE: "Why you blessed child, you've brought sunshine into our lives. Just tell me what you want and I'll gladly do it."

SNOOKS: [*Sexily*] Huh?

DIRECTOR: Cut! [*Lights go out*] Come here, Snooks. Now when your father says, "Just tell me what you want and I'll gladly do it" you just say, "Stay with Mummy tonight." Now will you please try and remember this simple line?

SNOOKS: Why?

DIRECTOR: Now look. Let's begin. Can you say "Stay?"

SNOOKS: "Stay."

DIRECTOR: "With Mummy."

SNOOKS: "With Mummy."

DIRECTOR: "Tonight."

SNOOKS: "Tonight."

DIRECTOR: Now can you say, "Stay with Mummy tonight?"

SNOOKS: Uh-huh.

DIRECTOR: [*Yells*] Well say it!

SNOOKS: [*Yells back*] I did!

DIRECTOR: All right. Camera. Turn them over.

CAMERAMAN: Lights!

[*Lights go on*]

GABLE: "You blessed child, you've brought sunshine into our lives. Just tell me what you want and I'll gladly do it." [SNOOKS *remains silent. The* DIRECTOR *pantomimes the line.* SNOOKS *pantomimes back.*] "Just tell me what you want and I'll gladly do it."

SNOOKS: Play "Post Office" with me.

DIRECTOR: There's no use. You're all dismissed. [*Lights go off.* GABLE *and* CRAWFORD *exit muttering.*] Snooks, come here. [*She does.*] I'm going to Santa Barbara for two weeks and when I come back I want you to know that line. Do you think you can learn it in two weeks?

SNOOKS: Maybe.

[PHOTOGRAPHER *and* OFFICIAL *rush on.*]

PHOTOGRAPHER: Oh, Mr. Bullfinch! We want to take a picture of Baby Snooks for the newsreels. We've got a big scoop.

[MRS. HIGGINS *enters*.]

DIRECTOR: All right. Mrs. Higgins, will you pose with your daughter?

MRS. HIGGINS: Yes, sir.

OFFICIAL: Baby Snooks, on behalf of the Academy of Motion Picture Arts and Sciences, I present you with this gold trophy for the most intelligent, spontaneous and inspired performance of the year.

SNOOKS: I don't want it.

OFFICIAL: What? Well just tell me what you want and I'll gladly do it.

SNOOKS: [*Looking at the* DIRECTOR] Awight, stay with Mummy tonight.

BLACKOUT

THE PETRIFIED ELEVATOR

by David Freedman

First produced in the *Ziegfeld Follies of 1936*, at the Winter Garden Theatre, on January 30, 1936, with the following cast:

OPERATOR Bob Hope
EVANGELIST Hugh O'Connell
BANKER John Hoysradt
WINSTON Everett West
ALICE Gertrude Neisen
DOCTOR Riques Tanzi
PICKPOCKET William Quentmeyer
TAX COLLECTOR Roger Davis
ALLEN Rodney McLennan
MISTRESS Lyn Leslie
ANXIOUS GIRL Judy Canova
HUSBAND George Church
GIRL Jean Moorehead

SCENE: *An elevator with thirteen people in it. Lights are out. A drop in back shows that the elevator is stuck between floors. As the lights come up, the passengers are murmuring fearfully.*

WINSTON: Let us out of here. Let us get out!

OPERATOR: You can't get out. We're stuck between floors.

GIRL: How high are we?

OPERATOR: Not high. Between the nineteenth and twentieth floors.

GIRL: How long are we going to be stuck here?

OPERATOR: Not long. Didn't you hear those steel cables rattle? When the last one breaks, down we go.

WINSTON: We'll be killed!

OPERATOR: It looks pretty bad. Thirteen people in the elevator; but it's lucky it's Friday. It's a funny thing; I could have told you this was going to happen. A year ago today my brother was killed in a falling elevator. It got stuck just like this one and after a couple of quivers it fell right to the bottom. [*The elevator jolts.*] That's the quiver.

BANKER: You've got to get this elevator going. Why don't you telephone and call for help?

OPERATOR: It's no use but I'll try it. [*Takes phone off hook*] Hello? Hello, Starter? Listen, we're stuck up here between the nineteenth and twentieth floors and the last cable is breaking. Yeah? Will you do that? You're a real pal, Bill.

[*Hangs up*]

251

BANKER: What did he say? Is he coming up?

OPERATOR: He said he'll wait for us in the cellar.

[*All groan.*]

BANKER: Oh, do something. I've got to go and settle a million dollar estate.

GIRL: I've got to go and sign a contract for pictures.

WINSTON: I've got to go and make a long distance call to Washington.

ANXIOUS GIRL: I've got to go. [*Elevator jolts again.*] Oooh, can't you keep the elevator still?

EVANGELIST: Quiet. We're all doomed. Let us leave this world with a clean conscience. Kneel and repent.

[*All start to kneel.*]

OPERATOR: Take a tip from me—kneel easy.

MAN: [*Faints*] Oooh.

GIRL: Good heavens, he's fainted. Is there a doctor in the elevator?

OPERATOR: That's the doctor.

[*Elevator jolts.*]

BANKER: [*On his knees*] I want to leave this world with a clean conscience. I'm Mansville Westinghouse, President of the Amalgamated Trust Company. I've amassed a fortune, but I'm a miserable man. I took a mortgage on a widow's home and charged her nine percent interest.

OPERATOR: Don't worry. From where you'll be, it'll look like six.

TAX COLLECTOR: I was just going to see you, Mr. Westinghouse, about tax evasion.

BANKER: You're right. For five years I've cheated the government and never paid a cent on my income tax.

OPERATOR: Stop bragging. Let's hear your sins.

BANKER: But the money is no use to me now. I've got fifty thousand dollars with me. You can have it. [*Reaches into his pocket*] My God, I've been robbed!

ALL: Robbed?

EVANGELIST: What, a robbery at this time?

PICKPOCKET: Aw, what's the use—I did it.

EVANGELIST: Who are you?

PICKPOCKET: Well, I used to be a counterfeiter. I used to make cheap money. Till the government went into competition with me and I had to turn to picking pockets.

BANKER: How did you dare to take my money?

OPERATOR: What's the difference? If he [*Meaning* PICK-POCKET] don't get it, he [*the* TAX COLLECTOR] gets it.

BANKER: Oh, no. I'd rather give it to charity. Here, brother, give it to the poor.
[*Starts to give the money to the* EVANGELIST *but the elevator jolts and he takes it back.*]

EVANGELIST: Why did you take the money back?

BANKER: I thought the elevator was starting. Here, give it to the poor.

EVANGELIST: Hallelujah. You won't regret it, brother. There comes a time sooner or later when we all have to go. [*To* ANXIOUS GIRL] Isn't that true, sister?

ANXIOUS GIRL: The sooner the better.

ALLEN: Good God, do something. I've got to get up there. I must get to the twentieth floor. I know that she's been deceiving me and that she's all alone up there on the twentieth floor with a man and I want to stop them. [*Buzzer sounds.*]

OPERATOR: Somebody wants to come down from the twentieth floor.

ALLEN: That's him! That's him!

EVANGELIST: Brother, you can't be angry with him now. He's leaving.

OPERATOR: They're probably changing shifts.

HUSBAND: Excuse me. This woman on the twentieth floor. Is her name Elizabeth Wendell?

ALLEN: Yes, and I love her madly.

HUSBAND: I'm glad to know you. I'm her husband.

ALLEN: Then forgive me, brother.

HUSBAND: I forgive you. [*Points up*] And I forgive him.

OPERATOR: Then you can forgive me too.

EVANGELIST: Hallelujah!

ANXIOUS GIRL: This is an outrage. [*To* OPERATOR] You should be tarred and feathered.

EVANGELIST: Sister, control yourself.

ANXIOUS GIRL: I'm doing the best I can.

ALICE: Oh save me, save me! I was going to be married today and now I'll die a virgin.

OPERATOR: Did you say you were a virgin?

ALICE: Yes.

OPERATOR: May I have your autograph?

[*Elevator jolts.*]

BANKER: I have one more thing on my conscience.

OPERATOR: Say, you'll be better off if the elevator falls down.

BANKER: I used to give parties on my yacht and twenty years ago a son was born to me out of wedlock. I've never seen the boy but his mother named him Ulysses after the yacht.

OPERATOR: His name was Ulysses?

BANKER: Yes.

OPERATOR: [*Falls into his arms*] Father!

OLD WOMAN (MISTRESS): Don't you remember me, Mr. Westinghouse? I was a maid on that yacht.

OPERATOR: Mother!

BANKER: Let me out of here!

[*Elevator jolts.*]

OPERATOR: Take it easy, Dad. Two more seconds and the agony will be over.

ANXIOUS GIRL: So far as I'm concerned, it makes no difference any more.

BANKER: No. No! I don't want to die. Let me get at that switch. This damned, bloody switch has got to work. Damn it, damn it, damn it.

EVANGELIST: Hush, my good man. I can't stand such blasphemy. Such language will only make matters worse. Why don't you kneel and seek spiritual aid?

BANKER: I'll try anything. [*Kneels and prays*] Forgive me for my profanity. Aid me in this moment of affliction. Save us from disaster and give me power to start this elevator.

[*He pulls the switch. The motor starts and the drop moves to give the illusion of the elevator moving.*]

ALL: It worked! We're saved! We're saved!

EVANGELIST: Well, what the hell do you know about that!

BLACKOUT

DR. FRADLER'S DILEMMA

by David Freedman

This sketch was added to a recast and slightly revised *Ziegfeld Follies of 1936* when it resumed performances in the Fall of 1936 following a summer hiatus [caused by an ailing Fannie Brice]. In its cast were:

MRS. BIGLEY Marjory Leach
NURSE Gypsy Rose Lee
DR. FRADLER Bobby Clark
MRS. PHOEBE SWARTZ Fannie Brice

SCENE: *The office of* DR. FRADLER, *a psychoanalyst. The office is more like a library—the walls are all covered with high book shelves. Right center is a door leading to an inner office. Downstage right, a door leading to the waiting room. There is a desk with a chair behind it and a telephone on the desk. On one side of the desk is a doctor's office operating table. It is set so it looks like it is a chair in sitting position—a crank on the side of the chair can be turned so that the chair can be made totally horizontal. On the other side of the desk is a heavily padded armchair. Downstage left is a couch. Over the right center door is a sign reading, "THE TRUTH SHALL MAKE YOU FREE." At rise, the* NURSE, DR. FRADLER, *and* MRS. BIGLEY *are in the office.* DR. FRADLER *and* MRS. BIGLEY *get up from their seats.*

DR. FRADLER: Mrs. Bigley, the whole secret of psychoanalysis is to get at the truth. [*Indicates her brow*] Think the truth, [*Points to her lips*] speak the truth, [*Pats her back*] and feel the truth.

MRS. BIGLEY: Oh, you're so marvelous, Doctor.

DR. FRADLER: [*Beams*] And don't forget every morning when you get up, wash your face with soap and water. That'll be two thousand dollars, please.

MRS. BIGLEY: [*Pays him*] Oh, thank you, Dr. Fradler, thank you. And you think I still have sex appeal?

DR. FRADLER: Oh yes, oh yes. I'm sure your husband did not run away—he was kidnapped. [*Ushers* MRS. BIGLEY *out. After she is gone he turns to* NURSE.] Call up her husband and tell him in four more treatments I'll have her convinced he's dead.

NURSE: [*Dryly*] Speak the truth, think the truth, feel the truth!

DR. FRADLER: [*Beaming*] Exactly. [*Phone rings. He goes to it.*] Hello? [*Coughs*] Yes—this is Dr. Fradler's office—the psychoanalyst! Oh, Dr. Fradler is not in. I'll let you talk to his nurse.

[*Motions* NURSE *to take phone*]

NURSE: [*On phone*] Yes . . . This is the Nurse . . . Who is this calling?

DR. FRADLER: [*Aside to* NURSE] If it's anybody but John Hutchins tell him I've gone out to lunch. If it's John Hutchins tell him I'm in Europe and if it's Mrs. Hutchins tell her I'll be right back.

NURSE: [*Into phone*] He's in Europe . . . Oh, I'm sorry, Mrs. Fradler. [*To* DR. FRADLER] It's your wife!

DR. FRADLER: [*With annoyed look—leering at* NURSE] Why didn't you tell me who it was so I don't have to be under this psychic tension! [*Into phone*] No—I can't be home to dinner. I'm taking a plane to the coast. Donald Duck is having bad dreams! . . . Keep your libido clean. Good-bye! [*Hangs up. Door buzzes. Quickly to* NURSE] If it's Mrs. Peasley tell her I'm sick and if it's George Brooks tell him I'm at the golf club and if it's neither tell them I'll be right back!

[*Exits door right center.* MRS. PHOEBE SWARTZ *enters—smartly dressed.*]

PHOEBE: How do you do?

NURSE: Oh, a new patient—may I have your name?

PHOEBE: Mrs. Swartz. Phoebe Swartz.

NURSE: The doctor will see you in a moment.

PHOEBE: Where do I undress?

NURSE: You don't have to undress.

PHOEBE: Oh, it's a fake!

NURSE: What psychological trouble have you?

PHOEBE: Well, my back hurts—you see I'm a gymnasium teacher in a settlement and I'm lifting heavy weights—oi! [*Holds her back*] And all night I'm playing with Indian clubs!

NURSE: What is that—a dream?

PHOEBE: [*Looks surprised*] No—it's a fact.

[DR. FRADLER *enters excitedly.*]

DR. FRADLER: [*Aside to* NURSE] Who is she? Which one? What did you tell her?

NURSE: It's a new patient.

[*Exits*]

DR. FRADLER: Then I can talk freely. [*Obviously to impress her*] The psychological phenomena of the subconscious complexes evidence themselves in the strangest manner. [*To* PHOEBE] How do you do? How do you feel?

PHOEBE: Say—if I felt good I wouldn't be here! I was recommended by Mrs. Weingarten.

DR. FRADLER: [*In a grand manner*] Oh yes! She and I were making splendid progress. She was almost cured when she committed suicide. Have a seat.

PHOEBE: Thank you.

[*Sits on operating chair*]

DR. FRADLER: [*Sits on desk*] Now what enjoyment are you not getting out of life?

PHOEBE: The usual thing.

DR. FRADLER: Are you married?

PHOEBE: In name only.

[*Bows her head*]

DR. FRADLER: [*Gets up—paces floor thinking—suddenly darts question at her like a district attorney*] Don't you and your husband quarrel all the time?

PHOEBE: [*Startled*] No—we like each other.

DR. FRADLER: I thought so. [*Same pacing up and down*] In the morning your husband rushes away to the office without kissing you!

PHOEBE: [*Startled*] No—we go to work together.

PHOEBE: Oi! May I use your phone? [*Dials on phone*] cious! Eh—I suppose he lives at the club and you at your mother's?

PHOEBE: No. We live in the same house.

DR. FRADLER: I thought so. [*Pensive*] Hmmm—a case of psychosis—neurosis—halitosis!

PHOEBE: [*Trying to be helpful*] One trouble I have—I walk in my sleep.

DR. FRADLER: [*Darts at her*] Nightmare, huh?

PHOEBE: No—twin beds!

DR. FRADLER: [*Trying to cover it up*] I thought so. Hmmm—a very baffling case. [*Takes down big book and opens it*] No—that's not it! [*Opens another book*] No! Not that! [*Opens third book made like box and takes out a piece of chocolate*] That's it! [*Chews chocolate*] You have a serious mental disturbance!

PHOEBE: I have no mental disturbance—I've got a pain in the back.

DR. FRADLER: Ah! A clue! ... Do you keep a diary?

PHOEBE: No—I just got an ordinary pain in the back! I'm a gymnasium teacher and I lift weights—

DR. FRADLER: [*Scornfully*] That has nothing to do with it! To cure your condition there must be a transfer from your subconscious to mine. You must relax and reveal your inner self.

PHOEBE: Well, I wanted to undress!

DR. FRADLER: No—no—you must relax—and let your thoughts flow—relax—[*Tries to loosen her up. She stiffens. He steals up behind her and shouts in her ear.*] RELAX!! [*She gets the jitters.*] Hmmm—just as I thought—a dope fiend!

[*She starts up. He makes her sit on chair—turns crank—chair flattens out like a bed—she gets up alarmed.*]

PHOEBE: What are you gonna do?

DR. FRADLER: I'm gonna psychoanalyze you.

PHOEBE: Well, I want to sit up while you do it. [*She gets up and goes over and sits in armchair. The back of the chair falls back and she's stretched out again.*] Is this your office or your bedroom?

DR. FRADLER: Now—have you had any dreams lately?

PHOEBE: No.

DR. FRADLER: You're sure? Think now!

PHOEBE: I'm sure—I had no dreams—but my cousin had a dream.

DR. FRADLER: Well, let's hear it.

PHOEBE: She didn't tell it to me.

DR. FRADLER: That makes it harder. Do you know any dreams at all?

PHOEBE: No.

DR. FRADLER: Would you like to hear some of my dreams?

THE READING OF THE PLAY

by David Freedman

First produced in *The Show Is On,* at the Winter Garden Theatre, on December 25, 1936, with the following cast:

MADEMOISELLE LEONORE Beatrice Lillie
FLYDE TWITCH Reginald Gardiner
THE PRODUCER Ralph Riggs
ARMAND Jack McCauley
ALPHONSE Willem Van Loon
PIERRE Andre Charise
WARREN BRUCE Mortimer O'Brien
SUPPORTING CAST Vera Allen, Marie Carrol, Hazel Bofinger

SCENE: *A theatre greenroom in the 1890's.*

TWITCH: [*Reading from script*] "The door opens slowly and Annabelle, a picture of pitiful despair, enters the room. She faces her husband, tears of repentance fill her weary eyes. He takes her in his arms and says, 'Annabelle, we need to suffer as we did. It will make us both clean in our hearts.' Annabelle rests her head on his shoulder and says, 'Rinaldo,' and slowly the curtain falls and so the play ends."
[*All "Bravo!" and applaud.*]
Well, Mademoiselle Leonore, what did you think of my play?

MLLE. LEONORE: I did not understand a goddamn word.

ARMAND: But why did you not say so. He read four acts. Why did you not say something?

MLLE. LEONORE: I look at all the faces and everyone is sad, sad, sad. So I say, "Oh hell, I go back to Paree."
[*She rises amid general ad lib.*]

PRODUCER: But, Mademoiselle Leonore, this is your first appearance in America. We have spared no expense to bring you here. Our outstanding playwright, Mr. Flyde Twitch, has written this play especially for you.

MLLE. LEONORE: Je regret beaucoup but this is no play for Leonore LeLait.
[WARREN BRUCE *enters.*]

BRUCE: I hope I'm not late.

PRODUCER: Mademoiselle Leonore, I want you to meet your new leading man, Warren Bruce.

BRUCE: [*Kissing her hand*] Charmed.

267

MLLE. LEONORE: How do you do? I want you to meet my husband, Pierre, who takes care of my business affairs, my previous husband, Alphonse, who takes care of Pierre; and this is Armand, my lover, whom I take care of. And now, I go back to Paree.

[*She says good-bye to all and starts to leave.*]

TWITCH: I am perfectly willing to change the play to suit your style.

MLLE. LEONORE: [*Crossing down center*] Ah, well, if you make little changements for me, I will stay.

[*They all sit down.*]

TWITCH: Now in this play there is a man and a woman.

MLLE. LEONORE: Too much plot.

TWITCH: But the entire story really centers about the woman. You see, in this play you are a young girl—a virgin.

MLLE. LEONORE: Oh, it is a comedy.

TWITCH: Not exactly; your husband is unfaithful to you.

MLLE. LEONORE: Oh, he is the hero.

TWITCH: But you get a lot of sympathy; in the end, you die.

MLLE. LEONORE: Oh no. I want happy ending. My husband dies. Now, how do I make my first entrance?

TWITCH: You are a simple country girl and you come in from milking a cow dressed very plain.

MLLE. LEONORE: Ah, that is good, very plain. Always I come in dressed very plain. When I was in the *Follies Bergere of 1891—2—3—4—5—6—7—8*, always I dress plain. I wear a simple tiara, with one simple twenty carat diamond, a brassiere, and no skirt. That makes me very plain!

TWITCH: But, Mademoiselle, this is not a musical comedy—this is a legitimate play.

MLLE. LEONORE: Oui, that is why I wear the brassiere.

TWITCH: I'm sorry, but in this play you will have to wear a skirt.

[*They form a huddle.*]

MLLE. LEONORE: [*After huddle breaks*] We can discuss the costumes later. Go on with the play.

TWITCH: Well, at the opening of the play, you are putting your little baby to sleep.

MLLE. LEONORE: Ah, that is good. I sing a little lullaby

and dance the can-can around the baby cradle and sing
Goose Mother rhymes. I once do that in night club in
Paree. Oh, I am so cute. I sing:
> "Petit Jacque Horner
> Assez dans le corner
> Petit Mademoiselle Buffet
> Assez à la tuffet."

Ah, that last line. It has twenty-five meanings—all
dirty.

TWITCH: [*Rises*] Now see here, Lawton, this is quite impossible.

PRODUCER: Calm down, Twitch. Mademoiselle Leonore,
we simply cannot permit you to recite a poem with
twenty-five dirty meanings.
[*They form a huddle.*]

MLLE. LEONORE: [*After huddle breaks*] Silence. We compromise.

PRODUCER: What is the compromise?

MLLE. LEONORE: I will not sing the song—if you let Armand sell post cards in the lobby . . .

PRODUCER: Well, she meets us halfway.
[*All return to positions.*]

TWITCH: Now, there comes a moment in the play when
your husband thinks you're dead.

MLLE. LEONORE: You mean I am off the stage?

TWITCH: Only for a little while.

MLLE. LEONORE: Oh, it is intermission.

TWITCH: No, no. There is one whole scene where they
talk about you. You don't come on at all.

MLLE. LEONORE: "Petit Jacque Horner . . ."

ARMAND: But, Leonore, you can fix that. Remember how
you fixed Romeo and Juliet?

MLLE. LEONORE: Oui, I fixed Shakespeare good. I make
Shakespeare big hit. When I go on the balcony I wear
a big feather.

TWITCH: You mean you wore a feather in your hat?

MLLE. LEONORE: In my hat! Crazy Americans! [*She
laughs and Frenchmen laugh with her. She falls off
seat with laughter and* ARMAND *helps her back.*] No,
that is not where I wear it.

TWITCH: But in Romeo and Juliet you were not on the
stage all the time.

MLLE. LEONORE: [*Rises*] I know that. But when the Montagues fight the Capulets, I stick out my feather from the wings and say, "Leonore will be back soon." That is very funny.

TWITCH: Well, you certainly fixed Shakespeare.

MLLE. LEONORE: [*Seating herself*] Don't worry, I fix you too. Go on with the play. Continue.

TWITCH: Well, at the end of the first act our heroine leaves the farm. She wants to go on the stage so she comes to New York and meets a producer. But he will not give her a part unless she becomes his mistress.

MLLE. LEONORE: So she gets the part. Go on.

TWITCH: No, it's not as easy as all that. She has the most terrific struggle.

MLLE. LEONORE: Why does he resist her?

TWITCH: No. She resists him.

MLLE. LEONORE: Crazy Americans!

TWITCH: But she knows nothing about acting so the producer deserts her and life deals her the first blow.

MLLE. LEONORE: Ah, I understand. She is just a little bit ... pre ... pre ... how do you say ... ah yes—prejudiced.

TWITCH: [*Wiping brow with handkerchief*] Be that as it may, she meets another producer and becomes his mistress; but he, likewise, deserts her and life deals her a second blow. [*She lifts two fingers.*] Then she meets another producer, the same thing happens, and life deals her a third blow.

MLLE. LEONORE: Too much prejudice in one play. But not to make it too sad, I put in little joke that was big laugh in Paree.

TWITCH: What was the joke?

MLLE. LEONORE: Well, I play the part of a maid and my mistress tells me she has caught her husband kissing the cook and I say to her, "Oh, you only tell me that to make me jealous." And they laugh and laugh and laugh. That is very funny, no?

TWITCH: No!

[MADEMOISELLE LEONORE *gathers things.*]

Then she meets another producer and another producer and another ...

MLLE. LEONORE: One minute. During all these affairs, she has a husband?

TWITCH: Oh yes, she has a husband!

MLLE. LEONORE: That is good. Keep it clean!

TWITCH: [*Rising*] Then when she reaches the top of the ladder, she has left behind her a trail of broken lives—a woman who has sold her honor for her career—a sham and a fraud—unscrupulous—sinful—without talent—and beneath all the glamour and glitter she is nothing but a woman of the streets—a common harlot!

MLLE LEONORE: [*Rising*] I have never been so insulted in my life.

TWITCH: Why, what have I done?

MLLE. LEONORE: You know very well what you have done. You have written the story of my life!
[*She starts to exit.*]

BLACKOUT

TAXES! TAXES!!

by David Freedman

First produced in *The Show Is On,* at the Winter Garden Theatre, on December 25, 1936, with the following cast:

BERT LARRIMORE Bert Lahr
MR. HIGGINS Reginald Gardiner
CRUNCH Ralph Riggs

SCENE: *A government office.* MR. HIGGINS *and* CRUNCH *are discovered.*

HIGGINS: We'll now take up income tax X-6200. Mr. Bert Larrimore—motion picture actor.

CRUNCH: Mr. Larrimore is waiting outside.

HIGGINS: Show him in.

[BERT LARRIMORE *enters.*]

CRUNCH: Mr. Larrimore.

BERT: It's about time. See here, Mr. Higgins, I flew in from Hollywood to make a protest against my income tax report for 1934. My lawyer told me that the government gypped me out of $197.58 and I demand a refund.

HIGGINS: Mr. Larrimore, if there has been any discrepancy, we will gladly rectify it.

BERT: $197.58. That's the discrep ... dis ... I want it.

HIGGINS: Have we Mr. Larrimore's income tax records here?

CRUNCH: Yes, but we haven't got much.

HIGGINS: Well, bring in whatever we have. [CRUNCH *exits.*] If there is the slightest doubt about your tax assessments we will refund all the money you paid the government—with interest.

BERT: It's time something happened.

HIGGINS: Why, Mr. Larrimore, you're not mad at the government?

BERT: Well, it's getting a little irksome. Say, how do you think up all these taxes?

HIGGINS: I have nothing to do with it. There's a scientific economist who spends all his time each year working out new and intricate taxes.

BERT: What does he get for doing that?

HIGGINS: Nothing. He does it for love of the work.

BERT: Just a natural born louse.

CRUNCH: [*Entering*] This is all I could find on the Bert Larrimore matter.

BERT: Wait a moment. I'm only thirty-seven years old. That looks like the Congressional Record.

HIGGINS: I don't think we shall have to go through all of it.

BERT: Well, I should hope not.

HIGGINS: Now, according to Schedule C, Item 1, I see you have deducted the following for servants—$350 a week for your cook. Now, Mr. Larrimore, don't you think $350 a week is a lot of money to pay a cook?

BERT: Well, there's certain complications there. She's also my mother-in-law.

HIGGINS: Of course, Mr. Larrimore. I understand that a man of your position must have the finest. I suppose you go out a lot to nightclubs and cafes?

BERT: No. I stay home every night with my wife and kids. I never go out at night.

HIGGINS: Then what's this item—$25,000 for nightclub entertainment?

BERT: Well, I went out a couple of nights. Once to the Colony Club.

HIGGINS: Let's get to Item 3.

BERT: Yeah, that's the item. That's where my lawyer says you made a mistake.

HIGGINS: Mr. Larrimore, I envy people in your profession. You must travel everywhere.

BERT: That's just publicity. I spent the entire year of 1934 in Hollywood making pictures.

HIGGINS: Then your lawyer is right. We did make a small error.

BERT: I told you you made a mistake.

HIGGINS: Yes. We allowed you $15,000 for traveling expenses.

BERT: Yeah, how do you come to allow a thing like that? [*Does a doubletake*] Say, where is the place you owe me $197.58?

HIGGINS: But of course, you can account for this $15,000 for traveling expenses?

BERT: Certainly. Buses and streetcars. A dime here and a quarter there—it counts up. Besides, I always forgot to take transfers.

HIGGINS: What's this item? $4,562.20 for a single trip from New York to California?

BERT: Well, I was in a hurry. I took a cab.

HIGGINS: To save time?

BERT: Yeah. Do you mind if I take a drink? I'm very thirsty. [HIGGINS *pours him a drink.*] Thanks. It's certainly a refreshing drink, water.

HIGGINS: Yes, we're very lucky to have such good water in this country, aren't we? The water over in Europe is very bad, isn't it?

BERT: How would I know?

HIGGINS: What about this deduction for a trip to Europe?

BERT: More water, please.

HIGGINS: Certainly. [*Pours water*] You know I envy you, Mr. Larrimore. Your family seems very gifted. It's marvelous how you can keep all the talent in one family.

BERT: Yeah, my sisters all want to be actresses.

HIGGINS: Now who is Hannah Larrimore?

BERT: That's my grandmother. She's about ninety-eight.

HIGGINS: You've got her down here as a gag-man.

BERT: [*Doubletake*] Well, she gives me nifties every now and then. Here's an original line she gave me the other day: "What hen lays the longest?"

HIGGINS: You mean a dead one?

BERT: Yeah. That's the one she gave me.

HIGGINS: Now, who is Enoch Larrimore?

BERT: Is that bastard in there? [*Rises*] Everywhere I go that tramp pops up. How did he get in there?

HIGGINS: I don't know, but he must be a very important man—he gets $250 a week.

BERT: What? That half-wit gets $250? Since when?

HIGGINS: Since the first of the year.

BERT: Where is the place you owe me $197.58?
[*Sits*]

HIGGINS: Of course, Mr. Larrimore, you must realize, that just as we must return you an overtax, ipso facto, you must make up to us all deficiencies we uncover no matter how much they amount to. [BERT *motions for water.*] And, ipso facto, if we are to allow that deduction for your business trip to Europe, we must have some definite proof that you made the trip.

BERT: You don't think I'd lie about it? Here's the proof. I bought this diamond ring in Paris—$5,000.

HIGGINS: Of course, you deducted the customs duty you had to pay on the ring.

BERT: Customs duty? I know a guy on the docks. I never pay any customs duty.

HIGGINS: That comes under another federal law which makes you guilty of smuggling.

BERT: Is that bad?

HIGGINS: It's not very good. Now, Mr. Larrimore, Item 4—contributions to charity.

BERT: That's the item. That's where I got you by the ipso facto.

HIGGINS: Under "Charity Deductions," you contributed $10,000 to the Arizona Foundling Home for Illegitimate Indians. You contributed to illegitimate Indians?

BERT: Yeah. I like to encourage things like that.

HIGGINS: I think you're going to have a little difficulty proving the existence of this organization.

BERT: Oh, no, I'm not. It's a secret enterprise and if I want to give my money to the Indians, do I have to make it public? Besides, I did it all for a girl—an Indian girl. A Sioux.

HIGGINS: Mr. Larrimore, we may be forced to extradite you to Arizona.

BERT: That's where I got you. The girl's not in Arizona. I took her to Hollywood. She was just a young girl—only seventeen—wanted a career. So I made her my prodigy.

HIGGINS: Can you prove that you took her to Hollywood?

BERT: Certainly I can prove it. I got evidence—hotel bills.

[*Does a "take"*]

HIGGINS: That is a violation of the Mann Act and you are liable to prison.

BERT: This whole thing is a frame-up. I got rights under the Constitution. I want to be represented by my lawyer, Wickersham Ginsberg.

HIGGINS: Is Wickersham Ginsberg your lawyer?

BERT: Yes.

HIGGINS: I know him well.

BERT: Then everything is all right.

HIGGINS: Well, hardly. I had him arrested last week.

BERT: I don't blame you.

[*Another "take"*]

HIGGINS: Now, Mr. Larrimore, your new taxes amount to $40,000.50 and if you'll sign right here . . .

[*Hands him pad*]

BERT: I won't sign. I haven't that kind of money.

HIGGINS: Sign it, or I'll turn you over to the federal authorities and you know what that means?

BERT: I'll sign, but you haven't heard the end of this. I'll take this up with the good will court.

[*Starts to exit*]

HIGGINS: One more thing. This cleans up everything for the year of 1934. Now we'll go into your taxes for 1935.

BERT: No you won't. No you won't. And even if you did you couldn't do a thing about it. You know why? You know why? Because you haven't got any evidence against me in that year.

HIGGINS: Why not?

BERT: Because in 1935 I didn't file any income tax.

BLACKOUT

GONE WITH THE REVOLUTION

by Moss Hart and George S. Kaufman

First produced in *Sing Out the News,* at the Music Box Theatre, on September 24, 1938, with the following cast:

W. S. VAN DYKE Will Geer
NORMA SHEARER Mary Jane Walsh
ROBERT MORLEY Hiram Sherman
TYRONE POWER Michael Loring
SCRIPT GIRL Daisy Bernier
ASSISTANT TO VAN DYKE Ben Ross
CAMERAMAN Chic Gagnon
MAID Elizabeth Dozier
A WRITER Charles Lawrence
ANOTHER WRITER Leslie Litomy
L. B. MAYER Philip Loeb

SCENE: *A large sound stage on the Metro Goldwyn Mayer studio. A scene from* Marie Antoinette *is in progress of being shot. The* CAMERMAN *and* CREW *are present.* NORMA SHEARER *as "Marie Antoinette" and* ROBERT MORLEY *as "Louis XVI" stand awaiting a signal from the director,* W. S. VAN DYKE.

VAN DYKE: Ready, Miss Shearer? Ready, Mr. Morley? [*They nod.*] All right! Camera!

SHEARER: [*A deep curtsey to* MORLEY] "Your Majesty!" [*She kisses his hand.*]

MORLEY: [*As she rises*] "You may go now!" [*He starts away leaving her standing there.* SHEARER *looks after him; heaves a deep sigh, and is about to speak a line.*] I'm most frightfully sorry, Miss Shearer—Mr. Van Dyke ... I say to her, "You may go now" and then *I* go instead. That's a bit of all wrong, isn't it?

VAN DYKE: [*Rises*] All right—cut! Let me see that script! [*A* SCRIPT GIRL *hands it to him.*] No, Louis XVI says to Marie Antoinette, "You may go now," then *he* goes.

MORLEY: Well, it's a bit on the balmy side, don't you think, Mr. Van Dyke? "You may go now," then *he* goes! I'm sure an English king would never do that!

VAN DYKE: Yes, I know, Mr. Morley, but you're playing a French king. Furthermore, we can't change this—it's history. The king *has* to go because Marie Antoinette must stay here to meet Count Fersen, her lover. Now that's history, Mr. Morley.

MORLEY: Well, to me it seems a very queer cup of tea.

[*He grumbles to himself as he moves away.*] "You may go now," and *I* go. Bloody nonsense!

VAN DYKE: All right, Miss Shearer—we'll cut to where Count Fersen comes in. [*Calls*] Are you ready, Mr. Power? Tyrone Power!

POWER: [*Off*] Ready, Mr. Van Dyke!

VAN DYKE: All right! Camera!

[SHEARER *takes a deep sigh.* TYRONE POWER *enters, stops and looks at her.*]

POWER: "Marie! Marie Antoinette!"

[*He goes to her; they embrace.*]

VAN DYKE: All right—cut! Swell, Miss Shearer! [MORLEY *reenters.*] Very nice, Tyrone. Now let me see . . . what's next?

[*He becomes absorbed in the script.*]

MORLEY: I say, Miss Shearer, I hope I was not being a bit of a cad. I didn't really *want* you to go, you know.

SHEARER: That's quite all right, Mr. Morley.

POWER: I know just how you feel, Mr. Morley. In *Alexander's Ragtime Band* I had to tell Alice Faye to go, but she stayed right there and sang thirty-five songs!

SHEARER: You know, when we were doing *The Barretts of Wimpole Street* I had to tell Flush to go once, and—

VAN DYKE: [*Leaping to his feet, staring at the script*] My God, what's this?

POWER: What?

SHEARER: What's the matter, Woody?

VAN DYKE: Why, it says here in the script that now comes a revolution. What the hell are they talking about?

POWER: Let's see!

SHEARER: Where is it?

[SHEARER, POWER *and* ASSISTANT DIRECTOR *crowd around* VAN DYKE *and look at the script.*]

VAN DYKE: Right here—see it? "Then comes the French Revolution." [*Yells to an* ASSISTANT] Get those writers down here right away!

ASSISTANT: Yes, sir.

[*He dashes away.*]

VAN DYKE: We can't do a picture with a revolution in it! The Hays office'll *never* allow it! Look what happened to that picture *Blockade*. And that was just a mythical revolution.

SHEARER: Woody, this is terrible! I certainly can't play in a picture with a revolution in it. I turned down Scarlett O'Hara, and all that had in it was the Civil War.

POWER: I can't play in it either. A revolution takes a long time and Mr. Zanuck doesn't want me to look old. Look at *Alexander's Ragtime Band.* If I didn't look old after thirty-five songs, I'm not going to look old for a revolution!

VAN DYKE: I know. I know! Wait till I get a hold of those writers!

MORLEY: I say, old chap, this lets *me* out too, you know. A revolution would completely change my characterization. I'm supposed to be impotent, you know.

VAN DYKE: I know, Mr. Morley. And you're swell.

MORLEY: It was understood when I was signed for the part in England that I was to be impotent. I made all my screen tests on that assumption.

VAN DYKE: It'll be all right, Mr. Morley.

[*He stops as the* TWO WRITERS *enter with the* ASSISTANT.]

1ST WRITER: Do you want us, Mr. Van Dyke?

VAN DYKE: Oh, here you are! Do you know what you've done? Do you know what you've done to this studio? What the hell do you boys mean by putting a revolution in a picture about Marie Antoinette?

1ST WRITER: Well, Mr. Van Dyke, we didn't want to, but every book we read about Marie Antoinette had a revolution *in* it!

2ND WRITER: In fact, some of them said more about the revolution than they did about Marie Antoinette.

[NORMA SHEARER, *with a moan, faints dead away.*]

VAN DYKE: [*To the* WRITERS] You see what you've done, you fools! Norma, Norma, it's all right!

2ND WRITER: It wasn't our fault, Mr. Van Dyke. The revolution . . .

1ST WRITER: We made it a carnival in one version, but then it was hard to get the guillotine in.

VAN DYKE: Get out! [*Turns to an* ASSISTANT] Ask Mr. Louis B. Mayer if he would mind coming down here for a minute!

ASSISTANT: Oh, Mr. Mayer's presiding at an important meeting.

VAN DYKE: What meeting?

ASSISTANT: It's that new committee—"Motion Pictures Are Your Best Entertainment."

VAN DYKE: Tell him it's important! Tell Mr. Mayer we've discovered a revolution in *Marie Antoinette*.

ASSISTANT: Yes, sir!

[*Exits*]

SHEARER: Woody, I have an idea! Suppose the revolution were sympathetic—lovely boys and girls, with the right people *leading* it—the censors wouldn't mind *then*, would they?

VAN DYKE: But, Norma, the right people don't *lead* a revolution!

SHEARER: Yes, but what I mean is, Woody, suppose *I* lead the revolution—Marie Antoinette. And win it for everybody! It makes the whole thing sympathetic!

POWER: That's wonderful! And it's a reason for my staying young, to help you lead the revolution.

MORLEY: Just a moment, though. Do I stay impotent right through it?

SHEARER: Why, certainly, Mr. Morley. I lead it *because* you're impotent. It becomes the *reason* for the revolution. The people of France appeal to Marie Antoinette. . . .

[*There is a flurry offstage, and the whispered word spreads: "Mr. Mayer," "Mr. Mayer," "It's Mr. Mayer!" Finally,* LOUIS B. MAYER *enters followed by* ASSISTANT.]

MAYER: What's the matter? What's the matter?

VAN DYKE: L. B.!

MAYER: [*The little father*] Boys and girls, what's this I hear about a revolution in *Marie Antoinette?* We've got three million dollars in it. You're playing a little joke on L. B., huh?

VAN DYKE: No, L. B., it's true!

MAYER: [*Screaming*] WHAT?

VAN DYKE: Yes, L. B. And you know what it does, don't you? It makes Miss Shearer unsympathetic, it makes Tyrone Power look older, and it changes Mr. Morley's characterization, right from the ground up.

MORLEY: I have a contract, you know, Mr. L. B., I have a contract!

VAN DYKE: To say nothing of the censors!

MAYER: [*Suave again*] Now, wait a minute, boys and girls, wait a minute! I am chairman of the committee, "Motion Pictures Are Your Best Entertainment." And a three-million-dollar picture, boys and girls, is not the time or place for a revolution!

VAN DYKE: But it's history, L. B., everybody *knows* it. The French Revolution!

MAYER: I didn't know it, and I am chairman of the committee, "Motion Pictures Are Your Best Entertainment." All right—make it the American Revolution. That gets you past the censorship. It makes Norma sympathetic—Tyrone Power can stay young. And what was the matter with Mr. Morley?

VAN DYKE: He wants to stay impotent.

MAYER: You don't say? Mr. Morley, could you stay impotent through the American Revolution?

MORLEY: I think it's a better period to stay impotent in, Mr. L. B.

VAN DYKE: It's no good, L. B.! We couldn't show it in England. They don't like the American Revolution.

MAYER: All right, make it the Russian Revolution. That only offends Russia, and there's no money there anyhow!

MORLEY: But dear old boy, I could hardly play a Russian and remain impotent. It wouldn't be cricket.

SHEARER: L. B., the whole picture's been shot in Versailles.

MAYER: [*Paces a moment, stuck. Talks as he walks*] Let me see that script. Where does the revolution come?

VAN DYKE: [*Handing* MAYER *the script*] Right there, L. B. Right after Tyrone Power says, "Marie! Marie Antoinette!" He takes her in his arms, they kiss, then comes the revolution!

MAYER: Right after the kiss, huh?

VAN DYKE: That's right!

MAYER: [*Paces a little as he considers this, talks half to himself*] "Motion Pictures Are Your Best Entertainment." "Motion pictures are your best . . ." [*He gets the idea.*] The revolution should not come *after* the kiss, but *during* the kiss. Then they will *not* look at the *revolution*, they will look at the *kiss!*

SHEARER: [*Ecstatically*] L. B.!

VAN DYKE: You've got it, L. B.!

MORLEY: That's what I call muddling through.

POWER: It's wonderful!

MAYER: Come on—where is the revolution? Bring in the revolution!

VAN DYKE: [*Claps his hands*] Pete, is the revolution ready?

ASSISTANT: Yes, sir. We've got four thousand extras waiting, right here.
[*Exits*]

MAYER: Four thousand? They'd notice that! Cut it to four. Now, do it once!

VAN DYKE: All right. Let's do it, folks! Tell 'em where to come in, Pete! Do it!
[SHEARER *and* MORLEY *take their original positions.*]

SHEARER: [*As she curtseys*] "Your Majesty!"

MORLEY: [*Crosses as she rises*] "You may go now!"
[MORLEY *goes, with a malevolent look at* VAN DYKE. SHEARER *turns, sighs.* POWER *enters.*]

POWER: [*Stops, looks at her*] "Marie! Marie Antoinette!"
[*He goes to her. They kiss.*]

MAYER: Now comes the revolution!
[*And it does. Four tattered extras rush across the scene, growling ferociously. The revolution is over but* TYRONE POWER *is still kissing* NORMA SHEARER.]

MAYER: Wait a minute! Wait a minute! What are you growling about?

VAN DYKE: Well, it's the revolution, L. B. And they're sore.

MAYER: Wait a minute. You are growling. You are sore. All right. Then what do you see? You see not only Marie Antoinette, but you see Norma Shearer, the first lady of the screen, kissing Tyrone Power, borrowed from Twentieth Century Fox. Now—are you sore?

1ST EXTRA: No, Mr. Mayer.

2ND EXTRA: No, sir.

MAYER: All right, now we do the revolution. Wait a minute! Get that woman a rose for her hair—this is a three-million-dollar picture. All right! [EXTRAS *go off.*] Norma, you are sympathetic; Mr. Power, you are young—

MORLEY: And . . . er . . .

MAYER: Mr. Morley, you are impotent! Is everybody happy?

ALL: Yes, Mr. Mayer.

MAYER: Now do the scene once!

SHEARER: [*As before*] "Your Majesty!"

MORLEY: [*As before*] "You may go now!"

POWER: [*As before*] "Marie! Marie Antoinette!"

[*The four* EXTRAS *come on again but stop at the sight and kiss each other.*]

BLACKOUT

LOCAL BOY MAKES GOOD

by George S. Kaufman

First produced in *Seven Lively Arts*, at the Ziegfeld Theatre, on December 7, 1944, with the following cast:

THE SECRETARY Billie Worth
THE PRODUCER Albert Carroll
THE AGENT Michael Barrett
THE STAGEHAND Bert Lahr

SCENE: *A theatrical producer's office. A desk, a few chairs, two or three pictures on the walls, a vase of flowers.* JACK MARTIN, *the producer, is at his desk, reading a script. His secretary, a gorgeous blonde, enters.*

SECRETARY: Mr. Martin.

MARTIN: Yes, Miss Freylinghuysen?

SECRETARY: Sam Clark's outside. He wants to see you about the new play.

MARTIN: Tell him to come in.

SECRETARY: Come in, Mr. Clark.

[MR CLARK *enters.*]

CLARK: Hello, Jack.

MARTIN: Hi, Sam. How's the busy little agent this morning?

CLARK: Fine! ... Well! So you're going to produce another play, huh? Got a pretty good script this time?

MARTIN: Think so. But I need a couple of darned good actors. Somebody like Lunt and Fontanne.

CLARK: [*Puzzled*] What?

MARTIN: I say that these two parts have to be played just right—I've got to find two good actors.

CLARK: Hey! Hold on a minute!

MARTIN: What's the matter?

CLARK: Haven't you heard? I'm not representing actors anymore. I'm in the big money now ... the really important end of it. I'm representing stagehands.

MARTIN: Stagehands. That's a break. I've been worried sick about getting some competent stagehands.

CLARK: Sure. They are the most important people in the-

atre today. They run the works. I've got some of the
biggest people in the business. Spike Kennedy, Butch
Hutchins . . . Spike Kennedy is out there waiting . . .
can he come in?

MARTIN: Sure thing.

CLARK: [*Going to door*] Hey, Spike! Come on in.

[SPIKE *enters, swaggering, looking around.*]

SPIKE: [*To* CLARK] Remember, I'm not promisin' nuttin'
. . . no commitments . . . Well, nice joint, pretty near
good as our clubrooms . . . [*At desk*] Ahh, Drunken
Fyfe!

CLARK: This is Spike Kennedy, Jack . . . Mr. Martin.

MARTIN: How are you, Mr. Kennedy?

SPIKE: Hello, Jack . . . sit down . . . Sam here says you
want to be a manager. What have you ever done?

MARTIN: Well, I've done quite a number of plays . . .

SPIKE: Speak up! Lemme hear you. What?

MARTIN: I say I've done a number of plays.

SPIKE: [*Suspicious*] You ain't the Shuberts?

MARTIN: No, no!

CLARK: Spike is one of the best stagehands there is. Had
a lot of experience. Tell him about yourself, Spike.

SPIKE: Did you catch me in *Our Town?*

MARTIN: *Our Town?* Yes, I saw that.

SPIKE: Great show! No scenery. Didn't have to do nothing. I hate scenery. Fellow named Frank Craven or
something—actor—he moved all the furniture. Great
show. Played cards down in the cellar all season . . . I
made a 450 pinochle hand in spades during the third
week . . . Great show!

CLARK: Spike played a solid season in that show. Didn't
you, Spike?

SPIKE: Every night, from eight to eleven. And you didn't
have to stop in the middle of the game on account of
scenery. I hate scenery.

CLARK: I don't think you'll make a mistake, Jack, taking
a man like this. He's a great talent. Tell him some more
about yourself, Spike.

SPIKE: Well, remember that show last season . . . it was
in the . . . Plymouth The-atre, and the manager wanted
to move it across the street to the Music Box?

MARTIN: Oh, yes.

SPIKE: Just across the street. Well, I'm the guy made him put in on trucks and take it all the way around the block.

MARTIN: You don't say?

SPIKE: Piled it all up on the trucks—got it good and scratched up. Then we throwd it off the trucks onto the sidewalk—got it all banged up. I hate scenery.

CLARK: It took twelve hours, didn't it, Spike?

SPIKE: Sixteen! Couldn't turn on Broadway . . . had to go all the way over to Sixth Avenue . . . made 'em postpone the opening . . . had to give 'em back all their money.

CLARK: He got a medal from the truckdriver's union, didn't you, Spike?

SPIKE: Aww, it wasn't anything!

CLARK: Spike's a great fellow, Jack. Of course, there've been some Hollywood nibbles, but Spike figures he wants to stick to the stage, don't you, Spike?

SPIKE: Sure . . . no pinochle. They just play gin rummy in Hollywood . . . Who's going to be in this play?

MARTIN: Well, I'm trying to get Lunt and Fontanne.

SPIKE: I don't know . . . little corny, ain't they? Now about billin' . . . my name has got to go up in electric lights.

MARTIN: Well, if we get Lunt and Fontanne . . .

SPIKE: Alright . . . if you think they're more important!

CLARK: Now, now, it'll be alright.

MARTIN: It'll be alright, Mr. Kennedy. We'll put your name in lights above the play.

SPIKE: Oh . . . okay . . . er . . . wait a minute . . . has it got any scenery? I hope it ain't got scenery. I hate scenery.

MARTIN: Well . . . a little.

SPIKE: Oh, well . . .

CLARK: Now I'm sure it hasn't got much, Spike . . . there'll be plenty of time for pinochle.

SPIKE: I hate scenery.

MARTIN: Just one light set.

SPIKE: [*To* CLARK] Just one light . . . oh . . . overtime!

MARTIN: May we call it a deal, Mr. Kennedy?

SPIKE: Maybe I better read the script before I say yes.

CLARK: Sure . . . you wouldn't mind, Mr. Martin?

MARTIN: Not at all.

CLARK: [*Handing script to* SPIKE] Here you are, Spike.

SPIKE: Needs cutting, don't it? [*Starts for door*]

MARTIN: Just a minute, Mr. Kennedy . . . Before he goes,

Sam, maybe you can get Mr. Kennedy to give me a little audition?

CLARK: You wouldn't mind, would you, Spike? Showing Mr. Martin what you can do?

SPIKE: For nuttin'? . . . Sure thing, Jack. What do you want me to do?

MARTIN: Let's see . . . suppose you pick up that chair right there and carry it across to the other side of the room.

SPIKE: [*Crossing to small chair*] Just me alone?

MARTIN: Yes, try it.

SPIKE: I ain't never seen the chair before . . . it's a strange chair. I'm kinda nervous.

MARTIN: It's nothing to be nervous about.

SPIKE: Well! [*Picks up chair all wrong*] No . . . let me start over again. [*Tries again*] Now, this time I'm going to do it. [*Grabs chair awkwardly, stumbles across room*] Sorry.

[*Wipes perspiration from face*]

MARTIN: Thank you very much.

SPIKE: I don't feel it yet! [MARTIN *starts to right the chair—*SPIKE *stops him.*] Hey! Where's your union card?

MARTIN: I'm very sorry.

SPIKE: O.K., O.K. . . . forget it.

MARTIN: There's just one thing, Sam . . . there's a quick change in the show. You know, in the dark. I wonder if Spike would be willing to show me just what he can do.

CLARK: Sure . . . wouldn't you, Spike?

SPIKE: All you got to do is name it. Just name it.

MARTIN: Well, now, let's say that when I say "Strike," the lights go out and this desk is to be put in that corner, this chair is to go over there and these two chairs up there. And this picture is to be taken down and that one put in its place. Is that clear?

CLARK: Got that, Spike?

SPIKE: Sure . . . photographic mind . . . desk over there . . . chair under desk . . .

MARTIN: No, no. Chair over there.

SPIKE: Chair over there. Picture down, other one up. I can do it! Gimme room!

MARTIN: And one more thing . . .

[MISS FREYLINGHUYSEN *enters.*]

SECRETARY: Oh, Mr. Martin . . .

MARTIN: Just a minute, Miss Freylinghuysen . . . let's say there's an audience out there and the whole thing has to be done very quietly, right?

SPIKE: Right!

MARTIN: Very quietly . . . out in front two lovers are whispering a tender farewell . . . I'll switch out the lights and yell "Strike!" Very quietly. Remember. Shhh . . .

SPIKE: [*Loud whisper*] Got you . . . I got you . . . a tender farewell.

MARTIN: STRIKE!

[*Lights out. Yelling and noise. "Goddamn it" . . . "Son of a —" . . . "Get out of my way, will ya" . . . "OUCH" . . . "For Christ's sake . . . you lousy . . . son of . . . a . . . (Scream) . . . goddamn"*]

MARTIN: LIGHTS!

[*Lights up. The place is a shambles. Desk upside-down, picture broken—hanging on one wire, the* SECRETARY *draped over the desk, vase in* MARTIN'S *hands, etc.*]

SPIKE: [*A chair hanging around his neck*] I HATE SCENERY!!

BLACKOUT

THE ARMY WAY

by Arnold Auerbach

First produced in *Call Me Mister*, at the National Theatre, on April 18, 1946, with the following cast:

SAM Alan Manson
SOLDIER Tommy Knox
CAPTAIN BAINES George S. Irving
PAUL REVERE George Hall
MASTER SERGEANT Harry Clark
CORPORAL Bill Calahan
DENTAL OFFICER Sid Lawson
INSURANCE OFFICER Glenn Turnbull
HYGIENE OFFICER Roy Ross

PROLOGUE

PROLOGUE: SAM, *a soldier, enters from the left followed by another soldier. SAM is extremely peeved. They cross the stage during the scene and exit right.*

SAM: Why shouldn't I gripe? Here I am, held up two weeks in this lousy separation center, just because some jerk lost my papers.

SOLDIER: Well, that's the army for you. If they don't shoot you with bullets, they strangle you with red tape.

SAM: Red tape! Paper work! I've had a belly full of it! You want a pair of shoe laces—fill out these eight-four forms! You can't even burp without doing it in triplicate!

SOLDIER: Aw, take it easy.

SAM: Why should I? Look at the way you have to stand in line for everything. Boy! What the army has done to my feet.

SOLDIER: I don't see anything wrong with a little standing in line—

SAM: A little standing in line! You want some chow, or a doctor, or a pack of cigarettes, and where are you? At the tail end of the crowd! This wasn't an army—it was an eight million man Conga line!

SOLDIER: Well, we won the damn war, didn't we?

SAM: I'm not sure. I bet the surrender papers didn't get through channels yet. Anyway, we won a lot of other wars, without all this hocum. Look at the American Revolution. George Washington fathered the whole country and never once used a mimeograph machine.

SOLDIER: Say, wouldn't it have been funny if they had all this red tape back in those days?

SAM: You said it. Take a guy like Paul Revere. Suppose
he'd had to go through channels before making that
ride? What do you think would have happened? Let
me tell you—
[*They exit right.*]

SCENE: *An orderly room, or army office, in 1775.* CAP-
TAIN BAINES, *clad in the costume of the period sits at a
desk, writing.* PAUL REVERE *dashes in through the door.
He is fumbling, eager, eternally frustrated—the revolu-
tionary counterpart of the sad sack.*

REVERE: [*As he enters, highly excited*] Captain! Captain!
[*Going to* BAINES] Captain, the British are coming!
They—
BAINES: Just a minute, Revere. Do you have the permis-
sion of the First Sergeant to see me?
REVERE: No sir, but—
BAINES: Well, suppose you go out that door and try com-
ing in like a soldier.
REVERE: But, Captain—
BAINES: [*Apoplectic*] Did you hear what I said!
REVERE: [*Feebly*] Yes, sir.
[*Dashes toward door, notices that* BAINES *has bent to
absorb himself in papers again, slams the door but
stays in the room. Knocks*]
BAINES: [*Not looking up*] Come in.
REVERE: [*Opens and closes the door, walks up to* BAINES,
salutes] Private First Class Revere reporting from Mes-
sage Center, sir.
BAINES: That's better. What's on your mind?
REVERE: The British are coming!
BAINES: Nonsense. Don't you know you're not supposed
to spread latrine rumors?
REVERE: But it's true, sir. They'll be here any minute.
BAINES: Phaugh! Anyway, they won't dare arrive until
tomorrow. There's a dance tonight at the officer's club.
REVERE: You don't understand, sir. They've broken
through near Lexington. Here's the bulletin from head-
quarters. [*He hands* BAINES *a scroll.*]
BAINES: [*Glancing at it, leaps up*] By gad! We've snafued
again! You'd better go out and warn the civilians.

REVERE: Yes, sir. I'll get a horse and leave right away.
[*Salutes briskly, starts out*]

BAINES: Just a minute—[REVERE *turns*, BAINES *is hurriedly writing an order.*] You'll have to clear with transportation first.

REVERE: Yes, sir.
[*Salutes, turns*]

BAINES: And check with intelligence.

REVERE: Yes, sir.
[*Salutes, turns*]

BAINES: And contact Quartermaster.

REVERE: [*He's caught in the middle of his turn and whirls back.*] But the British may be here any minute!

BAINES: Do as you're told. We don't get paid to think in this man's revolution.

REVERE: But all I want is a horse.

BAINES: Never mind. [*Handing* REVERE *the order he has written with a quill pen*] Here's a set of orders assigning you to Middlesex on temporary duty. Take these over to the supply room right away.

REVERE: [*Taking the orders*] But the British are coming! Why do I have to go through all this? Can't I just take your horse?

BAINES: No, he's off limits to enlisted men. Get going.
[REVERE *runs out the door as a roller curtain falls on the scene. This curtain is painted with posters: "Keep Your Muskets Clean," "Free Beer—Bunker Hill USO," "Sign Here For Weekend Passes."* REVERE, *on his way to the supply room runs past this curtain frantically seeking his way. The orchestra is playing "Yankee Doodle." As he runs off left, the roller curtain rolls up and we are in a quartermaster depot. A* CORPORAL *stands back of a counter that is piled high with equipment of the period. The* SERGEANT *is standing in front of a counter holding a batch of forms. They are dressed in the costumes of the period.* REVERE *dashes in and past the counter, stops himself and runs up to the* SERGEANT.]

REVERE: Is this the place where I get a horse?

SERGEANT: Yeah. Are you Revere?

REVERE: Yes.

SERGEANT: Good. We're expecting you. [*To the* CORPO-
RAL *behind the counter*] Okay, Sam. Ready for issue.

CORPORAL: Right.

[REVERE *hands the* SERGEANT *a scroll of his order and
requisition.*]

SERGEANT: Never mind that. I ain't learned to read yet.
One M-1 saddle! [SERGEANT *throws the scroll back of
the counter.*]

CORPORAL: One M-1 saddle.

SERGEANT: [*Handing* REVERE *a form and quill*] Sign
here.

REVERE: Wait a minute. All I want is—[CORPORAL *picks
up a heavy saddle and slings it over* REVERE'*s shoulder.*
REVERE *buckles under its weight.*] All I want is a horse.

SERGEANT: So what? You can't ride a government horse
bareback. One pair stirrups.

CORPORAL: One pair stirrups.

SERGEANT: Extra heavy.

CORPORAL: Extra heavy. [*Slings stirrups around* RE-
VERE'*s neck*]

SERGEANT: Sign here.

REVERE: What is this?

SERGEANT: One oat bag.

CORPORAL: One oat bag.

SERGEANT: With oats.

CORPORAL: With oats.

[*Hands the oat bag to the* SERGEANT]

SERGEANT: Sign here.

REVERE: Just get me a horse. I don't care if he goes hungry.

SERGEANT: Listen, bud—the rules say take oats, so oats
is what you get. You don't like it, eat 'em yourself.
[*Places oat bag around* REVERE'*s neck*] One pair boots.

CORPORAL: One pair boots.

[*Hands the boots to the* SERGEANT]

SERGEANT: Sign here.

[*A* DENTAL OFFICER *carrying a bag of dental tools enters hurriedly from right.*]

DENTAL OFFICER: Private Paul Revere?

REVERE: [*By now he can scarcely stand under his load.
Salutes. The others return the salute.*] Yes, sir?

DENTAL OFFICER: I'm here to give you a dental checkup. Open your mouth!

REVERE: Hey, what's the idea?

DENTAL OFFICER: What's the idea? You're going out on a combat patrol, aren't you? Suppose you're found dead with a cavity in your teeth? How'll it look for me?

REVERE: But I don't see—

DENTAL OFFICER: Quite. [*He shoves* REVERE *to a sitting position on a small barrel and begins working on his teeth.*]

SERGEANT: One powder horn.

CORPORAL: One powder horn.

SERGEANT: Without powder.

CORPORAL: Without powder.

[*Hands powder horn to* SERGEANT]

SERGEANT: Sign here.

[*A* HYGIENE OFFICER *carrying a large scroll enters hurriedly from the right.*]

HYGIENE OFFICER: Private Paul Revere?

REVERE: [*Salutes—all return the salute*] Yes, sir?

HYGIENE OFFICER: I'm from the Chief Surgeon's office. Before shipping out of this post, you're to receive a sex hygiene lecture.

REVERE: [*Extricating himself*] Sex lecture, what for?

HYGIENE OFFICER: Your orders call for you to visit every Middlesex village and farm. Farmers have daughters. Daughters lead to fraternization. Do you want to catch— [*Pointing an accusing finger in* REVERE's *face*] you-know-what?

REVERE: But all I want is a horse! How can I catch you-know-what from a—ow!

[*This last as* DENTAL OFFICER *taps a particularly sensitive tooth.*

An INSURANCE OFFICER, *carrying a large scroll, enters hurriedly from the left.*]

INSURANCE OFFICER: Private Paul Revere? [REVERE *salutes and all return the salute.*] Our records show that you haven't taken out the full ten-thousand-dollar GI insurance. [*He unrolls the scroll and begins to read. At the same time, the* HYGIENE OFFICER *reads from his scroll and the* DENTAL OFFICER, *working on* REVERE's

teeth, *exclaims at all the defects he is finding.*]
"Government insurance is not compulsory. Still, it is
in the best interests of the average soldier to sign up
for the full amount, because it affords protection to his
dependents in the event of—"
[*He continues to read in the same vein.*]

HYGIENE OFFICER: [*Simultaneously*] "The army realizes
that the sex impulse is an urge that is normal to everyone. Still, for the sake of his loved ones at home, the
soldier should try to practice continence. He should
realize that the casual acquaintance, or pick-up, is
fraught with danger."
[*He continues to read in the same vein.*]

DENTAL OFFICER: Slight cavity in the lower left incisor—
loose filling in rear molar—occlusion of upper right ca-
nine—etc.
[*The* SERGEANT *has, during this, been calling for and
piling on* REVERE *other paraphernalia, calling out each
item as before with the* CORPORAL *repeating the orders.*]

REVERE: [*Through all this making an attempt each time
to escape the clutches of the men*] Let me out of here—
Get me a horse—I'm supposed to be a Minuteman—I
wanna desert!

DENTAL OFFICER: [*Having finished, salutes*] Carry on!
[*Exits*]

INSURANCE OFFICER: [*Salutes*] Carry on!
[*Exits*]

SERGEANT: One riding crop.

CORPORAL: One riding crop.
[*Hands it to* SERGEANT]

SERGEANT: Sign here.

REVERE: [*Loaded to the hilt with equipment*] Now can
I get a horse?

SERGEANT: Sure. Get him a horse, Sam.

CORPORAL: We're all out of horses.

SERGEANT: Gee, that's right. Some big shot took them all
away for a parade in Washington.

REVERE: But I have to—

SERGEANT: T.S., pal. Come back tomorrow at three.
[*He and* CORPORAL *go off.*]

REVERE: But the British are coming! [*Getting up slowly,* *hardly able to under the weight*] Help! [*Calling for all to hear, moving down stage*] The British are coming! The British are—

[*Muffled drums are heard off left and a* BRITISH CAPTAIN, *carrying a sword, enters, followed by four* RED COAT SOLDIERS *carrying muskets.* REVERE *turns, sees them, shrugs.*]

They're here!!

BLACKOUT

BETTER LUCK NEXT TIME

by Moss Hart

First produced in *Inside U.S.A.*, at the New Century Theatre, on April 30, 1948, with the following cast:

MARY SHELTON Jane Lawrence
GLADYS Beatrice Lillie
THE STAGE MANAGER Rendell Henderson

SCENE: *The dressing room of Miss Mary Shelton. It is a star's dressing room. On the upstage wall is a costume rack on which hang several costumes of various kinds. There is a dressing table down left, a chair right of center, and a small table up right, near the door.* MARY SHELTON *sits at the dressing table. She wears a dressing gown, a towel wrapped around her hair and she is about half-finished with her makeup.*

SHELTON: [*Calling*] Gladys! [*No response*] Gladys!
  [GLADYS, *the maid, enters. She is ever so efficient, ready for any situation and master of it. She carries a tray with hairbrush, comb and powderpuff.*]
GLADYS: Coming!
  [*She crosses to* SHELTON, *singing and whistling.*]
SHELTON: [*Sharply*] Gladys! [GLADYS *stops her whistling but then emits one last peep. She hands* MISS SHELTON *the comb, then the brush, which* MISS SHELTON *uses.*] Powderpuff.
GLADYS: Hm?
SHELTON: Powderpuff!
  [GLADYS *pats her own face with the puff and then hands it to* MISS SHELTON. *There is a knock at the door.*]
GLADYS: Come in!
  [GLADYS *crosses to center above chair. The door opens and* MR. MERRICK, *the Stage Manager, comes in.*]
MERRICK: Eight-fifteen, Miss Shelton. I hope we have a big hit—and good luck.
SHELTON: Thank you, Mr. Merrick. [MERRICK *goes out*

311

and closes the door. GLADYS *stares after him.* SHELTON
looks at her with annoyance.] Oh God! I've never been
so nervous in my life. What's the matter, Gladys? What
are you staring at the door for?

GLADYS: He never should have said it—[*She turns.*] He
never should have said that. Once they say it, it's the
kiss of death. [*She crosses to left center.*] Not quite so
much blue on your eyelids, dear. You look like Anton
Dolin.

SHELTON: Who shouldn't have said what? What are you
talking about, Gladys?

GLADYS: Whenever the stage manager wishes you good
luck at eight-fifteen on opening night, you can figure
we close in about three weeks. Never saw it fail, dear.
[*She whirls up center, singing.* SHELTON *is very upset.*]
      "Blue skies, shining on me,
      Nothing but blue skies, do I see."
[*She gets higher and louder.*]

SHELTON: Stop that singing, Gladys! I never heard such
nonsense. I don't believe it for a minute.

GLADYS: Oh, well—Vivien Leigh—I mean—Lady Oli-
vier—[*She genuflects as before royalty.*] said the same
thing as I was dressing her, dear. We didn't even come
into New York with that one. [*Crosses to her*] And I
looked at my watch just now. It was eight-fifteen on the
dot. Wouldn't give you two cents for this clambake
now. [*She whirls away again, singing gaily.*]
      "Money is the root of all evil
      Money is the root of all evil
      Money is the root of all evil
      Take it away! Take it away!
      Take it away! Take it away!
      Take it away! Take it away!"

SHELTON: Gladys! Will you for God's sake stop that singing. I'm nervous enough as it is. If there's one thing
I'm not, it's superstitious. Never have been and never
will be.
[*She turns to her table again.*]

GLADYS: Wouldn't do you any good if you were, dear.
This show's got the kiss of death written all over it.

SHELTON: What on earth do you mean?

GLADYS: Well, dear, I worked out your name in my numerology book yesterday—"Mary Shelton"—you know what I got?

SHELTON: What?

GLADYS: The Titanic. That's how it worked out. According to my numerology book you should have been dead about three years ago. A little more rouge on your cheeks, dear. You look a little pale.

[*She whirls away and sings again.*]

"She died of a fever
And no one could save her
Singing cockles and mussels
Alive—Alive-o—"

SHELTON: [*Jumps up in a fury*] Gladys! Gladys! Come here! [*She points to the floor before her. She stands rigid as* GLADYS *slowly goes to her and stands quietly.*] Now you listen to me. I don't want to hear another word about numerology, astronomy or anything else. I want you to be absolutely quiet until they call "curtain." Understand?

GLADYS: Yes, ma'am. You want quiet.

SHELTON: Yes.

[SHELTON *sits.* GLADYS *tiptoes to chair center and sits; crosses her knees and folds her arms over her knees. There are a few moments of silence and then* GLADYS, *struck by a memory, bursts into gales of laughter, which she checks as* SHELTON *whirls on her.*]

GLADYS: I'm very sorry, madam. You wanted quiet.

SHELTON: Well, if it's that funny, I wouldn't mind hearing it. What is it?

GLADYS: Well, it might not strike you funny, dear, but it *killed* me. I nearly burst a gut.

SHELTON: Well, what is it?

GLADYS: [*Rises*] Well, dear, you remember when I was dressing Gertrude Lawrence in *Lady in the Dark*—you know—

[*She sings and dances.*]

"Jenny made her mind up when she was three
She herself was going to trim the Christmas tree
Christmas Eve she lit—"

SHELTON: Gladys!

GLADYS: [*Stops and continues the story*] Well, dear, you remember in *Lady in the Dark* they had all these revolving stages?

SHELTON: Yes.

GLADYS: Well, one night, the wardrobe woman—a silly bit if ever there was one—she was on stage eating a banana—and she slipped up and got caught between two of the revolves. [*She laughs again.*] Funny thing was, I'd been reading her palm not five minutes before and I told her that if I was her I wouldn't set foot out of the house. That's how bad her palm was. I've never read your palm, have I, dear?

[SHELTON'*s right hand is on the back of her chair.* GLADYS *lunges for it.* SHELTON *pulls it away.* GLADYS *falls forward on her hands and then rises.*]

SHELTON: No, you haven't.

GLADYS: Don't really have to. I read faces, too. Now these lines—[*She starts to trace lines on* SHELTON'*s face.*]

SHELTON: But what happened, Gladys? The story—what's the funny part?

GLADYS: Oh, yes, the funny part. Well, the funny part of it was, after she got out of the hospital, she came back to the theatre and slipped up and got caught between the same two revolves. [*Waits for a reaction that doesn't come*] Caught her in the same places, too. Of course, it doesn't seem very funny when you tell it— but I nearly burst a gut—

[*There is a knock at the door.* GLADYS *doesn't move.*]

SHELTON: Answer the door, Gladys.

GLADYS: Hm?

SHELTON: Answer the door!

GLADYS: What's the magic word?

SHELTON: [*Resigned*] Please.

[GLADYS *goes to door.*]

GLADYS: Come in.

[*The door opens and* MR. MERRICK *enters with several telegrams which he hands to* GLADYS *as he speaks.*]

MERRICK: Telegrams.

[*He exits.*]

SHELTON: Oh, thank goodness! Telegrams always take my mind off the opening somehow. Give them to me, Gladys.

GLADYS: Oh, they're not for you, dear. They're for me. So relax. I've got friends, you know. Oh, this is very interesting—it says, "Dear Gladys, The stars are absolutely wrong for your show tonight, but I hear Helen Hayes is looking for a new maid. Better luck next time. Love, Min." That's Cornell's maid. She's never been wrong yet. She's very psychic. [*Opens another*] Oh, listen to this—this is *very* interesting and no-vel. It says, "Dear Gladys, Last night I dreamt about Gilbert Miller. You know what that means, dear. Love, Sophie." That's Tallulah Bankhead's maid. The last time she dreamt about Gilbert Miller, you know what?

SHELTON: What?

GLADYS: The Normandie caught fire. Of course, I knew it the minute [*She rises.*] he opened the door and said, "Good luck."

[*She sings gaily.*]
  "In your Easter bonnet
  With all the frills upon it
  You'll be the grandest lady—"

SHELTON: [*Jumping up fiercely*] Gladys! Gladys! [*She repeats the gesture, pointing to the floor in front of her.* GLADYS *walks to the spot slowly.*] Now, listen to me! I don't want one word out of you until that door opens and they say, "Everybody on stage." Understand?

GLADYS: Yes, madam, I was only trying to cheer you up.

SHELTON: Well, don't.

[SHELTON *sits again.* GLADYS *goes very quietly to center chair and sits, mumbling to herself. Then she is quiet for a moment. She looks around the room in her boredom and spies her Ouija board on the table. She clears her throat rather pointedly.* SHELTON *turns slowly.*]

GLADYS: Madam, would you mind if I used my Ouija board, very quietly?

SHELTON: No. Providing it keeps you quiet. [*She turns back to her dressing table.*]

GLADYS: Thank you, madam.

[GLADYS *rises and starts toward her table.* SHELTON *sneezes.* GLADYS *stops, gives* SHELTON *a scathing look, returns to her chair, sits, rises again and goes to her*

*Ouija board; picks up the table and board and carries
them down to center, sits on the chair center and, with
her hands on the Ouija, begins to summon the spirits.*]

GLADYS: Ouija—Ouija, this is Gladys. Can you hear me?
Thank you, Ouija. Are you ready to give me control,
Ouija? Thank you. Is there a spirit in the room? [*The
"mover" jumps off the table.* GLADYS *dives after it.*
SHELTON *whirls around.* GLADYS *picks up the "mover,"
curtseys, returns to place.*] Y—E—S. Dear spirit, who
are you? What is your name? [*The "mover" spells a
name.*] Good God!

SHELTON: Well, who is it?

GLADYS: Booth—the man who shot Lincoln.

SHELTON: Nonsense.

GLADYS: Please, Miss Shelton. The night I got Jack the
Ripper, Ina Claire said "Nonsense" and she hasn't
been in a play since! How're you keepin', Mr. Booth?
Nicely, thanks, musn't grumble. Tell me, Mr. Booth,
what do you know about this show that's opening tonight? [*She moves her hands.*] Yes, I think it stinks,
too. But what else? What about Miss Shelton? Miss
Mary Shelton. Yes, yes, go on. Yes, that's right. Yes,
that's his name. Ritz Hotel, Boston. That's right.
Mmmmm? No? No, really! Well, whaddya know!
[*When the "Ritz Hotel" is mentioned,* SHELTON *rises
and crosses to* GLADYS' *left.*]

SHELTON: What is it, what's he saying?

GLADYS: Just a minute, Mr. B. [*To* SHELTON] That doctor
was all wrong. You *are* pregnant!

[SHELTON *screams and falls over backward.*]

BLACKOUT

I COULD WRITE A BOOK

by Max Wilk and George Axelrod

First produced in *Small Wonder*, at the Coronet Theatre, on September 15, 1948, with the following cast:

THE NORMAL NEUROTIC Tom Ewell
1. MOM Alice Pearce
   JOEY Jonathan Lucas
   GABBY Joan Mann
2. EDDIE Chandler Cowles
   DOLORES Marilyn Day
3. JOY POLLOI Mary McCarty
   CZAR NICHOLAS Mort Marshall

SCENE: *At rise, the* NORMAL NEUROTIC, *a harried, vaguely distraught young man, enters in front of the curtain, carrying three books.*

NORMAL NEUROTIC: Books, books, books. I just came out of Womrath's. I've been in there for four hours. All I wanted was something good to read. According to the *Times* these three are the country's best sellers. The *Trib* had another called *I Typed the Atlantic Charter*. Best sellers . . . everybody hates them and everybody reads them. The trouble is they're so predictable. Take this first one, for instance. *Mama Was a Mess Boy.* This'll be one of those warm, endless chronicles about somebody's family. I don't even have to read it. [*He tosses it away.*] I know exactly how it goes.

I remember my family . . . and most of all, Mom. Gee, Mom . . . she'd run away to sea when she was a girl . . . and the stories she used to tell. She was always full of good humored advice. I can see her now on the front porch . . .

[*The curtains part, revealing* MOM *staring off through a telescope.*]

Joey, the youngest, was always full of get-up-and-go. If it hadn't been for Mom, he might have turned out badly.

JOEY: [*Dashing on*] Mom, I betcha gonna be mad with me—I just killed the boy next door.

MOM: That's three this week.

JOEY: But all I did was hit him with a rock.

319

MOM: Well, young man, it's no supper for you tonight. Now you go right upstairs to bed.

JOEY: Yes, Mom.

[*He exits.*]

MOM: And Joey, before you do another thing—wash that blood off your hands.

NORMAL NEUROTIC: My sister, Gabby, was the darling of the house. She was always full of the Old Nick. If it hadn't been for Mom, she might have turned out badly.

[GABBY, *a bouncing redhead, enters.*]

GABBY: Mom!

MOM: Mom's been frettin'. Where you been these last three days?

GABBY: The fleet's in.

MOM: Oh, the Navy. It takes me back to when I was a girl. What mad times we used to have on the poop.

GABBY: And Mom, it's pretty hot in the engine room too.

MOM: Well, young lady, it's no supper for you tonight. Now you go right upstairs to bed—alone!

[GABBY *exits.*]

NORMAL NEUROTIC: I was the eldest, named after Papa. I was a dreamy kid, always full of love and hope. If it hadn't been for me, Mom would've never married.

[MOM *laughs, picks up telescope and resumes looking off.* NORMAL NEUROTIC *goes around curtain into scene.*] Mom, you'll never guess. I got "A" in all my subjects and they've made me Saint Joseph in the Christmas pageant and here's $112 I earned helping old ladies across the street.

MOM: Well, young man, I ain't playin' favorites, it's no supper for you tonight. Now you go right upstairs to bed.

NORMAL NEUROTIC: Yes, Mom.

[*He stamps off.*]

MOM: I ain't playin' favorites aboard this ship. [*She picks up a megaphone.*] Now hear this . . . now hear this . . . there will be no supper served aboard this ship.

[*Blackout on* MOM]

NORMAL NEUROTIC: That was Mom's quaint way of punishing us. Sometimes she would go six months at a stretch and never serve supper once. [*He examines sec-*

ond book.] Then there's this next one, *Anger Is My Brother.* The story of disillusioned youth, told through clenched teeth. I know what it's like.

[*Drops book*]

It was the summer after the autumn after the war. He was drinking too much. It was that kind of summer. He was trying to forget IT. He never talked too much about IT. Not him. Not Eddie. IT was all locked up inside him, quiet, see? Only to Dolores he sometimes talked. He had known too many women too well, and Dolores he knew best of all. It was that kind of relationship. Tonight she seemed particularly close. Not far off and gone away, but close.

[*Curtains part.* EDDIE *and* DOLORES *discovered in tight embrace on deck of ferry boat.*]

See? He turned away, and in that throaty voice which thrilled her deeply, inwardly, downwardly, he said—

EDDIE: Oh, Christmas!

DOLORES: You been through hell, honey.

EDDIE: On a one-way ticket, and I paid the fare in dreams.

DOLORES: Your face is young, honey, but your eyes is old.

NORMAL NEUROTIC: Dumb little dame, he thought.

EDDIE: [*Moving to rail*] C'mere.

DOLORES: Who?

EDDIE: You.

DOLORES: Me?

EDDIE: Yeah.

DOLORES: Oh!

[*She rushes to him and they stand nose to nose.*]

NORMAL NEUROTIC: But again the old tension was there. IT! He was only his old self when he met an old buddy from his old outfit.

[*He goes around curtain and enters scene.*]

EDDIE: Baby! Baby! It's me, Eddie.

NORMAL NEUROTIC: Eddie! Oh, ho, ho!

EDDIE: Ha, ha, ha!

NORMAL NEUROTIC: Remember the calisthenics on the beach? [*They execute a few.*] Take it easy, Eddie.

EDDIE: [*Pounding* NORMAL NEUROTIC *on the back*] Take it light, Baby!

NORMAL NEUROTIC: [*Back in front of the curtain*] But

again there was the memory of IT. The brutal training in Miami, the long wait in New York, the NOT going over.

DOLORES: What's gonna be, honey?

NORMAL NEUROTIC: And suddenly they were together—

[DOLORES *and* EDDIE *go into a tremendous clinch as center curtains close.*]

—and not apart, and IT didn't matter, and he was her and she was him and they were one and—afterwards moonlight spilled on the bed. He looked gently down at her and fled into the night. Tomorrow he would need his clothes, but he wouldn't think about that tonight. Not him, not Eddie.

[*Blackout on* EDDIE]

And look at this. A nine-hundred-page historical novel. *Wild Blow the Winds for Lust.* Three-and-a-half pounds. Know just how it goes ... It was snowing flakes in Russia. Napoleon camped cozily by the gates of St. Petersburg while the czar reveled at a state ball in the winter palace. Joy Polloi, the tempestuous little Confederate girl, a pretty baggage with all Europe at her feet, danced tempestuously out on to the balcony.

[JOY POLLOI *enters.*]

She caught the czar's eye, and there was a tight throbbing sensation in her alabaster bosom.

JOY: Whatever can that cute ol' czar see in li'l ol' me? [CZAR *enters.*] Good evenin', czar of all the Russias. [*They bow deeply to one another.*]

NORMAL NEUROTIC: He looked at her and he knew. Something inside clicked.

CZAR: [*Attempting to embrace her, although her figure makes it difficult*] Sometimes I think there's a barrier growing up between us.

NORMAL NEUROTIC: From somewhere there was a low rumbling sound ...

[*Several rumbles of drums are heard.*]

JOY: But hark! Ah hear gunfire to the left.

CZAR: Thunder, my dear.

JOY: It's gunfire, suh! Leave me go. Imperial Majesty. Ah wanna die in bed—the way ah lived!

NORMAL NEUROTIC: A shadowy figure loomed in the distance—

[*He goes around curtain and enters scene on his knees, wearing Napoleon hat. As* NAPOLEON—]

Attention! I demand the surrender of Moscow.

CZAR: Napoleon Bonaparte!

JOY: Fiddlededee—if it isn't the Little Corporal!

NAPOLEON: Joy Polloi!

CZAR: You two know each other?

JOY: Know each other? Shall I tell the boy where we really were Bastille Day?

NAPOLEON: Up the Seine—without a paddle. I know when I'm licked. *Je vais*—I go!

[*He exits on knees and comes in front of curtain.*]

JOY: Napoleon is in full retreat, Nick.

CZAR: [*Embracing her*] Never have so many owed so much—to so much.

[*Curtain closes on* JOY *and* CZAR.]

NORMAL NEUROTIC: Thus a czar and a little Southern girl cemented a firm friendship between the two countries which continues to this very day. [*During the following speech, he picks up the books and exits slowly as he starts to read the one about* MOM.] Afterwards, Joy becomes Bismarck's housekeeper and the mother of five men in President Harding's cabinet. Best sellers—huh! I could write one myself if I had the time. [*Reads*] "Mom had gone to sea when she was a girl, and the stories she used to tell—" Ha, ha, ha.

BLACKOUT

DO IT YOURSELF

by Charles Gaynor

First produced in *Lend an Ear*, at the National Theatre, on December 16, 1948, with the following cast:

ANNOUNCER William Eythe
ALVIN BLODGETT Al Checco
BESSIE BLODGETT Jenny Lou Law
JUNIOR Hal Hackett

BESSIE: You come here. [JUNIOR *crosses to her.*] Now you look me straight in the eye. [*He does so.*] Drop dead, what?

JUNIOR: [*Sulkily*] Drop dead, Mother.

BESSIE: [*Patting his cheek*] That's better. We mustn't forget our manners. Now you just run upstairs and get washed up for supper, like a good boy.
[JUNIOR *crosses with bag.*]

ALVIN: What's in that bag, son?

JUNIOR: It's my schoolbooks.

BESSIE: Now, now, Junior, we know your school burned down yesterday, don't we, Daddy?

JUNIOR: Ah, so I went to anudder school.

ALVIN: Put the bag on the table. [JUNIOR *does so.* ALVIN *takes out large packages of bills.*] I'll just see what he's got in here. Hey now, where did this money come from?

JUNIOR: It's the payroll for the Granby Machine Works.

BESSIE: How did you get it?

JUNIOR: I stuck 'em up. How else?

BESSIE: Is that the truth?

JUNIOR: [*Mimicking her*] Is that the truth?

ALVIN: [*Indignantly*] Of course it's the truth. Junior's never told a lie in his life. [ALVIN *crosses to* JUNIOR.]

BESSIE: With what did you stick them up?

JUNIOR: Wid a rod.

BESSIE: Wid a wat? I mean, with a what?

JUNIOR: A rod. [*Holding up gun*] A pistol, stupid.

BESSIE: Well, why didn't you say so in the first place? Now where did you get the rod?

ALVIN: [*Taking gun from* JUNIOR *and putting it in his pocket*] You remember, Bessie, Santa Claus gave it to him for Christmas last year—for being a good boy.

BESSIE: [*Starting to cry*] And now look what's happened; our only son a robber.

JUNIOR: I'm not a robber. I'm a stick-up boy.

BESSIE: [*Corrected*] Oh. Our only son a stick-up boy.

ALVIN: Why did you do it, son, after all the advantages we've given you?

BESSIE: [*As* JUNIOR *pauses*] Yes, why, Junior, why?

JUNIOR: All right, you asked for it, so now you're gonna get it like it is. It's because I'm a . . . J. D.

BESSIE: What in the land of Goshen is a J. D.?

JUNIOR: *Juvenile Delinquent!*

[JUNIOR *exits.* ALVIN *and* BESSIE *freeze with expressions of horror which they hold throughout the next speech.*]

ANNOUNCER: A juvenile delinquent! The admission from the lips of their only son. Alvin Blodgett and his wife were confronted by the greatest problem of their lives. This scourge that is sweeping the country had struck into their own home. What's to do, Alvin? Face facts, man. Face facts!

ALVIN: What's to do, Bessie?

BESSIE: Face facts, man. Face facts.

ALVIN: [*Calling*] Junior, you come in here.

JUNIOR: [*Entering*] Whaddaya want now?

ALVIN: You're going to be punished, young man, so you'll never forget it.

JUNIOR: Ah, go blow it.

BESSIE: [*Automatically correcting him*] Junior, go blow it, *Father.*

ALVIN: Now you march yourself in there, and I'll be with you in a minute. [JUNIOR *exits. To* BESSIE] It's the first time I've ever punished him, and I'm afraid it's going to hurt me more than it does him.

BESSIE: Leave your ivory tower, Alvin, and be strong.

[ALVIN *exits.* BESSIE *crosses to chair, picks up newspaper from floor, straightens chair, humming softly. A shot is heard offstage. She listens, with no change of expression, crosses to table, picks up silver, plate and napkin from one of the places and takes them to sideboard. She moves third chair away from table.* ALVIN *enters with smoking gun.*]

ALVIN: Well, Mother, I guess he'll never do that again.

BESSIE: [*Crossing to table*] You only did your duty, Daddy. [*Taking gun from his hand*] Spare the rod and spoil the child.

BLACKOUT

GORILLA GIRL

by Jean and Walter Kerr

First produced in *Touch and Go,* at the Broadhurst Theatre, on October 13, 1949, with the following cast:

DIRECTOR George Hall
ASSISTANT DIRECTOR Art Carroll
MISS HILTON Kyle MacDonnell
SKEETS Jonathan Lucas
TRAINER Lewis Nye
CAMERAMAN Nathaniel Frey

SCENE: *An African jungle location. Palm trees, coco-nuts, a suggestion of a beach on which a rotting boat—a small lifeboat—is seen. At opposite side of stage are a camera, camp chairs, and the usual paraphernalia. On stage are a* CAMERAMAN, *working over the camera and getting it ready, and an* ASSISTANT DIRECTOR *who is act-ing as supervisor of props, details, etc. At rise, the* AS-SISTANT *is finishing the process of making the boat look weatherbeaten as the* DIRECTOR *strides on.*

DIRECTOR: [*To audience*] You have no doubt seen a great many animal films, and perhaps enjoyed them. What you may never have stopped to consider is how difficult it is to make such pictures—what back-breaking work goes into the shooting of any film involving members of the animal kingdom. To make this clear to you, we now take you on location. [*To the* ASSISTANT] Got that boat battered up enough, Mike?

ASSISTANT: [*He and the* CAMERAMAN *move the boat and chairs downstage.*] Good and rickety, sir. Almost falling to pieces.

DIRECTOR: [*Crosses below boat and snatches up rope*] Ye gods, man! Look at this rope. Miss Hilton's been adrift in this boat for ten days. That rope should be in ribbons. Fix it.

ASSISTANT: Yes, sir.

DIRECTOR: [*Sees suitcase*] Wait a minute! Is this the suit-case she has in the boat?

ASSISTANT: Yes, sir.

DIRECTOR: [*Picks it up*] What's the matter with your eyes? It's too new! I tell you Miss Hilton and everything in that boat have been exposed to rain, sleet, hail and the hot sun. [*Throws down the suitcase, turns to his chair and picks up script*] It's got to look it.

ASSISTANT: [*Kicks suitcase*] I'll beat the hell out of it. [*He places suitcase right of boat and puts a new rope on the boat.*]

DIRECTOR: Is she ready? Is Miss Hilton ready?

[MISS HILTON *enters.*]

MISS HILTON: Coming!

DIRECTOR: Good morning, Miss Hilton.

ASSISTANT: Good morning, Miss Hilton.

CAMERAMAN: Good morning, Miss Hilton.

[MISS HILTON *nods, crosses to her chair and sits.*]

DIRECTOR: Miss Hilton, we can start shooting just as soon as the trainer gets here with his animal. Now, I'm going to have to ask you to be patient today. It'll be slow work. Slow and tricky. Any time you're working with animals, there's bound to be a lot of re-shooting. But I'm sure you understand. [MISS HILTON *nods.*] Now where's that gorilla? Anybody seen his trainer? [GO-RILLA *and* TRAINER *enter. Ad lib sounds*] Oh, there you are! [*He goes to them*] Now, this gorilla—does he need any special handling?

TRAINER: [*Removes chain from gorilla*] Oh, no, he's done a lot of picture work.

DIRECTOR: Fine. I'm always glad when they've had experience.

TRAINER: You'll love Skeets. [*Pats* SKEETS *on back and pushes him towards* DIRECTOR] Frank Buck never shot a picture without Skeets.

[SKEETS *sits.*]

DIRECTOR: [*Crosses to* SKEETS] Now, Skeets—he understands his name, does he?

TRAINER: [*Nodding*] Sure.

DIRECTOR: Now, Skeets, watch me carefully. [*Backs up*] Now you come from over here, cross around in front of this tree, pick up a coconut, break it open, drink some milk out of it, throw it away, turn around, see the suitcase, pick it up, open it, take out a looking glass, look at yourself, laugh a couple of times—that'll kill them—notice the rope over there, chew on it, follow the rope over to the boat, look surprised when you see there's a girl in the boat, then tiptoe very carefully over to her, and then start to rock the boat very gently. Okay? [*Crosses to his chair*] He'll never get it. We'll be all day on this scene. [SKEETS *executes all business quickly and precisely, then pauses.*] Well! Could be a lot worse. [*Goes to boat with* MISS HILTON] Now, Miss Hilton, when he comes toward the boat and starts to rock it; let him rock it about three times. Then you come to. We see that because your hand slowly comes up and falls over the side of the boat. Okay?

[MISS HILTON *is now in the boat, out of sight. The* DIRECTOR, *back to his chair, signals* CAMERAMAN.] All right. Skeets, let's start back a little.

[SKEETS *picks up rope, does business, moves toward boat, starts to rock it. He rocks it three times, pauses, nothing happens. He rocks it some more. Nothing happens.*]

Miss Hilton! Miss Hilton!

MISS HILTON: [*Her head pops from boat, brightly.*] Yes?

DIRECTOR: Where's your hand?

MISS HILTON: Here.

DIRECTOR: But I didn't see it.

MISS HILTON: [*Thinks a minute*] When didn't you see it?

DIRECTOR: [*Patiently*] I didn't see you put it over the side of the boat.

MISS HILTON: I didn't put it over the side of the boat.

DIRECTOR: [*Rises*] But I want you to put it over the side of the boat.

MISS HILTON: Oh, well, all right.
[*Drops hand over the side*]

DIRECTOR: Not now. I want you to lie down in the boat and put your hand over.

MISS HILTON: [*Turns to do it, then hesitates*] Won't that be awkward?

DIRECTOR: That's all right. It should be awkward. You've been knocked out. You've been drifting in an open boat for ten days.

MISS HILTON: Oh. [*Pause*] How did that happen?

DIRECTOR: Think back, Miss Hilton. The scene we shot yesterday. You were shipwrecked.

MISS HILTON: In this picture? I know I had a shipwreck at Paramount, but—

DIRECTOR: Let's try it now, shall we? Have you got it?

MISS HILTON: Yes, I put my hand over the side although I'm lying down.

[*She lies down in the boat with her hand already over the side.*]

DIRECTOR: [*Over-patiently*] After he rocks it. After the third time he rocks it. [*Sits in his chair*] All right, Skeets. Take it back a little bit. From the rope.

[SKEETS, *a little wearily, goes back to rope.*]

He's coming now, Miss Hilton. And he'll rock it three times.

[SKEETS *rocks it once.* MISS HILTON *pops up.*]

MISS HILTON: Was that three?

[SKEETS *throws rope down in disgust, walks away.*]

DIRECTOR: Not quite three, Miss Hilton.

MISS HILTON: Well, could somebody count it for me? It's awfully dark down here.

DIRECTOR: [*Signaling* ASSISTANT] Oh, Mike, would you—

[*But before he can give the instruction to his* ASSISTANT, SKEETS *has held up his paw and crosses to the boat. He rocks it three times, holding up fingers to indicate one, two, three.* MISS HILTON *smiles.*]

MISS HILTON: Oh, thanks. You're a peach.

[*She ducks under again.*]

DIRECTOR: [*Crosses and sits in his chair*] Fine, fine. Take it again, from the boat this time, Skeets.

[SKEETS, *starting from the boat, rocks it, indicating one, two, three, and* MISS HILTON's *hand flies into the air, flops heavily over the side. Her head pops up immediately.*]

MISS HILTON: Was that it?

[SKEETS *walks down right, sits down, dejectedly.*]

DIRECTOR: Not exactly, Miss Hilton. [*Crosses to boat*] It should be a slow, groping movement of the arm.

[SKEETS *taps her on shoulder, shows her how to do it, limply.*]

MISS HILTON: Say, that's effective. [*To* DIRECTOR] Do you mind if I do it his way?

DIRECTOR: That would be lovely, Miss Hilton.

MISS HILTON: I'll tell you. Give me a couple of days to work on it.

[*Rises in boat*]

DIRECTOR: All right, boys. We'll jump to the next sequence. [*He helps* MISS HILTON *out of the boat.*] This is a lot easier, Miss Hilton. You don't have to do anything. You're unconscious. Now, the gorilla picks you up over here, looks to see if anyone is around, and then carries you over here. [*Indicates area*] Then stares into your face. Now, all you have to do at this point is open your eyes and scream.

ASSISTANT: [*Crossing to* MISS HILTON *with a slip of paper*] I've written it down for you, Miss Hilton.

DIRECTOR: Now, Skeets, your part in this is to—
[SKEETS *waves him away to indicate he already has it.*]
Oh, all right.

MISS HILTON: [*Reads paper*] "Open my eyes. Scream." Okay.

DIRECTOR: We can shoot this the first time, Joe.
[*He sits enthusiastically.* SKEETS *approaches* MISS HILTON, *picks her up, carries her down right. Just before scream*, MISS HILTON *whips out paper and reads directions.*]

DIRECTOR: Oh, no! Cut, cut! [SKEETS *puts her down.*] Miss Hilton, dear, you can't look at the paper in camera range. It would show in the picture.

MISS HILTON: Well, all right. I'll just have to keep it in my head.
[SKEETS *looks heavenward, crosses to* MISS HILTON, *pinches her as a cue. She squeaks.* SKEETS *gestures* "See?"]

DIRECTOR: Oh, that's fine! Get that, Miss Hilton? When the time comes for you to scream, he'll pinch you.

MISS HILTON: Thanks a lot.
[*She crosses to boat.* SKEETS *follows.*]

DIRECTOR: [*Sits*] Joe, let's do it this time.
[SKEETS *picks her up, repeats business, arrives at position, pinches her. She giggles.*]

DIRECTOR: [*Jumps up*] Cut!
[SKEETS *puts her down, crosses right, sinks to knees, beats his hands on the ground in despair.*]

MISS HILTON: I'll bet I spoiled that, didn't I?

DIRECTOR: You giggled, Miss Hilton. You're supposed to scream.

MISS HILTON: Mr. Portman, would you tell me something?

DIRECTOR: Of course, Miss Hilton.

MISS HILTON: Why do I scream?

DIRECTOR: Miss Hilton, you're in his arms. [SKEETS *crosses to* MISS HILTON.] You wake up. You see him. You're afraid of him!

MISS HILTON: [*Dawning*] Oh! Could he make a face? [SKEETS *looks front.*]

DIRECTOR: Miss Hilton. He's a gorilla. A beast of the jungle. Savage. Ferocious. Look at him! [SKEETS *and* MISS HILTON *face each other.*]

MISS HILTON: Did you know my first husband? [SKEETS *walks away.* TRAINER *goes to him quickly.*]

TRAINER: Oh, Mr. Portman.

DIRECTOR: Yes?

TRAINER: Skeets would like to take a look at the script.

DIRECTOR: [*Very matter-of-factly*] Oh, sure. [ASSISTANT *hands script to* SKEETS *who leafs through.* SKEETS *tosses script upstage angrily and starts to leave.*]

TRAINER: Skeets! Where are you going?

DIRECTOR: What's the matter?

TRAINER: He says too many scenes with Miss Hilton. He quits.

DIRECTOR: But he can't quit! What'll I do with my picture?
[SKEETS *lifts his arm angrily, expressively in response.*]

TRAINER: No, Skeets!
[*Tries to come between* SKEETS *and* DIRECTOR.]

DIRECTOR: Skeets, you just don't understand Miss Hilton. She's a lovely girl. She just hasn't had your opportunities.
[SKEETS *gestures to* TRAINER]

TRAINER: He says all right.

DIRECTOR: Wonderful!

TRAINER: On one condition. [SKEETS *pantomimes his requests*—TRAINER *interprets them.*] Private chauffer back and forth from his cave.

DIRECTOR: Certainly.
[SKEETS *pantomimes next demand.*]

TRAINER: Soft focus lens in all his close-ups.

DIRECTOR: Right!

   [SKEETS *pantomimes "Feature billing," etc.*]

TRAINER: Feature billing, over the title. In letters four times as large as Miss Hilton's.

   [MISS HILTON *screams—success! They go into action.*]

DIRECTOR: She's screaming! Camera! We've got it!

   [SKEETS *picks* MISS HILTON *up while she's screaming, carries her up center.* CAMERAMAN *dollies in.*]

BLACKOUT

CINDERELLA

by Jean and Walter Kerr

First produced in *Touch and Go,* at the Broadhurst
Theatre, on October 13, 1949, with the following cast:

STEPMOTHER Jean Handzlik
NEIGHBOR Helen Gallagher
1ST SISTER Nancy Andrews
2ND SISTER Peggy Cass
CINDERELLA Kyle MacDonnell
NEWSBOY Jonathan Lucas
PRINCE Lewis Nye
PAGE Larry Robbins

ANNOUNCER: As everyone knows, Mr. Elia Kazan is one of the foremost directors of our time. If we examine the plays he has directed—notably *A Streetcar Named Desire* and *Death of a Salesman*—we see that they contain that mixture of passion, guts and poetic realism which has become his stamp in the theatre. Now we would like to show you what might happen if Mr. Kazan ever decided to direct a production of *Cinderella*.

SCENE: *One of those sets, interior and exterior combined, with an outdoor stoop at one side. Its design, however, is fairy-taleish and period. At rise, the* STEPMOTHER *and a woman* NEIGHBOR *are seated on the stoop, fanning themselves. Much mood. A tinkling piano is heard in the distance. Sounds of a cat fight come from offstage.* STEPMOTHER *rips open the bosom of her dress and fans it furiously. A cat meows over the microphone system.*

STEPMOTHER: Sure is hot.
NEIGHBOR: Sure is.
  [WOMAN's *scream comes from offstage.* WOMAN *and* MAN *in nightgowns run across stage at back of the scrim.*]
STEPMOTHER: [*Rises on scream*] Yes, it's rape weather. [*Sits*] That scurvy wench, Cinderella, skipping off somewhere and leavin' me to do the chores.
NEIGHBOR: Cinderella's all right.
STEPMOTHER: She's liked. But she's not well-liked. [*Fans herself under the arms*]
NEIGHBOR: Where's your two lovely daughters?

STEPMOTHER: Went to the ball, down at the Palace.

NEIGHBOR: How'd they look? Lovely?

STEPMOTHER: Lovely. Make you feel proud to see 'em getting ready for the ball shaving together, in the bathroom.

NEIGHBOR: [*Rises*] Twelve o'clock. [*Starts off*] Jim'll be comin' home. I'd better get the stomach pump ready. [STEPMOTHER *gets watering can and waters imaginary plants.*] Wha'cha doin'?

STEPMOTHER: Waterin' the beans.

NEIGHBOR: I don't see no water.

STEPMOTHER: See any beans?

[NEIGHBOR *exits over ladder.* CINDERELLA *floats in.* STEPMOTHER *meets* CINDERELLA *center.*] Cinderella, you been drinkin'?

CINDERELLA: [*Crosses in front of her, goes into the house*] Just a little taste, honey. Nothin' more than just enough to be sociable.

STEPMOTHER: [*Has followed her in*] How many? [*Puts watering can in fireplace*]

CINDERELLA: Well, I can tell you that, honey. I can tell you exactly how many. I saved the olives so I could keep count. [*Takes olives out of her pocket, puts them on a plate on the table and counts.*]

STEPMOTHER: [*Pacing*] You're shiftless. You're just a no-good. Trash—nothin' but trash. How do you expect me to keep you around here when you're nothin' but trash?

CINDERELLA: You're shakin' the olives, honey. If you're going to shake the olives I'll never get to know my limit. [NEWSBOY *enters—knocks on door*]

STEPMOTHER: Answer the door. [STEPMOTHER *exits to bathroom.* CINDERELLA *goes to door.*]

NEWSBOY: Collect for the *Evening Gazette*.

CINDERELLA: Why sure, honey. [*Kisses him*]

NEWSBOY: Thank you, ma'am. [*Exits*]

CINDERELLA: [*Crosses to bathroom door*] Honey, I had

twenty-seven. You goin' to be in there long?

[STEPMOTHER *enters from bathroom door, shoots a dirty look at* CINDERELLA, *who exits through bathroom door.* TWO SISTERS *enter, cross the stage and stop outside door. They take two deep breaths and enter.*]

1ST SISTER: Hey, Mom.

[*Throws hat through bedroom door.*]

2ND SISTER: There's our Mom!

STEPMOTHER: [*Applying headlock to* 2ND SISTER, *vigorously slaps* 1ST SISTER] Were you popular? Were you liked? Were you well-liked?

[*Pushes* SISTERS *away, sits*]

2ND SISTER: Go on, Sis. Tell her about the Prince. Tell her.

1ST SISTER: Listen, Mom. [*Sits on* STEPMOTHER*'s knee*] Y'know Prince Charming?

STEPMOTHER: He is a very respected man. A good connection.

1ST SISTER: Well, Mom, you won't believe it of one of your daughters—I no sooner get inside the joint than he gives me the glad eye. [*Rises*] An' I was dancing, Ma. I was dancing with some other fella, see? An' we danced past the Prince, see? An' I feel this pinch.

[*Kneels at her mother's feet*]

STEPMOTHER: [*Rises, clasps her daughter's head to her*] My girl. He pinched my girl. I can see it all now—he's gonna be coming to this house. He's gonna be coming to this house and making you a very nice proposition.

1ST SISTER: [*Rises*] Aw, what's the use? Tell her the truth.

2ND SISTER: [*Rises*] He didn't give me no glad eye, Ma. She ain't been pinched.

1ST SISTER: Why don't we face it? Why don't we face the truth? He didn't pinch me. I pinched him!

[*Sits and sobs, head on table*]

STEPMOTHER: [*Takes chair from under* 1ST SISTER] What kind of talk is this? He was crazy about you.

1ST SISTER: No. No.

STEPMOTHER: I know how it was. He was crazy about you. Burning up. He took you out on the balcony—

2ND SISTER: Ma, will you shut up?

STEPMOTHER: [*Takes* 2ND SISTER *by the shoulders*] Don't you take that tone with me.

[*Starts to shake her*]

1ST SISTER: [*Shakes* STEPMOTHER] Ma, wake up. Wake up, Ma! I'm just trying to tell you how it was.

STEPMOTHER: [*Throws* 1ST SISTER *off and follows*] You're no good. You're shiftless and no good. [*Slaps her on behind*] Forty-five years old and you ain't been pinched. When you gonna settle down and be pinched?

1ST SISTER: [*Slaps* STEPMOTHER] Get away from me. [*She and her sister look at each other and sob.*] I'm sorry, Ma.

[*She crosses to her mother and places her head under* STEPMOTHER'*s shoulder.*]

STEPMOTHER: [*Throws her off. To* 2ND SISTER] She likes me. That girl likes me. She cried over me.

2ND SISTER: [*On her knees, takes* STEPMOTHER'*s hand*] Sure, Ma, you're well-liked.

1ST SISTER: [*Exercising against door jamb*] Look, Ma, I'm losin' weight all the time.

STEPMOTHER: Are you girls keepin' in trim?

2ND SISTER: You know we are, Ma.

STEPMOTHER: [*Picks up beanbag and throws it to both sisters*] Everybody's crazy about a girl who keeps her figure.

[WOMAN *in nightgown—same as before—enters followed by a different* MAN. *She is screaming, runs off.* PAGE *enters, blows bugle.*]

PAGE: Make way for Prince Charming. Make way for the Prince.

[PRINCE *enters. Stops, flexes muscles, enters house, takes out shoe. Speaks in Marlon Brando rhythms.*]

PRINCE: I got a shoe. A shoe belongin' to some dame. This dame I am stuck on. Whose shoe?

STEPMOTHER: Prince, I don't think you've been introduced to my two lovely daughters.

PRINCE: How are you? Who else around here?

STEPMOTHER: Why, no one. Just my two lovely daughters.

[*The* PRINCE *is about to leave. Just as he reaches the door, from bathroom offstage comes the sound of a toilet flushing. The two* SISTERS *sit up.*]

PRINCE: Who's in there?

STEPMOTHER: Oh, just Cinderella.

PRINCE: [*Goes to bathroom door and beats his fists on it passionately*] Cinderella! Cinderella!

CINDERELLA: [*Enters from bathroom*] Prince. You musn't look at me just now. My little old face all hot and steamy—and nothin' but this mangy old bathrobe on. [PRINCE *starts removing his clothes while* CINDERELLA *primps before a mirror.*]
My goodness, honey, a girl don't expect a man to walk in this way without no warning. Not giving her a chance to do all those nice little things a girl does to herself before a man comes to call. [*Turns and sees* PRINCE] My goodness, honey, I ain't dressed. And now you ain't dressed.

PRINCE: How come you run away from the ball, baby? How come?

CINDERELLA: Oh, I had to—

PRINCE: You come along with me. I'm going to take you to the Palace. I like your style, baby. [*Picks her up over his shoulder. Glances back at* STEPMOTHER, *referring to earlier toilet flush*] I knew all the time that wasn't Niagra Falls.
[*They exit.*]

STEPMOTHER: Sure is hot!

1ST SISTER: Sure is.
[*Same* WOMAN *in nightgown enters, screaming, followed by the first* MAN *who chased her. The two* SISTERS *spit on their hands and chase him off.*]

BLACKOUT

I NEVER FELT BETTER

by Joseph Stein and Will Glickman

First produced in *Alive and Kicking,* at the Winter Garden Theatre, on January 17, 1950, with the following cast:

WIFE Louise Kirtland
BARNEY Jack Gilford
CHARLIE Carl Reiner

SCENE: *A living room. There is a small sofa, an endtable at each end, a small radio and other props to dress the set. At rise,* BARNEY *is idly picking at candy in a box on an endtable. He samples one, decides against it. Takes another.* WIFE *enters, dressed to go out.*

WIFE: I'm going shopping, Barney.

BARNEY: Okay.

WIFE: I'll be back in about an hour.

BARNEY: Take your time.

WIFE: Now don't forget! No cigarettes!

BARNEY: When I make up my mind, I make up my mind. I gave up cigarettes for good.

WIFE: And don't you feel better?

BARNEY: Better? I feel like a new man!

WIFE: And you *look* so much better since you've stopped smoking.

BARNEY: I know I do ... [*Glances at wristwatch*] It's been almost thirty-eight minutes!

WIFE: Darling, I'm proud of you ...

BARNEY: Look, I'm putting on weight already! [*Feeling his thigh*]

WIFE: Now, if you're tempted to take a cigarette, what are you going to say to yourself?

BARNEY: [*Springs to attention and recites stiffly*] Tobacco is a filthy weed ... And from the devil doth proceed ... It stains your fingers, burns your clothes ... And makes a chimney of your nose!

WIFE: [*Pats him fondly on head*] That's a good boy ... it hasn't made you nervous or anything, has it?

BARNEY: [*Laughs casually*] Nervous? Ridiculous! Run along, dear.

WIFE: Bye, Barney.

[WIFE *exits.* BARNEY *seats himself on couch, picks up newspaper, casually reads for a moment. Then he folds the newspaper, and without a facial expression he very deliberately tears it into strips; as the strips get smaller and smaller, he tears more and more viciously. Then, dead-pan, he sits and drums for a moment with his fingers and stares. The doorbell rings.* BARNEY *leaps up as if hit by an electrick shock; he stares at the door, horrified.* CHARLIE *enters.*]

CHARLIE: Hello, Barney!

BARNEY: [*Dazed*] Charlie? Oh ... Oh ... [*Earnestly*] Charlie, don't *ever* ring a doorbell like that! You can give a guy a heart attack!

CHARLIE: What's the matter with you? Don't you feel well?

BARNEY: [*Relaxed again*] Me? I've never felt better in my life. Gave up cigarettes, you know.

CHARLIE: Gee, I wish I could.

BARNEY: There's nothing to it. You feel like a cigarette, just take a piece of candy instead.
[*Motioning to candy on table.*]

CHARLIE: I smoke like a fiend, two packs a day.

BARNEY: That's murder ... [*Picks up magazine*] Know what it says in this article? They tested two hundred smokers and two hundred non-smokers at the University of Pennsylvania. The two hundred non-smokers all have good jobs, are happily married and have an average of two and a third well-adjusted children ...

CHARLIE: No kidding? What about the two hundred smokers?

BARNEY: [*Meaningfully*] Everyone of them has dandruff!

CHARLIE: Well, that certainly is interesting ... Now, about that house you want to buy ... I took a look at it ... [*Takes out a pack of cigarettes—puts one in his mouth.*]

BARNEY: Yes?

CHARLIE: Well, I'd think it over if I were you ... [*Lights the cigarette—*BARNEY *watches every move.*] You see, it's in a good location ...

BARNEY: [*His eyes on the cigarette*] What is?

CHARLIE: The house . . .

BARNEY: Oh . . . [*Jams piece of candy in his mouth; offers box to* CHARLIE]

CHARLIE: It's not far from the station, and the grounds are beautiful, but there's a hitch . . .

BARNEY: What?

CHARLIE: [*Leans over, confidentially*] They're gonna build a garbage disposal plant right across the street. [*He blows a big cloud of smoke right at* BARNEY.]

BARNEY: [*Breathes ecstatically, following the trail of smoke with his nose*] Oh, that's lovely . . .

CHARLIE: You really think so? Anyway, let me give you some more details . . .
[*Puts out cigarette.* BARNEY *watches him hungrily, snatches a piece of candy and falls back, exhausted.*]

BARNEY: [*Muttering to himself*] Tobacco is a filthy . . . and from the devil . . .

CHARLIE: What'd you say?

BARNEY: Nothing.

CHARLIE: Another thing . . . the road leading up to the house, nothing but sand.

BARNEY. Sand?

CHARLIE: Yeah. That road wasn't built for cars, it was made for camels!

BARNEY: Camels, *so* mild . . .
[*Starts twitching.*]

CHARLIE: And the inside of the house needs a paint job. The living room is sort of a dingy yellow . . .

BARNEY: Yellow?

CHARLIE: Well, it's more of an old gold . . .

BARNEY: Old Gold . . .
[*Laughs maniacally*]

CHARLIE: I don't blame you for being happy. You're lucky you didn't put a deposit on it . . . *LUCKY!* [BARNEY *reacts; his feet shoot up rigidly.* CHARLIE *puts another cigarette in his mouth and searches for a match.*] Got a match?

BARNEY: I . . . I think so . . .
[*He lights a match and his hand trembles more and more as it nears* CHARLIE'S *cigarette. He lights it and is shaking as he tries to blow out the match.*]

CHARLIE: [*All through this, he is unaware of what* BAR-
NEY *is going through.*] Thanks. Look, Barney, if you
want to get a real idea of what the place is like, I'll
draw you a little diagram.
[*He puffs on the cigarette.* BARNEY *puts his finger into
the smoke then licks it.*]

BARNEY: [*In a trance*] Yeah, yeah . . .

CHARLIE: [*Takes out pencil and paper; hands cigarette
to* BARNEY] Here—hold this a second.
[*As* CHARLIE *draws a diagram,* BARNEY *holds the cigarette at arm's length like a snake, jams candy into his
mouth, etc., then fights cigarette and finally brings it
to his lips. At the last second,* CHARLIE *takes it from
him and gives him the drawing.*]

CHARLIE: There! [BARNEY *stares close to* CHARLIE's
face.] You want to know something? One strong wind
and that house'll blow away like a puff of smoke. [*He
says this right into* BARNEY's *face exhaling smoke the
while.* BARNEY *jumps up, rigid.*] I'd forget that house
if I were you. What do you think?

BARNEY: Hah? Hmmmm? What?

CHARLIE: What do you think?

BARNEY: [*Staring into space*] Tobacco is a filthy weed!

CHARLIE: And it's a big investment. Where can you raise
the money?

BARNEY: From the devil doth proceed!

CHARLIE: Now, Barney, you gotta make a decision!
[*Touches* BARNEY's *shoulder*]

BARNEY: Don't touch me! Don't touch me! [*Rushes
around room*] I can't stand it! [*Rushes to* CHARLIE,
pleading] Charlie . . . please . . . [*Pantomimes for cigarette*] Please . . .

CHARLIE: Ohh . . . What a boor I've been! You're off cigarettes and I've been smoking!

BARNEY: [*Gibberish*] Please . . . please . . . I'm dying . . .

CHARLIE: How could I do such a thing! You want to stop
smoking and I'm going to *help* you!
[BARNEY, *still talking gibberish, falls to his knees.*]
Yes, sir! I'll throw them away!
[BARNEY *tries to stop him*—CHARLIE *breaks away,
flings his pack out the window.* BARNEY *is frozen,
hands outstretched.* CHARLIE *makes as if he snuffs his*

lit cigarette out but really keeps it in his hand (palm)
out of sight of the audience.]
No more cigarettes!
[*He fans smoke out of the room with his hat.* BARNEY
starts to search frantically—finds gun in endtable
drawer.]
Barney, what are you doing?
[*Struggles with him*]
Don't!

BARNEY: Lemme alone!

CHARLIE: Don't!

[*During struggle,* BARNEY *surreptitiously takes a drag*
from the cigarette concealed in CHARLIE's *palm—un-*
seen by audience]

BARNEY: [*Pushing* CHARLIE *away*] Get away from me!
[*He shoots the gun in the air then puts barrel in his*
mouth as if to smoke it. Then he ecstatically exhales
the smoke.]

BLACKOUT

BUCK AND BOBBY

by James Kirkwood and Lee Goodman

Produced in *Dance Me a Song*, at the Royale Theatre, on January 20, 1950, with the following cast:

BUCK Lee Goodman
BOBBY James Kirkwood
SECRETARY Ann Thomas

ANNOUNCER: Ladies and gentlemen. Undoubtedly some of you are parents. And we like to think that most of you have at one time or another been children. If you fit into either one of these categories you've probably been exposed to the kind of radio program that floods the airwaves in the early evenings—to the delight of thousands of kiddies and to the consternation of their parents. We'd like to take you behind the scenes and show you what goes on just before and during one of these programs. We take you now to Studio Number Four.

SCENE: *A small radio station. There is a table with a couple of chairs and two standing mikes right and left of the table. At rise,* BUCK *is seated at the table with an ice bag on his head. He is obviously hung over.*

BUCK: [*Looking at watch, feeling head*] We're on the air in five minutes. Where is that little monster?
[SECRETARY *enters with arm-load of fan mail.*]
SECRETARY: [*Very loudly*] Did you call me, Buck? Here's the Buck and Bobby fan mail.
BUCK: Softly, please, Miss Finch. There are those of us who have hangovers this evening. I merely said, "Where is that little monster—we're on the air in five minutes."
SECRETARY: I'm afraid he'll make it as usual. It's just another one of his big days. Today he's in the clutches of the Boy Rangers of America. They're making him an honorary Spotted Horse Brave, Second Class of the Purple Panther Division.
BUCK: Bully. Miss Finch, do you realize that today's pro-

gram will make my 7,560th broadcast of the *Adventures of Buck and Bobby* with that perennial child radio star. And people wonder why I drink.

SECRETARY: What are ya crabbin' about? You got a sponsor, ain't ya? Ya makin' money. Look at all the fan mail.

BUCK: Miss Finch, this is strictly a moral issue. Just read one of those letters.

SECRETARY: [*Opens letter*] This one's from Jackie Schnitzer, Milwaukee, Wisconsin. Age nine. "Dear Buck and Bobby: Last week, thanks to my 'Buck and Bobby Junior Taxidermist Kit' I stuffed our pet canary and got a spanking from Mother. Next week—MOTHER."

BUCK: See what I mean. [*Trumpet blares offstage.* BUCK *winces, holding head.*] That would be Spotted Horse Brave, Second Class.

SECRETARY: Brace yourself.

[BOBBY *enters wearing knickers, sweater, feather; carries tomahawk.*]

BOBBY: [*Gives Indian whoop*] Hiya, Buck. [*Slaps* BUCK *on the back*] How.

BUCK: How.

BOBBY: Boy, what a keen shin-dig. They made me a Spotted Horse Brave, Second Class . . . of the Purple Panther Division. And then we had a jim-dandy tribal banquet. Buttermilk and fish-balls. And you know what they tattooed on my chest?

BUCK: What?

BOBBY: Hair.

SECRETARY: Hey, you're on the air in ten seconds.

[*All three scramble for scripts. Theme music of "Boola-Boola" up and out.*]

BUCK: [*At microphone*] Hello, boys and girls, it's five o'clock.

[BOBBY *picks up cymbals and crashes them together.* BUCK *winces.*]

And time again for the *Adventures of Buck and Bobby* presented by Choco-crunchies. That yummy candy.

[*Bell note*]

ALL THREE:

    Yummy, yummy, yummy

    Yummy, yummy, yummy

    That's Choco-crunchies

Won't upset your tummy
Won't upset your tummy
That's Choco-crunchies
A taste that will thrill yahse
But won't make yah bilious
Yummy, yummy, yummy
Yummy, yummy, yummy
Choco-crunchies
CHOCO–CRUNCHIES.

BOBBY: It's yummy.

BUCK: Yes, mothers, it's yummy, and nutritious too. Here's a delicious candy made from dextrose, glucose, dried egg albumen, raw beef muscle, lecithin curds, amoniated sulphate, sulphated amonium and containing that new secret ingredient.

[*Fanfare*]

Sugar. And topped with a rich chocolate-colored covering made from glucose, dextrose, dried egg albumen, raw beef muscle, lecithin curds.

[BUCK *and the* SECRETARY *become ill*—SECRETARY *staggers offstage.* BUCK *turns back to audience.*]

BOBBY: Hiya kids, this is Bobby! Buck and I want you to drag your mothers down to the grocer's today and make them buy you Choco-crunchies. They come in three sizes: small, medium and the large economy box which you can plaster and use as a summer home.

BUCK: [*Returning to the microphone—weakly*] So yummy eating, kids.

BOBBY: Yeah, yummy eating, kids.

BUCK: Did you say yummy?

BOBBY: Yes, I said yummy.

BUCK: Say it again.

BOBBY: Yummy, yummy, yummy, yummy . . .

BUCK: [*Stopping him*] And now, kids, for—

BOBBY: Yummy!

BUCK: And now, kids, for Buck and Bobby's Daily Good Manners Jingle.

BOBBY:

A child should be polite
His habits should be sweet
A child should help old ladies
When they try to cross the street.

> Always help a lady
> Whose leg is in a cast
> 'Cause when you snatch her pocketbook
> She cannot run so fast.

BUCK: And now for the *Adventures of Buck and Bobby*. As you will remember, Buck and Bobby are in darkest Africa engaged in the frantic search for Goona, the ash-blond Queen of the Ant-eaters, who has in her possession a formula for a weapon more deadly than the atomic bomb, which if it falls into the hands of a group of secret agents known only by the sinister initials Baton, Barton, Durston and Osborne may well mean the end of civilization as we know it today.

BOBBY: Buck and Bobby have reason to believe that this secret formula which if it falls into the wrong hands may well mean the end of civilization as we know it today . . . is tattooed underneath the tongue of Emmy Lou Mitlock, the only girl in Bobby's gym class.

BUCK: Yesterday, as you will remember, Emmy Lou Mitlock had fallen into the hands of the evil witch doctor Varga, who had given her a secret potion which was making her grow smaller every minute. Buck and Bobby had been tied to a stake by a tribe of man-eating headhunters who were doing a savage death dance around them. Shall we listen?

[BOBBY *starts beating on tom-tom.*]

BOTH:

> Umbaga-boogie-woogie
> Umba rhumba
> O yo to ootchie coo matsumba
> Tumba uh—das is dein schnitzelbaum.

BOBBY: Gloriosky, Buck, that was a close shave.

BUCK: Right, Bobby. But I was able to get our hands loose. Thanks to our genuine Buck and Bobby magnifying glass, bolo knife and pastrami slicer.

BOBBY: Gloriosky, Buck, here comes a tiny little pygmy. Maybe he knows where Emmy Lou Mitlock is. You talk to him.

BUCK: Right, Bobby. We wantum find Emmy Lou Mitlock. Gotum secret formula tattooed underneath tongue and battleship Wisconsin tattooed on chest. You savvy.

BOBBY: Gloriosky, Buck, it's not a pygmy at all. It's Emmy

Lou Mitlock and she's getting smaller every minute.

BUCK: Right, Bobby, and that battleship tattooed on her chest has shrunk to the size of a rowboat.

BOBBY: Gloriosky, Buck, we better get into our Buck and Bobby Rocket Ship and get out of here.

BUCK: Right, Bobby, while I get this crate off the ground, you contact headquarters on the two-way atomic phone.

BOBBY: Buck and Bobby to headquarters. Buck and Bobby to headquarters. Over.

BUCK: Headquarters to Buck and Bobby. Headquarters to Buck and Bobby. Go ahead.

BOBBY: Buck and Bobby to headquarters. The savages are surrounding the plane. Not much time. What'll we do? Over.

BUCK: Headquarters to Buck and Bobby. Mercy—you better get that crate off the ground. Over.

BOBBY: Buck and Bobby to headquarters. The savages have jammed the motors with poison arrows. Emmy Lou Mitlock has just disappeared. There's a forest fire and Goona the ash-blond Queen of the Ant-eaters still has the secret formula which if it falls into the wrong hands may well mean the end of civilization as we know it today. There's not much time. What'll we do? Over.

BUCK: Headquarters to Buck and Bobby. Repeat after me. "Now I lay me down to sleep . . ."

BOBBY: Well, it looks like trouble for Buck and Bobby. And now it's health-time. All you kids, join Buck and I in a glass of wholesome pasteurized milk. Get your milk while I pour one for Buck and me.

[*Pours two glasses of milk*]

BUCK: Just look at that rich, creamy color.

BOBBY: So nourishing and so good.

BOTH: Here's to you kids.

[BOBBY *drinks milk*—BUCK *puts glass down. Takes pint bottle of whisky out of pocket and drinks it.*]

BOBBY: Gloriosky . . . that's real milk, eh, Buck?

BUCK: Right, Bobby.

BOBBY: And now, kids, for Buck and Bobby's secret surprise offer of the week. Send Momseys and Dadseys out of the room.

BUCK: Now, kids, here's all you have to do to get for your

very own to have and keep for the rest of your natural lives, a genuine human shrunken head. Merely pry the diamond loose from mother's engagement ring and send it to us together with not more than three well-chosen, four-letter words on why you like Choco-crunchies.

BOBBY: And, kids, as an extra added premium, if you get your order in the mails early, we will send you a booklet on how you can breed a whole family of deadly poisonous water moccasins right in your very own bathtub.

BUCK: Ahhh, don't tell Momseys and Dadseys—surprise them.

BOBBY: Say, kids, remember that Choco-crunchies is not only yummy to eat, but also serves many other useful purposes. Tell Mom that Choco-crunchies is good for scouring pots and pans. And tell Dad, in case he's losing his hair, that Choco-crunchies is good for the scalp. Here's a testimonial from one of thousands of satisfied fathers.

BUCK: I've been rubbin' Choco-crunchies into my scalp for nigh on to twenty-eight years and I can truthfully say that I've got the hairiest fingertips you ever saw.

BLACKOUT

HIGHLIGHTS FROM THE WORLD OF SPORTS

by Abe Burrows

Produced in *Two on the Aisle*, at the Mark Hellinger Theatre, on July 19, 1951, with the following cast:

PRODUCER Loney Lewis
ANNOUNCER Elliott Reid
CAMERAMEN Richard Gray and Robert Gallagher
LEFTY HOGAN Bert Lahr

SCENE: *A television studio. The* ANNOUNCER *is sitting at a table looking at scripts—bored. A* PRODUCER *with earphones is standing poised over him. There is a microphone, boom and a camera.* PRODUCER *throws a cue. The* ANNOUNCER *is galvanized.*

ANNOUNCER: *(Very sharp)* Good evening, sports fans everywhere . . . [*Music in and out*] Yes, sports fans, this is Bill Burns. Your old sportscaster bringing you highlights and spotlights from the world of sports on the spot. This program is completely . . . [*He turns a page of the script.*] spontaneous and unrehearsed. These sportscasts are telecast to you through the courtesy of our sponsors, the makers of Sawsie Dusties, the cereal that gives you that quick extra energy. And now, friends, for our guest tonight. Sawsie Dusties is proud to present our guest on tonight's parade of sports stars . . . Sports fans, here's a real . . .

[PRODUCER *signals to wings. Nothing happens.* PRODUCER *signals again more urgently.* LEFTY HOGAN *comes out in uniform. The lights get him.*]

old timer . . . a great ball-player and a great man.

LEFTY: [*Crosses to front of table, backside to camera*] Now, now?

ANNOUNCER: Lefty Hogan. Hiya, Lefty. Sit right here, Lefty.

LEFTY: [*Trying to look happy*] Hiya, Buster.

ANNOUNCER: Well, Lefty, say hello to our TV audience.

367

[LEFTY *waves to camera.*] Now, Lefty, tell the folks—
how long have you been donning those old spiked
shoes?

LEFTY: Huh?

ANNOUNCER: How long have you been donning those old
spiked shoes?

LEFTY: [*Crosses legs, looks at shoes*] Well, I've had these
shoes about two, three years.

ANNOUNCER: How long have you played big league baseball?

LEFTY: Huh?

ANNOUNCER: How long have you played big league baseball?

LEFTY: Well, let's see now . . . I started in 1920 and this
is . . . 'bout fourteen, fifteen years.

ANNOUNCER: If you started in 1920, that would make it
more than twice as long as that.

LEFTY: Well, I ain't counting the time the other side was
batting.

ANNOUNCER: Well, you were a great symbol of American
sport all these years . . . and you're still a great pitcher.

LEFTY: No, I'm a coach—been a coach for ten years.

ANNOUNCER: Oh, I'm sorry . . . what with covering sports
I never get a chance to see a game. [*He chuckles—
LEFTY imitates him.*] Of course you're a coach . . . and
a coach is very valuable. Errr—exactly what does a
coach do?

LEFTY: [*Doing a double take*] Well, I try to learn the
young players all my experiences just like they was
once teached to me.

ANNOUNCER: Where did you first play baseball?

LEFTY: At college.

ANNOUNCER: You went to college?

LEFTY: Sure I went. Do I look like a diseducated guy?
I played college football, basketball and baseball. I
went to college for six years.

ANNOUNCER: Why six years?

LEFTY: I had a contract. So like I said I played college
football, basketball, baseball . . .

ANNOUNCER: And finally, Lefty, you became a professional—you had to. You had to because of that deep

love you possessed for this great sport! Because of that you wouldn't rest until you became part of this beloved game.

LEFTY: No, I wanted to make some dough.

ANNOUNCER: Magnificent sportsman that you are . . . and what a great pitcher you were. Tell me, Lefty, after being so great, what made you decide to take off your armor and cease to do active battle on the field of honor with the other knights of baseball?

LEFTY: I never played night baseball . . . only daytime.

ANNOUNCER: No, I mean why did you quit pitching?

LEFTY: Whyn't you say so? You talk like an umpire. Well, why I quit pitching was I hurt my hand. Busted it. Couldn't pitch no more.

ANNOUNCER: Hurt your hand in the service of the great game! But you went down in action. How'd it happen, this tragedy of a great athlete?

LEFTY: Well, it was back in 1948 . . . I was pitching against the Red Sox . . . and in the first inning I got a tough break.

ANNOUNCER: What was it?

LEFTY: They made nine runs. I never missed a bat. So anyway . . .

ANNOUNCER: But you hurt your hand.

LEFTY: No! No—I didn't hurt my hand. So anyway, in the second inning I was a little better—they only made six runs. But still the manager turned me out, anyway.

ANNOUNCER: But all the time your pitching hand was hurt and sportsman and gentleman that you are you made no mention of it.

LEFTY: No, my hand was all right . . . so then later I got dressed and went home and when I came in the door, my wife said, "Well, they certainly made a bum out of you today." So I socked her and busted my hand.

ANNOUNCER: Broke it defending your reputation as a pitcher! Tell me one more thing, Lefty. What advice would you give to young boys who are eager to become future ball-players?

LEFTY: Well—I'd tell 'em—

ANNOUNCER: What would you tell these future diamond greats?

LEFTY: Well, I'd . . .

ANNOUNCER: Let's hear what an old timer has to say to the new generation. What yesterday has to say to today.

LEFTY: Well—

ANNOUNCER: What's your advice to these young, young kids?

LEFTY: [*Exasperated*] They'll be old men before I get to tell 'em. [*Stops*] Now what was the question?

ANNOUNCER: What's your advice to these young kids?

LEFTY: Well, I'd say they should practice a lot . . . work hard . . . stay away from girls . . . live clean lives . . . don't take baths, that softens up their hands . . . eat good healthy meals . . .

ANNOUNCER: Now, that's what I wanted to hear you say.

LEFTY: It is?

ANNOUNCER: Yessiree—ladies and gentlemen, those meals are mighty important. Especially breakfast. Now tell me, Lefty, what's your favorite breakfast?

LEFTY: Pizza.

ANNOUNCER: And what do you take for that quick, extra energy?

LEFTY: A hook 'a rye.

ANNOUNCER: What a grand sense of humor. But seriously, Lefty, now that it's almost time to go, how about those Sawsie Dusties?

LEFTY: How about what?
    [*Squinting quizzically*]

ANNOUNCER: Sawsie Dusties—you remember, you were going to tell the young folks something about them.

LEFTY: Oh yeah, now I remember, Buster. Now, kids, listen.

ANNOUNCER: That's right, Lefty. Tell the kids about those great Sawsie Dusties.

LEFTY: Well, listen—

ANNOUNCER: Tell them about that quick extra energy.

LEFTY: When you go to the grocery—

ANNOUNCER: Tell them about Sawsie Dusties' rich, tangy goodness.

LEFTY: —buy some—

ANNOUNCER: Tell them what's the most important thing to remember about Sawsie Dusties.

LEFTY: [*Glaring at the camera disgustedly*] Don't eat 'em—THEY'LL KILL YA!

BLACKOUT

SPACE BRIGADE

by Betty Comden and Adolph Green

First produced in *Two on the Aisle*, at the Mark Hellinger Theatre, on July 19, 1951, with the following cast:

HODGEKINS Richard Gray
HOTCHKISS Robert Emmett
HITCHCOCK Robert Gallagher
CAPTAIN UNIVERSE Bert Lahr
HIGGINS Stanley Prager
RADIO VOICE Walter Kelvin
QUEEN CHLOROPHYL Gloria Danyl
DENIZENS OF VENUS Arthur Arney, John Raye, Victor Reilley, Buford Jasper, Roscoe French

SCENE: *The planet Venus. It's a weird-looking scene. Suddenly a roar of engines is heard. The engines stop. Three members of the Space Brigade enter. They're equipped Buck Rogers/Flash Gordon style.*

HODGEKINS: This way, Captain Universe.
[CAPTAIN UNIVERSE *enters. He's* really *equipped; he wears a hat with an antenna coming out of it.*]
CAPTAIN UNIVERSE: Men of the Spa-a-ace Brigade ... This is a great moment.
HODGEKINS: Where are we, Captain?
CAPTAIN UNIVERSE: What's our stellar orientation?
HODGEKINS: 38 over 74 South by East Space.
CAPTAIN UNIVERSE: Our orbitary retraction?
HOTCHKISS: Zero over zero plus ten.
CAPTAIN UNIVERSE: Our gravitational quotient?
HITCHCOCK: 200 CC's centigrade.
CAPTAIN UNIVERSE: Longi-space-itude?
HODGEKINS: 72 Space East.
CAPTAIN UNIVERSE: Lati-space-itude?
HOTCHKISS: 34 Space North.
CAPTAIN UNIVERSE: Making our distance factor ... [*Looking at his instruments*] Men, as I calculate it, we're in Perth Amboy.
HODGEKINS: [*Looking around*] Captain Universe, haven't you made a slight error?
CAPTAIN UNIVERSE: What's that? Are you saying that I have made an error? I, Captain Universe, leader of the Spa-a-ace Brigade, which asks no quarter and gives no quarter in its struggle against the malicious forces of interplanetary evil?

HODGEKINS: Oh no, sir. It's just that your detrolecticalter may be off a little.

CAPTAIN UNIVERSE: Mmm . . . [*Shakes instrument*] That's right. Shows you when you use cheap plutonium. This is two degrees off which means . . . [*Does mental calculation*] Men, this is the planet Venus.

HOTCHKISS: [*Awed*] Venus?

CAPTAIN UNIVERSE: If this isn't Venus, I'll eat my antenna . . . Venus! And what a day to discover it. This is October 12, 2492 . . . exactly one thousand years since Columbus said the earth was round. Took us quite a few years to correct that little error, eh?

HODGEKINS: Venus! Captain Universe, if this is Venus, we of the Spa-a-ace Brigade have accomplished our mission!

HITCHCOCK: Yes! Venus has the richest deposits of neutrocraniplatium in the entire secondary galaxy.

HOTCHKISS: And with the right supply of neutrocraniplatium we can continue the polarization of syndrovasalobregen in unlimited quantities . . . and you know what that means . . .

CAPTAIN UNIVERSE: You mean . . . [HOTCHKISS *nods.*] Men, this means that we can finally wipe out the disease that has been plaguing mankind for 500 years . . . Penicillin poisoning! And we've done it—we of the Spa-a-ace Brigade.

ALL:
> [*Sing to the tune of the Cornell song*]
> We're all noble Space Brigadesmen
> Through the skies we race
> Nothing else is on our minds
> Our hearts are full of space.

CAPTAIN UNIVERSE: Quickly! Let's tell our headquarters on Earth.

[*They set down a radio-like machine or panel board.*]

HODGEKINS: Space Brigadesman Hodgekins calling Earth . . . Calling Earth . . . Come in Earth . . . Hmm, I'm going to have to use the Super-powerizer to call them, sir . . . We're over sixty million miles away.

CAPTAIN UNIVERSE: Sixty million miles, eh? Well, use whatever you think but make sure you reverse the charges.

[HODGKINS *busies himself connecting wires.*]

How are you making out, Hodgekins?

HODGEKINS: I'm having some difficulty with the capillary detonatizer.

CAPTAIN UNIVERSE: They don't make 'em like they used to.

[HIGGINS *enters.* CAPTAIN UNIVERSE *sees him.*]

I thought I told you to wait in the rocket.

HIGGINS: Well, sir, I . . . sir, I was all alone and . . . I'm ashamed to say this but I believe I'm suffering from a decrease in my bravery factor.

CAPTAIN UNIVERSE: You? Higgins? Afraid? You? Afraid? Higgins? You?

[HIGGINS *hangs his head.*]

Have you forgotten your oath? The Oath of the Space Brigadesman! Hodgekins, Hitchcock, Hotchkiss. The oath! . . . Repeat after me . . . "As a member of the Spa-a-ace Brigade . . ."

TRIO: "As a member of the Spa-a-ace Brigade . . ."

CAPTAIN UNIVERSE: "I promise . . ."

TRIO: "I promise . . ."

CAPTAIN UNIVERSE: "To do anything . . ."

TRIO: "To do anything . . ."

CAPTAIN UNIVERSE: "No matter how crazy."

TRIO: "No matter how crazy."

CAPTAIN UNIVERSE: You took the oath, Higgins, and here you are showing the white electron.

HIGGINS: I'm sorry, Captain, but . . . I felt as though I were being watched . . . that the rocket was surrounded by strange-looking creatures with green heads and . . .

HOTCHKISS: Strange creatures?

HITCHCOCK: Green heads?

[*Two* CREATURES *enter. They have pointed green heads and goggle eyes. As they enter, the* SPACE BRIGADESMEN *see them and begin backing away in horror.* CAPTAIN UNIVERSE, *however, doesn't see them. As he says the following, the two* CREATURES *walk up on either side of him.*]

CAPTAIN UNIVERSE: Listen to you, men—you know I can't stand cowardice. Oh, well, I understand. This is a new planet . . . [*Puts his arms around the two* CREATURES *affectionately*] But really, I can assure you that Higgins

is wrong. It has been conclusively proven that there
are no living creatures on the planet Venus. This fact
was established during a lecture at the Massachusetts
Institute of Technology by Dr. Cedric Goltvasser. And
boys, you know that when Cedric Goltvasser says
something, it's ... [*He looks at each of the* CREA-
TURES.] ... That lousy Goltvasser. [*A big realization.
He runs toward his men.*] Mama!

MEN: [*Grab the* CAPTAIN] Steady, Captain ... Easy there.

CAPTAIN UNIVERSE: Sorry, men. I guess I suffered a touch
of altitude poisoning ... but I could swear I saw ...
[*Points toward* CREATURES. *Sees them. Tries to run*]
Mama! [CREATURES *approach the cowering group
talking code-style.*] Listen to them. They ain't people,
they're storage batteries.

[*Suddenly the* CREATURES *get noisier and four others
join them.*]

HOTCHKISS: Captain, I think they're going to attack.

CAPTAIN UNIVERSE: Members of the Spa-a-ace Brigade!
Formation G! Use your disintegrator guns.

[MEN *shoot guns.*]

HODGEKINS: No effect, Captain.

CAPTAIN UNIVERSE: Try your paralizerifles.

[MEN *shoot again. No effect*]
The superatomizers!

HOTCHKISS: Captain, what do we do now?

CAPTAIN UNIVERSE: Run like hell!

[*The* CREATURES *rush off.*]

HITCHCOCK: Look, they're leaving.

CAPTAIN UNIVERSE: Another victory for the Spa-a-ace Brigade. Good work, men.

[*The* CREATURES *come back carrying a box.*]

HIGGINS: Here they come again!

HODGEKINS: They're carrying a box ...

[*The box slowly opens.*]

HIGGINS: Look, it's ... it's a thing!

HOTCHKISS: It's a ... a vegetable!

[QUEEN CHLOROPHYL *emerges. She has green hair.*]

CAPTAIN UNIVERSE: It's a tomato ... It's all right, men,
she's a woman.

[QUEEN *approaches with two of her* CREATURES. *They*

all talk in code. QUEEN *addresses the* CAPTAIN *in code.*
CAPTAIN *listens, puzzled.*]

CAPTAIN UNIVERSE: [*Pokes her*] Me Tarzan.
[*Two of the* CREATURES *angrily talk to the* CAPTAIN
and he backs away. The QUEEN *says something to them
and they back off. The* QUEEN *approaches the* CAPTAIN
regally, stops near him and speaks.]

QUEEN: What the hell are you doing up here?

CAPTAIN UNIVERSE: Well, we were ... You talk English?

QUEEN: [*Phony regal*] Of course I do. I am Queen Chlorophyl of Venus. My grandfather was an Earthman—an
American.

CAPTAIN UNIVERSE: An American? Up here?

QUEEN: Yes, he was an actor. He came here with the
interplanetary company of *Oklahoma!* ... What are you
staring at?

CAPTAIN UNIVERSE: Are you the only woman on this
planet?

QUEEN: I am.

CAPTAIN UNIVERSE: [*Pointing to* CREATURES] No wonder
their eyes are popping out ... Now, if your majesty
will ...
[*Radio starts making sounds.*]

VOICE: Earth calling Captain Universe ... Come in Captain Universe ...

HOTCHKISS: [*As the above starts*] Captain, we've gotten
through to them.

QUEEN: Do not answer that.
[*She points her finger at* HOTCHKISS *and makes a
sound.*]

HOTCHKISS: [*Transfixed*] Captain, I can't move.

QUEEN: [*Snaps her fingers and* HOTCHKISS *moves.*] That
was my finger ray ... right under my finger nail is an
infinitesimal piece of cathode neutronic prototon.

CAPTAIN UNIVERSE: [*Aside to his men*] Men, don't move.
This woman is dangerous.

HODGEKINS: But, Captain ...

CAPTAIN UNIVERSE: Quiet, or she'll give you the finger.

HIGGINS: [*Bursting out wildly*] I can't stand it. I'll go
mad. I can't stand it ... No ... No ... No ...

CAPTAIN UNIVERSE: Quiet or she'll give you the finger.

I'll go talk with the Queen and see if I can't get the neutrocraniplatium ... Look, your majesty, I am Captain Universe of the Spa-a-ace Brigade and I ...

QUEEN: You are very handsome, Captain.

CAPTAIN UNIVERSE: Huh? [*The* QUEEN *comes close and touches his cheek. Stern*] Please, your majesty ... I am here purely in the interest of science-fiction. [*The* QUEEN *comes even closer.*] Please, your majesty, we Spa-a-ace Brigadesmen don't go in for that sort of thing.

QUEEN: [*Her arms around him*] I get so lonely up here ... [*The two* CREATURES *approach her. They talk in angry code. She answers. They back away.*] They're jealous. Oh, Captain Universe ... you're so virile ... so ...

[CAPTAIN UNIVERSE *begins to melt.*]

HOTCHKISS: [*Coming up behind him*] Captain Universe ...

CAPTAIN UNIVERSE: Please, I'm negotiating.

HOTCHKISS: But, Captain ... this is a woman and ... well, sir, you know our rules.

CAPTAIN UNIVERSE: Hotchkiss, at a moment like this, we must use our initiative and I haven't used mine in a long, long time. Trust me, Hotchkiss. [*To the* QUEEN] Now where were we?

QUEEN: Captain Universe, you must stay here with me. We'll live here and be so happy ...

CAPTAIN UNIVERSE: [*Coming out of it*] What am I doing? I can't. I must go back to Earth. My home ... my work ... my research ... my electric trains.

QUEEN: [*Hard*] You will stay here. I command it! If you try to leave I will destroy you and your men. Now, I will make you a proposition. You are searching for neutrocraniplatium. Well, as you know, this planet is lousy with the stuff. So I will permit your, as you laughingly call them, men, to leave taking all the neutrocraniplatium they want. But you must stay. [*There's a pause.*] Well, Captain?

CAPTAIN UNIVERSE: One moment. I am thinking rapidly.

HODGEKINS: You can't do it, Captain!

HOTCHKISS: We won't let you!

HITCHCOCK: I won't hear of it!

HIGGINS: Let's get going.

CAPTAIN UNIVERSE: Men. I know how you all feel. But

the Earth needs ... that stuff ... [*The* QUEEN *puts her arms around him.*] And I feel that I should make the sacrifice. After all, there are four of you and only one of I. So if I give my life ...

HOTCHKISS: I'd rather give mine.

CAPTAIN UNIVERSE: The Queen asked for mine!

QUEEN: [*Arms still around the* CAPTAIN] My men will help load your rocket. [*She gives command in code. The* CREATURES *leave.*]

CAPTAIN UNIVERSE: Believe me, men. This is for the best.

HODGEKINS: We'll try to get help to you.

CAPTAIN UNIVERSE: Fine, fine ... Now, on your way, boys.

HOTCHKISS: The solar system won't seem the same without you. I feel like a traitor ...

CAPTAIN UNIVERSE: Go, lads ... leave ... and don't turn around ... I want you to remember me as you last saw me. Brave and smiling.

[*The* MEN *turn and go. As soon as they do, the* CAPTAIN *dashes for the* QUEEN. *They walk behind a rock. The radio on the stage starts up.*]

VOICE: Earth calling Captain Universe. Are you in trouble? Come in, Captain Universe. Come in, Captain Universe. Can we send help?

[*As this is going on, the* CAPTAIN *comes back on stage. He is wearing the pop-eyed goggles the* CREATURES *wore.*]

Captain Universe, do you need help? Come in Captain Universe!

[*The* CAPTAIN *talks to radio in code and clicks it off.*]

BLACKOUT

TRIANGLE

**An old-fashioned burlesque sketch
with two variations
by Betty Comden and Adolph Green**

The music, not included here, was by Jule Styne.

First produced in *Two on the Aisle*, at the Mark Hellinger Theatre, on July 19, 1951, with the following cast:

PART ONE
HUBBY Elliott Reid
WIFEY Dolores Gray
LOVEY Bert Lahr

PART TWO
HUSBAND Elliott Reid
WIFE Dolores Gray
CLOSE FRIEND Bert Lahr

PART THREE
HE Elliott Reid
SHE Dolores Gray
HIM Bert Lahr

PART ONE—BURLESQUE

SCENE: *Bedroom. Has bed, door, large oval window, closet and chest of drawers or couch about hip height. At rise,* HUBBY *and* WIFEY *are embracing. She is in a negligee, he is in a suit and hat. They are standing behind the couch. This is to be played in typical brisk, stylized burlesque manner.*

HUBBY: Honey-wonny, oo woves oo's dweat big daddy?

WIFEY: Me! Me woves dweat big daddy! Mmmmmmmmmmmmmmmm. [*She covers him with kisses.*]

HUBBY: Gee, I hate to go, honey! But I gotta play golf with Mr. Bixby, the diaper king. Wanta stick him with a big order! Ha!

WIFEY: Oooo, honey, you're the only one in the world I really love. Wifey's gonna be so lonely with hubby away!

HUBBY: You won't be lonely. Why don't you curl up with a good book. Here's one—hot off the press—*Strange Interlude.*
[*Hands her book*]

WIFEY: All right, honey—I'll be here all alone with my book!
[*At this point* LOVEY's *face appears in the window. She motions him away.*]

HUBBY: You'd better be. Why, if I found anyone hanging around you I'd—I'd—

WIFEY: What would you do, honey?

HUBBY: [*Working into a fury*] What would I do—? I'd give him this!

[LOVEY *appears in window—but just as* HUBBY *wheels around with a gun he disappears.*]

And this!

[*He pulls a knife.* LOVEY *appears and disappears just in time again.*]

And this!

[*Brandishes a hammer. Same business repeated.*]

WIFEY: [*Nervously gay*] Now isn't that silly?

HUBBY: [*Snapping out of it*] Of course it's silly—'cause you're the truest, bluest little gal a man ever married! Good-bye, sweet stuff! [*He steps out from behind couch and we see he has no pants on. He exits.*]

WIFEY: Good-bye, Joe, dear.

[*Knock on window. She opens it.* LOVEY *steps in.*]

LOVEY: Dis muss be de plaze! What a night for spooning. Have these cleaned and pressed.

WIFEY: Sam, darling!

[*They embrace.*]

LOVEY: Poopsie pie!

[*They kiss. He goes behind couch and is removing his pants.*]

Say, how long's the hubby-wubby gonna be gone?

WIFEY: He said long enough for me to read *Strange Interlude.*

LOVEY: Well, let's not read it. Let's have one! You got anything on tonight?

[*He goes toward bed—his pants off.*]

WIFEY: Not a thing.

LOVEY: The flies are gonna bother the hell out of you.

WIFEY: Oh, honey-wunny, you're the only one in the world I really love!

[*Knock at door*]

HUBBY'S VOICE: Darling, it's me! Let me in!

LOVEY: What was that?

WIFEY: It's Joe! My husband!

LOVEY: Why didn't you say so. Say, I gotta get outa here! Where'll I hide? What a night for spooning.

[*Looks around wildly. Tries window. Window stuck.* WIFEY *motions him into closet. More knocking at door. Through all this* LOVEY *keeps repeating frantically in a sing-song manner:* "Where'll I hi-i-i-de?" "Where'll I hi-i-i-de?"]

HUBBY'S VOICE: Hey, lemme in! What is this!

WIFEY: Coming, darling!

[*She opens door.* HUBBY *steps in and goes behind couch.*]

HUBBY: Funny thing— forgot my pants!

WIFEY: Why, honey—you didn't have to come back for those. That's a perfect sports outfit!

HUBBY: [*Putting on* LOVEY's *pants*] Just for indoor sports! Well—here we are—I'll be off in just a minute. Say— [*He steps out in* LOVEY's *pants which are much too small.*]

Say—what *is* this? These fit me last night!

WIFEY: [*Nervously*] Sam, that was twenty-four hours ago. Why—why—you're just a growing boy, Sam!

HUBBY: [*Going toward door*] Sure—that's it! [*Double take*] Wait a second! My name's Joe. Who's SAM?!

WIFEY: Why—why—my aunt! Aunt Sam!

HUBBY: [*Suspiciously*] Aunt Sam, eh? O.K., this is it! [*Pulls open closet door.*]

WIFEY: No! No! No!

[*Out of closet comes* LOVEY *in* HUBBY's *pants which are much too large—and wearing a huge, flowered woman's hat.*]

HUBBY: [*Threateningly*] Are you Aunt Sam?

LOVEY: Certainly.

HUBBY: What are you doing in these! AUNT SAM!

LOVEY: Perfectly simple! You got aunts in your pants!

BLACKOUT

PART TWO—T.S. ELIOT

SCENE: *Same bedroom set.* HUSBAND *and* WIFE *discovered standing a bit apart. In the room also are three people holding cocktail glasses. They say nothing throughout the entire sketch but get in the way of some of the action, having to be walked around, etc. They merely look reserved and disinterested during the proceedings. This part is to be played in clipped British style.*

HUSBAND: Here it is the appointed teatime, the teatime.
    Except that in this suspended hour
    Between morning and nowhere
    We require stronger dreams and stimulation
    Brewed from the decomposed bodies
    Of dried vegetation.
    Another gin and bitters, Olivia—
WIFE: [*Coolly*] Gin and bitters would be equally pointless or pointed
    Before or after your departure, Joseph.
    For whether you are here or not
    The void is the same—
    The gin is the same—
    And you are always the same—
HUSBAND: So our parting is not a parting at all
    But just a continuation
    Of that which has never happened.
    Picture him then—the average suburban husband
    Swaddled in his emptiness—
    Going forth in the space-time continuum to his business appointment.

Golf—Mr. Bixbee—
The ball the green and cup—
Perhaps that is the end of everything—
The cup, the ball—the—
[*During this the* CLOSE FRIEND'*s face has appeared
at the window. The* WIFE *sees him and turns to the*
HUSBAND, *yawning.*]

WIFE: Your observations are extremely interesting, Joseph—
But it is getting late—

HUSBAND: Perhaps it is getting early.
You must amuse yourself in your faithful loneliness
With some hilarious readings
From Spengler's *Decline of the West.*
[*Hands her book. Pushes past the three other peo-
ple. Puts on bowler hat and takes umbrella.*]
Pardon me—but I am summoned—
[*He steps out from behind couch and we see he is with-
out pants. He exits. Knock at window. She opens it.
The* CLOSE FRIEND *steps in casually.*]

CLOSE FRIEND: This must indeed be the location.
[*Pats the bed*]
The center of my faintly smoldering desires.
Amid the clinking of the glasses—
I see in your face
A difference to the indifference.
Gin and bitters, Olivia?

WIFE: Samuel—gin and bitters or not
The void is the same—
The gin is the same
And you are always the same.

CLOSE FRIEND: Forgive me—
The most refreshing thing about you, Olivia,
Is your ability to see through the nothingness
Which surrounds us all—
By what ticking of the clock
Shall we hear the returning footfalls of your golf-
playing husband
Dragging his clubs behind him?
[*During this he is behind the couch removing his
pants.*]

WIFE: Should I so desire I should have the time

To read the entire *Decline of the West*—
Between these covers—

CLOSE FRIEND: [*Going toward bed*] And how about between *these* covers?

WIFE: Samuel—from decline to recline—
A simple change of a letter—
A mere alphabetical—

CLOSE FRIEND: [*Interrupting*] Shall we cut out the alphabet soup
And get on with it—
[*Knock at door*]

HUSBAND'S VOICE: Olivia!

WIFE: I hear an accustomed knock at an unaccustomed time.

HUSBAND'S VOICE: Olivia!

CLOSE FRIEND: There is a time for showing oneself—
A time for revealing oneself—
Time for facing other faces one meets—
There is also the time for hiding.
Where is it?
[*Tries window. It is stuck.*]
Time is standing still—
The universe is suspended in—

HUSBAND'S VOICE: Olivia!

WIFE: The closet.

CLOSE FRIEND: [*Sardonically*] The closet.
The final ignominy of the fool and the wiseman—
The final shroud—the room of darkness—
The all-enveloping pitch which—
[WIFE *pushes* CLOSE FRIEND *impatiently in closet. She opens door.* HUSBAND *enters.*]

HUSBAND: [*Pointing to his legs*] Olivia—

WIFE: I know, Joseph.

HUSBAND: Convention demanded it. My trousers—
Those willing shields that hide the shrieking truth—
Pink skin beneath brown tweed—
[*He is putting on pants.*]
But what is this!
[*He steps out. They are much too small. Looks at her.*]
I know—

WIFE: You know?

HUSBAND: Yes, Olivia—it would seem you have deceived
me.
You have deceived me—
But perhaps I in some way have deceived you.
For between the deceived and the deceiving
The deception and the consequence—
The plotting and the victim
There is always you—Olivia—
And I—Joseph Samuel and he—Samuel Joseph.
Perhaps it doesn't matter very much—
The being or the not being—
The seeming and the not seeming—
The reality and the non-reality—
I know your secret—it is my secret too—
It is everybody's secret—
The figure in the closet—
Perhaps the skeleton—perhaps the flesh—
Olivia—
[*Indicating the closet*]
Who?
WIFE: My aunt.
[HUSBAND *opens the closet door.* CLOSE FRIEND *is
wearing a woman's hat and dress.*]
CLOSE FRIEND: From Brazil—where the nuts come from!

DIMOUT

PART THREE—COLE PORTER MUSICAL

SCENE: *Same set.* HE *and* SHE *are breezily sophisticated.*

HE: Who do you love?

SHE: Who do you think, idiot child?

HE and SHE: [*Sing*]

> Like Hippocrates loved Socrates
> Aphrodite loved to woo
> Like Terpsichore loved chicory
> That's how I love you—idiot child.
> Like Melpomene loved hominy
> Dionysus loved his brew
> Like Odysseus loved his misseus—
> That's how I love you—
> You drive me wild—idiot child.

[*They dance.*]

HE: [*Stopping suddenly*] What time is it?

SHE: Don't stop, Joe—when you dance like that—you're like a Greek god.

HE: You'll have to read all about them, angel, right here in Bullfinch's mythology. [*Gives her book*] Have to go to the office—idiot child.

SHE: Bye-bye, idiot child.

[HE *exits.* SHE *sits down with the book. The lights change. There is ethereal music and* HIM *enters.* HIM *is dressed normally but is sprinkled with sequin dust.*]

HIM: [*To audience*] 'Tis I, Jupiter—king of the gods. I have fallen madly in love with this mortal so I have come to earth and will appear to her in this disguise— as simple Samuel Schmidt.

SHE: By Jupiter, where's Sam—he's late.

HIM: [*As the lights come up full*] Here I am, beloved!

OF FATHERS AND SONS

by Mel Brooks

First produced in *New Faces of 1952*, at the Royale Theatre, on May 16, 1952, with the following cast:

MAE Alice Ghostley
HARRY Paul Lynde
STANLEY Ronny Graham
POLICEMEN Jimmy Russell, Allen Conroy

SCENE: *A tenement kitchen. A door right to the outside, a door left to the rest of the apartment. Center, a cheap, broken-down kitchen table with a few badly mismatched and decrepit chairs around it. In back, a table from which* MAE *will take food and, painted on backdrop, a stove and old-fashioned icebox. The whole must look tawdry.*

At rise, MAE *is setting the table with some chipped dishes and, after a beat,* HARRY, *a beaten-down little man, enters from right.*

MAE: Hello, Harry.

HARRY: Hello, Mae.

MAE: What's the matter, Harry? You look tired. How did it go today?

HARRY: [*Throws himself in chair*] Oh, what's the sense of talking! The little man ain't got a chance. Today, in order to get someplace, you gotta be a big operator.

MAE: What happened, Harry?

HARRY: [*With quiet desperation*] I made eight dollars ... a big eight dollars. Is that what a man should bring home to his wife? Mae, I'm fifty-three years old and I made eight dollars ... and I was lucky to make that. Thank heaven for the parade today! I might have ended up with a lousy two bucks.

MAE: Then you made six dollars at the parade, huh? Tell me about it.

HARRY: Well, there were a lot of cops around ... and I was nervous. Mae, something's happening to me. I'm getting so I can't pick pockets when cops are around. I was never like that, was I, Mae?

MAE: No, you were never like that, Harry.

HARRY: *Tell me*, I was never like that.

MAE: You were never like that.

HARRY: I was *never* like that.

MAE: You were *never* like that.

HARRY: [*Turning, then quietly*] I was never like that. By the way, where's the kid?

MAE: [*Hesitating, afraid to tell him*] Oh . . . he's around.

HARRY: Around where?

MAE: He's . . . he's . . . he's in the playground playing baseball with the other children.

HARRY: [*For the first time we see anger in this ostensibly gentle man.*] Baseball! This is how a boy amounts to something? This is where my teaching and training go? Wasted? All wasted! On a boy who takes a bat in his hand and smashes his father's hopes and dreams.

MAE: Eat your spaghetti, Harry, it'll get cold.

HARRY: Mae, I tell you this country is going insane. All a boy thinks about is becoming a Mickey Mantle. I talk to him, but he doesn't listen. I've failed, Mae. I've failed as a father.

[*Tears find their way to the gentle eyes of this poor, crushed father.*]

MAE: No, Harry, and he won't fail you. I know he won't . . . he has your blood in him.

HARRY: I'm not a well man. I'm not a well man.

[*STANLEY enters right. He is about fourteen and when you see his honest, almost angelic expression, you can see why he's such a disappointment.*]

STANLEY: [*Putting away baseball paraphernalia*] Hello, Mom. Hi, Dad.

[*STANLEY slaps his father on the back.*]

HARRY: You're not ashamed to say "hello" to your father?

STANELY: [*Repeating slap on back*] No, I'm not ashamed. Am I, Mom?

HARRY: [*Outraged*] You're not ashamed to waste your time in playgrounds, when you should be learning your craft? When I was your age I was breaking into candy stores already.

STANLEY: Why does he gotta holler?

HARRY: You're no good! You're well-liked!

[STANLEY *turns quickly, stands tense, with his back to his father. He is embarrassed and ashamed.* HARRY *walks to him and puts his gentle arm around the boy.*] Stanley, I'm your father and believe me, I know what's best for you. I'll help you, I'll teach you. Stanley, you're all I've got. Don't you ever want to be a criminal?

STANLEY: [*Obviously touched*] Sure, Dad, but . . .

HARRY: Then in the name of Dillinger . . . why don't you listen to me?

STANLEY: 'Cause you holler.

HARRY: Stanley, I know how hard it is to start. I don't ask you to do impossible things. Begin at the bottom. Start small. Put slugs into pay telephones. Steal a fountain pen from school. Punch your teacher in the mouth.

MAE: [*Firmly*] Stanley . . . listen to your father.

STANLEY: Yeah, Dad, yeah!

HARRY: Say, that reminds me. This is the end of the term, isn't it?

STANLEY: Uh huh.

HARRY: Okay, where's your report card?

MAE: Oh, oh.

STANLEY: [*Suddenly spins and walks downstage—stands tensely with back to father. Over his shoulder*] I . . . er . . . I . . . uh . . . I lost it.

HARRY: What's this nonsense? Show me your report card.

MAE: Stanley, show your report card to your father.

STANLEY: [*Reluctantly handing* HARRY *report card*] Here. Gee, Dad, I wish you wouldn't . . .

HARRY: [*Looks at card. Does a double take. Looks at card again. Very carefully, almost not believing what he sees*] A? B-plus? A . . . B-plus . . . A . . . A . . . A . . . a . . . a . . . a . . . a.

[HARRY *goes shrieking offstage left, still shouting.* STANLEY *reacts to the first couple of A's. He is ashamed and says, "I'm sorry. I didn't mean it, etc."*]

MAE: [*After a slight pause*] You're killing that man. He's a sick man. Pay attention. Oh, Stanley, follow in his footsteps or you'll put your father in his grave.

[STANLEY *sits on chair facing away from her, head in his hands.* MAE *walks to him, pulls his head up and says directly in his face.*]

Stanley, you're an only son and you mean so much to us. Please, Stanley, for his sake and mine, steal something! Anything! I know you can. I know deep down inside, down where it really counts, you're rotten.

[MAE *puts her hand on his shoulder.* STANLEY *looks around and then puts his hand over hers and looks into her eyes; a tableau.*]

STANLEY: Thanks. Mom, I love him . . . and I love you, too. You know that. But something went wrong with me. I've got crazy blood in me. I'm a misfit. You know, like Uncle Fred, the cop.

MAE: [*Putting her hand over his mouth*] Ohhhhhh! You must never mention that man's name in this house.

STANLEY: I'm sorry. Mom . . . [MAE *is seated.* STANLEY *leans over her, speaking slowly and with great effort and conviction. He pounds with one fist on the table to punctuate his conviction.*] I've got to tell you something. I know this is gonna sound strange, but you've gotta listen to me. Mom, I got a job . . . an honest job!

MAE: [*Giving him a big hit in the face, knocking him to the floor*] I told you never to use that kind of language in this house.

STANLEY: But, Mom . . . I bought something with the money. Something I love. Something I want to spend my whole life doing.

[STANLEY *exits right and returns with a violin case. He begins walking toward his mother with it when* HARRY *comes running in from left and sees it.*]

HARRY: Stanley, oh, son! You've come through. A tommy gun. My boy's got . . . a tommy . . . [*He snatches case from boy's hands, excitedly, and begins to open it. Looking in the case, he speaks in wonder.*] What . . . on . . . earth . . . is . . . this?

STANLEY: [*Firmly*] It's a violin. I want to play the violin. I want to be a great musician.

HARRY: You want to be a . . . [HARRY *wavers, clutches his heart.* MAE *catches him, holds him up. In a moment he recovers. Goes over to table and smashes violin in case.*] There'll be no musicians in his house. I'll not have it. Do you hear me? I'll not have it. I'll not have it!

STANLEY: [*Horrified*] No!

[*He recoils, then runs three steps toward the door right, looks back and makes an unbelieving, horrified noise, as he reels off.*]

MAE: Stanley, come back . . .

HARRY: Let him go. He's not my son. We'll go on together. Alone. Get my stuff. I'm going to work tonight. Only when I am lost in my work can I forget the pain of life.

MAE: [*Gets a black leather bag and begins stuffing tools into it. Glass cutters, wrenches, nitro, sandpaper and a couple of sandwiches. Still shaking, she speaks in a nagging tone.*] Now remember what we went over, Harry. It's a Thompson safe with a four-point, four-tumbler combination. Don't use too much nitro and don't forget to eat the sandwiches, and remember the watchmen are changed at 10:15 now. And, Harry, don't look suspicious.

HARRY: [*Interrupting*] Nag, nag, nag, nag, nag . . .

[*Just then the door right bursts open.* STANLEY *stands there, gloating, between two* POLICEMEN.]

STANLEY: There's the man! Harry, the eel. My father. Okay. Where's the reward?

[*One* POLICEMAN *grabs* HARRY *while the other pays* STANLEY.]

COP: There you are, son. Five hundred dollars.

[*The* POLICEMAN *then walks over and grabs* HARRY'*s other arm.*]

HARRY: [*Finally finding his voice*] Mae! Mae! The boy turned in his own father, his own flesh and blood, for a filthy reward. [HARRY *reaches out and takes her hand.*] Mae, our boy's a stool pigeon. He's gonna be all right! He's gonna be all right!

[*The* POLICEMEN *lead him out.* HARRY *is triumphant, laughing hysterically.* MAE *has a happy mother's smile on her face, and* STANLEY *is gleefully counting his reward as the curtain comes down.*]

BLACKOUT

UPPER BIRTH

by Ira Wallach

First produced in *Phoenix '55*, at the Phoenix Theatre, on April 23, 1955, with the following cast:

MORROW Kenneth Harvey
MIKE Harvey Lembeck
ANNIE Nancy Walker
UNCLE WILLIE Bob Bakanic
DELIVERY MAN Jay Harnick

SCENE: *Downstage left,* TED MORROW *is seated in an armchair.*

MORROW: Good evening. This is Ted Morrow inviting you to join him in another face-to-face interview with people in the public eye. Tonight we take you to Mr. and Mrs. Michael Snodgrass's efficiency apartment in lower Manhattan. This couple symbolizes a trend in American life that no one could foresee ten short years ago: the trend back to large families. Both college graduates, Mr. and Mrs. Snodgrass began years ago to anticipate the leap in the national birthrate. Mrs. Snodgrass, a Hunter College graduate, has the unique distinction of being the mother of twenty-seven children between the ages of two and seventeen—a feat that is barely possible. But now, let us go into the living-room of Mr. and Mrs. Michael Snodgrass.
[*Lights up on* SNODGRASS *living room. Refrigerator upstage on which stand cans of beer; clotheslines crossing the room, each line jammed with diapers. Upstage right a baby's gate that when closed cuts off the corner.*]
Good evening.

MIKE: Good evening, Mr. Morrow.

ANNIE: Hi.

MORROW: Mr. Snodgrass, we're grateful to you for allowing us to bring our cameras into your living room tonight, and we'd like to begin our interview—
[UNCLE WILLIE *enters. He takes a can of beer off the*

405

*refrigerator and opens it with a can opener that is on
a string around* ANNIE's *neck.*]

UNCLE WILLIE: Good evening, Mr. Morrow.

  [*He exits with beer.*]

MORROW: Good evening. May I ask who that was, Mr.
  Snodgrass?

MIKE: That's our eldest.

ANNIE: Are you sure?

MIKE: Sure I'm sure.

MORROW: He looks like a fine upstanding lad.

MIKE: He stands up fine now and then.

ANNIE: To get the beer.

MIKE: He's morose. He's been overwhelmed with sib-
  lings.

ANNIE: Every new sibling was a trauma.

MORROW: I see. Perhaps, Mr. Snodgrass, you'd tell—

  [DELIVERY MAN *enters, leaves package, exits.*]

  Perhaps you'd tell me where your children are now?

MIKE: The older ones are in Milwaukee, Detroit, Dallas,
  San Quentin, Cleveland, Seattle, Boston, New Orleans,
  San Francisco, Portland, Minneapolis, Keokuk, and—
  Rochester? [ANNIE *nods.*] Rochester!

ANNIE: But the little ones are still with us.

MORROW: Could we say hello to a few of them?

ANNIE: I'm sorry, Mr. Morrow, but Betty, Mary, Peter,
  George, Harry, Louise, Donald, Jean, Fred, Lola, Susquehanna, Acheson, and Bethlehem Steel are all at the
  movies.

MORROW: Well, I'm sorry to hear they're out of the house.

ANNIE: Look who's sorry!

  [DELIVERY MAN *enters. Leaves more packages and exits.*]

MORROW: Now, Mr. Snodgrass, may I ask what your work
  is?

MIKE: I'm an author. I write children's books. I wrote
  Little Bobby and His Floating Soapdish. That was a
  best seller.

ANNIE: You must have seen it. It was printed on water-
  proof paper and bound with a shoelace.

MIKE: That way the kids got something to read and
  learned to tie their shoelaces at the same time.

MORROW: And you, Mrs. Snodgrass, what do you do?

ANNIE: [*Drawing herself up*] I'm retired. I devote myself to my family.

MORROW: I believe you had an unusual scholastic record when you were a student at Hunter. What did you study?

ANNIE: I majored in biology.

MIKE: And Annie has never let her interest in biology flag for a moment.

MORROW: I'm sure, Mrs. Snodgrass, you have a message for the girls in America's colleges.

MIKE: Oh, Annie has a message, all right. Tell the girls, Annie.

ANNIE: Girls, major in English!!

MORROW: Uh— Thank you—now I'd like to ask you—
[DELIVERY MAN *enters, leaves packages, exits.*]
I'd like to ask you, Mrs. Snodgrass, if you'd be kind enough to show us around the house.

ANNIE: Certainly. [*Yawns, rises, picks up* MIKE's *feet from the table*] This is our kitchen table. It's chippin'. If the camerman would like to come in closer—

MORROW: That's all right, thank you.

ANNIE: [*Goes to upstage right corner*] And this is a corner.

MORROW: A corner.

ANNIE: Yeah—sometimes I like to take off my shoes and just stand here. I call this my quiet corner.

MIKE: Nobody but Annie is allowed to use that corner.
[ANNIE *heads for the beer on top of the refrigerator.*
DELIVERY MAN *enters, leaves his packages, kisses her.*]

DELIVERY MAN: Oooh, you!
[*Exits*]

MORROW: May I ask who that was?

ANNIE: Diaper service.
[*Takes two beers to table, opens them. They squirt. Sits down.* MIKE *and* ANNIE *toast with the cans.*]

MORROW: Now, Mr. Snodgrass, may I ask if you have any hobbies?
[ANNIE *chokes on her beer.*]

MIKE: Well—you may not believe this, but I like to sit back and watch Annie fold diapers. Not too many women can hold a candle to Annie when it comes to folding diapers.

ANNIE: And I don't want any women holding candles to me when I'm folding diapers.

MORROW: And may I ask what your hobbies are, Mrs. Snodgrass?

ANNIE: In my spare time—I like to watch Mike watch me—fold diapers.

MORROW: Well, it certainly is good to see a couple that know how to share. Mr. and Mrs. Snodgrass, what you have done is an inspiration to all of us. But I see that our time is up and we have come to the end of another face-to-face interview. Thank you very much, Mr. and Mrs. Michael Snodgrass. Good night, and good luck. [MORROW *studio blacks out.*]

MIKE: It's all right now, Annie, we're off the air. [*He crosses to her. She leaps up, staggers to corner, pulls the baby's gate between them, leans against wall and smiles at* MIKE.]

BLACKOUT

SELL, SELL, SELL

by Herbert Hartig and Herbert Reich

Originally entitled "Oh, Sell Me, Pretty Maiden," this sketch was optioned for inclusion in the revue *Pleasure Dome*, which went into rehearsal on October 10, 1955. The show has become something of a Broadway legend, though it never saw the light of an opening night, as it folded after three weeks of rehearsals because of "financial difficulties." The sketch, which was to have had Kaye Ballard as Miss Kreel and Jimmy Komack as Cranshaw, was subsequently leased by *The Martha Raye Show*, and aired on NBC-TV on April 17, 1956, with Martha Raye as Miss Kreel and Paul Lynde as Cranshaw. It contributed the catchphrase "What are you, some kind of nut?" to popular idiom.

Characters

J.W. CRANSHAW
MISS PITMAN
MISS KREEL
OPERATOR
SLADE

SCENE: *The office of J.W. Cranshaw, General Manager of Marcy's Department Store. There is a desk, upstage right, on which are three telephones and a thermos set. A swivel chair is behind the desk and a straight-backed chair is beside it. The upstage left wall displays the store motto: "Marcy's Sells Everything." An ornate cash register sits on a table beneath the sign. At rise,* CRANSHAW *is on the phone.* MISS PITMAN, *his secretary, sits in the deskside chair with pencil and stenopad.*

CRANSHAW: [*Into phone, distraught*] Yes, I *know*, Mr. Marcy. I *know* business has fallen off, but, sir—I'm only your general manager, you *can't* hold me personally responsible ... You *can* hold me personally responsible?? ... *My job???* But, sir, I—Hello? [*Cradles receiver; half to himself*] I've got to think of something quickly. What can I do? [*Paces*] What can I do? I must find a way to increase our sales ... [*Stops abruptly. A look of crafty desperation*] There is, of course, *one* way ...

PITMAN: [*Appalled*] Mr. Cranshaw! You don't mean ... *Miss Kreel?* [*He shudders and looks away.*] You *do* mean Miss Kreel! [*Shakes her head darkly*] I hope you know what you're doing, Sir.

[MISS PITMAN *exits.* CRANSHAW *crosses to thermos bottle on the desk, pours water, shakes a handful of pills from a small dark bottle and downs them.* MISS PITMAN *reenters. With her is* MISS KREEL, *a young woman with a dismaying amount of energy.* MISS KREEL *wears a slip—no dress—and carries a small brown paper bag.*]

KREEL: Whaddya want *now?* Hurry up. I gotta get back

411

and sell! Whaddya want? This is awready the fifth time you sent for me this week—and it's only Monday! [*Looks at her watch*] Quarter past ten!!??!?

CRANSHAW: Miss Kreel, I—

KREEL: [*Impatiently*] Whaddya want, *what?* Speak up!! I gotta get back and sell!

CRANSHAW: [*Realizing*] Miss Kreel, where is your dress?

KREEL: A lady said she liked it! I sold it!

CRANSHAW: And you've been walking around the store in—*that slip?*

KREEL: Whatsa matter with this slip? You don't like it? I think it's a nice slip! [*To* PITMAN] Isn't it a nice slip?

PITMAN: It's a very nice slip, Miss Kreel, but—

KREEL: You like it? It's yours. $3.50! A steal!

[MISS KREEL *starts to take her slip off. In horror,* CRANSHAW *rushes to her side to forestall her.*]

CRANSHAW: Miss Kreel!!

KREEL: Not now! Not now! You're lousing up my sale!

CRANSHAW: [*Trying to calm her*] Miss Kreel, shh, nice. Nice, Miss Kreel, shh, easy! Easy!

KREEL: I can't help myself, Cranshaw—I'll do anything to sell! There's a little voice inside me that keeps saying: "Sell! Sell! SELL!!" Alla time that little voice keeps repeating it, over and over, day in, day out . . . [*She grabs* CRANSHAW'*s lapels.*] Oh, Cranshaw, it's an insidious thing! [*Bends him back over the desk*] It's like—[*With dreadful import*] like a sickness! [*She releases him and turns aside, her arm thrown theatrically across her brow.*]

PITMAN: [*Moved*] Oh, the poor thing!

KREEL: You wanna fire me, go ahead and fire me! But fire me *quick,* 'cause I gotta get back and *sell!*

CRANSHAW: [*With an avuncular cackle, building to Knute Rockne exhortation*] Fire you, child? No! Marcy's *wants* you! Marcy's *needs* you as an example to the other salesgirls. I want you to get out there and sell! Sell the hell out of them! Sell anything you want, but sell! Sell! SELL!!

KREEL: [*To* PITMAN] He's sicker than I am! [*Pinches* PITMAN'*s cheek*] But you're a good kid. See ya! [*She starts to go. Hands him paper bag*] Oh! Here: the money I made this morning!

CRANSHAW: *In a paper bag?* Miss Kreel, didn't the Marcy training program teach you to work a cash register?

KREEL: I don't remember. All I remember is "Sell! Sell! Sell!"

CRANSHAW: [*With a despairing gesture*] Miss Pitman, please ... ?

PITMAN: [*Miss Efficiency*] The register works quite simply, Miss Kreel. You enter the first letter of the item—let us say it's a book—you ring up "B" [*She does.*] then the amount [*Ditto*]—then your own initials [*Ditto. The drawer pops out. She closes it.*] Now *you* try it. Ring up the money you just brought in.

KREEL: [*At the register, operating the keys*] "L," for lotsa things ... [CRANSHAW *moans*] $87.52 ... "E-K" ... [*Drawer opens, she deposits money.*] Hey, that was fun! But no time for fun! I gotta sell!! Thanks, Pitman. [*Pinches* CRANSHAW'S *cheek*] You're a good kid! [*At the door, momentously*] Oh boy, I learned how to work a cash register. Now there's *no stopping me!* [*She exits.*]

CRANSHAW: [*Stares at doorway for a moment*] Pitman, did you ever have the feeling you'd created a monster? [*He swallows another handful of pills. Phone rings. He picks it up.*] Cranshaw here ... *What?* ... That's *impossible* ... Well, search the store! [*Cradles phone*] Our timeclock? Missing??? [*To* PITMAN] Call Mr. Marcy. I'm calling the store detective. [*Picks up phone*] Get me Slade!

[PITMAN *takes the phone.* KREEL *rushes in with handful of money.*]

KREEL: Mr. Cranshaw ... Miss Pitman ...

PITMAN: [*Into phone*] Mr. Marcy, please. Mr. Cranshaw calling.

CRANSHAW: Miss Kreel, can't you see we're busy?

KREEL: Mr. Cranshaw, I made a sale. I got money!

CRANSHAW: Put it in the cash register, for heaven's sake! [KREEL *crosses to register. Into phone*] Hello, Slade? Our timeclock seems to have disappeared. Look into it and report to me immediately! [*Cradles phone*] What could happen to a timeclock???

KREEL: [*Ringing up on register*] "T" ... $75 ... "E-K" ... [*Drawer opens, she deposits money*] Gotta sell!

Gotta sell more!!

[*Exits*]

CRANSHAW: [*Noticing she has been there*] What was it you wanted, Miss Kree—? [*To* PITMAN] Did you reach Mr. Marcy?

PITMAN: [*Cradling receiver*] He's not in his office, sir. He must have just stepped out for a moment. I left word for him to ring back. [*Phone rings.*] That must be him now.

CRANSHAW: [*Picks up phone. Into it*] Mr. Marcy? . . . Oh, it's you again, Slade. Did you find the timeclock? . . . What do you mean, "*WHAT DOES IT LOOK LIKE?*". . . It's a *timeclock*. It's got a . . . sort of thing, with a—Do the best you can. [*The other phone rings. He hangs up one as he picks up another.*] Cranshaw here . . . What?? Are you *sure?* . . . We'll do what we can. [*Hangs up*]

PITMAN: Have they found the timeclock?

CRANSHAW: No! Now four watercoolers are missing from the seventh floor.

PITMAN: Watercoolers?

CRANSHAW: Who would want our watercoolers? This is fantastic!! Who could—[*Snaps fingers*] Trimbull! Trimbull's Department Store across the street. They've been trying to ruin Marcy's for years! That would explain the timeclock, too! [*To* PITMAN] Try Mr. Marcy again.

PITMAN: [*Picking up phone*] Yessir. [*Into phone.*] Mr. Marcy, please.

[MISS KREEL *enters with greenbacks.*]

KREEL: Mr. Cranshaw, I got more money.

CRANSHAW: [*Bitterly*] That Trimbull! Not content with sabotaging our schedule, now he's trying to cut off our water supply!

KREEL: [*Trying to get a word in*] I sold something else, Mr. Cranshaw!

PITMAN: [*Into phone*] Thank you. [*Hangs up*] Mr. Marcy hasn't returned yet, sir.

CRANSHAW: [*Into another phone*] Get me Slade.

KREEL: You should be proud of me, Cranshaw. I dumped a lot of things this store has been stuck with for years.

CRANSHAW: [*Impatiently*] Good, good! Don't bother me!

Ring it up; I have my own problems! [MISS KREEL
shrugs and crosses to register.] Hello, Slade? Never
mind the timeclock. Four of our watercoolers are missing ... What do you mean, *"WHAT DO THEY LOOK
LIKE?"*... They look like—four watercoolers!
[*He continues to ad lib exasperatedly under the following.*]

KREEL: [*At register*] "W" ... $30 ... "E-K," ... "W"
... $30 ... "E-K," ... "W" ... $30 ... "E-K," ... "W"
... $30 ... "E-K." [*She deposits money in drawer.*]
Gotta sell more! More! MORE!!
[*Exits*]

CRANSHAW: [*On phone*] Slade, you're an idiot! (*Slams
receiver down*] Was someone in here just now? [*Begins
pacing again*] Where is Mr. Marcy when we need him
most? Must I do everything myself? All right, if I must,
I will! I'll fight fire with fire! [*Into phone*] Get me the
shipping department. I'll show Trimbull and his *schlock
outfit!* ... Hello, shipping department? I want a dozen
of our biggest truckdrivers—with monkeywrenches.
Have them report to me immedi—Hello? Hello??
[*Jiggles cradlebar*] Hello???
[TELEPHONE OPERATOR *enters, phone apparatus on
chest, earphones on head, holding one switchboard
wire by its jack.*]

OPERATOR: Mr. Cranshaw?

CRANSHAW: [*Into phone*] Yes, hello, Operator ... I was
cut off.

OPERATOR: *You* were cut off! [CRANSHAW *does a double
take.*] I connected you with the shipping department,
then I went out for a drink of water. Not only I couldn't
find the watercooler, but I come back and my switchboard is missing!
[MISS KREEL *enters, money in hand. She makes a bee-
line for the register.*]

KREEL: [*En passant*] Hi, Cransh! Hi, Pitman! [*At register,
puzzles a moment, then turns to* CRANSHAW] Hey,
whaddya call that gizmo, like a big box, with a dial and
a lotta wires stuck in it ... ?

CRANSHAW: [*A black dawn*] Wires?

KREEL: [*Seeing* OPERATOR] Yeah, like the one *she's* got!

[*Points to* OPERATOR'*s hand*]

CRANSHAW: You mean—a switchboard?

KREEL: Yeah, that's right! Switchboard. [*Rings it up*] "S" ... $235 ... "E-K."

[*Deposits money in open drawer and beams. She leaves the register drawer open.*]

CRANSHAW: [*Aghast*] You sold—the switchboard ... and—four watercoolers? [MISS KREEL *nods.*] And the time-clock?

KREEL: I had a real good day. I shoulda been working on a commission. I sold them things, and also [*Pressing keys and depositing money*] two delivery trucks ... an escalator ... and all the counters on the mezzanine floor ... [*Looks at remaining bills in her hand, trying to remember*] There was something else ...

CRANSHAW [*Weakly*] But, Miss Kreel ... our fixtures ...

KREEL: [*Indicating sign*] "Marcy's Sells Everything."

[MISS KREEL *looks questioningly at the money in her hand.* CRANSHAW *groans. A man* (SLADE) *enters in a rush, wearing a derby and smoking a cigar.*]

SLADE: Mr. Cranshaw!

CRANSHAW: [*Wheels around*] Oh, it's you, Slade!

SLADE: Hey, Mr. Cranshaw, there's some kinda nut runnin' around the store in her slip. [*Sees* KREEL] Hey, there she is! What are you—some kinda nut? Runnin' around the store in your slip?

CRANSHAW: I've had it! That's all—I've had it! I quit! [*Picks up phone*] Get me Mr. Marcy ... [*Near hysteria*] What am I doing? I forgot, our switchboard was sold! My God!! [*To* SLADE] Slade, go find Mr. Marcy and bring him back here ... please?

SLADE: Sure! What does he look like?

CRANSHAW: [*Appealing to the heavens*] What does he look like? [*Patiently, as if explaining to a child*] Mr. Marcy, the man who owns our store, is about so big [*Hand from floor*] has grey hair ... and little round cheeks ... and he was last seen wearing a grey pin-stripe suit ...

[MISS KREEL *looks at him, then at the money in her hand, then turns to the register.*]

KREEL: [*Operating keys*] "M" ... $450 ... "E-K."

[*The drawer opens. She turns to the others with a little shamefaced smile.*]

BLACKOUT

TALLULAH FINDS HER KITCHEN

**A Monologue for Miss Tallulah Bankhead
by Joseph Stein, Danny and Neil Simon**

This monologue was written for Tallulah Bankhead and was presented by her on the summer stock circuit in 1956 in the show, *Welcome, Darlings!*

SCENE: *A kitchen with a table, chair, sink, stove and cabinets.*

TALLULAH: [*Directly to audience*] Darlings, I must tell you what a thoroughly bewildering time I had this morning. For one thing, I got up rather late—even for me. I thought I had really overslept but then I looked at the calendar and saw it was still February. Well, from that minute on nothing seemed to go right. Oh, what a time I had. I will never go through that sort of experience again. Never. Whatever possessed me to stay home alone and crochet?

I kept ringing for my maid, ringing for her to bring my breakfast, but she didn't answer. Then I realized that she said she had to go to the employment agency to hire a new chauffeur. Personally, I didn't see what was wrong with her *old* chauffeur. And then I found this note from her on my dressing table. She said: "Dear Miss Bankhead: I hereby resign as your maid. Having worked for you for several weeks I am now prepared to go out on a lecture tour." Such ingratitude! To think I sold her a copy of my book wholesale.

Well, I decided to go into the kitchen and make my own breakfast. [*Looks around*] Kitchen? Kitchen? That foolish girl! Where does she keep the kitchen? [*Sees the set*] Why, it's charming, isn't it? I thought it was a closet. Oh, isn't this exciting? A little restaurant in my own home. A refrigerator of my own. A stove and a darling baby's bath.

[*She picks up a cup and saucer from the sink, takes them to the table and sings.*]

"I'll be seeing you in all the old familiar places
  That this heart of mine embraces . . ."
[*She sits at the table.*]

Well, that part was easy. Now what do I do next? Oh,
I know what is missing! Food!
[*She goes to the refrigerator and takes out frozen food
packages.*]

Beans, peas, spinach . . . oh, that foolish girl. Everything is ruined. She let everything freeze. [*Takes
dressed chicken out*] Oh, that poor chicken! It must
have wandered in here by itself and smothered to
death. I'll bury it later. [*Takes out can of tomato juice*]
Oh, tomato juice! That will be all right. Oh, dear, it's
all locked up. [*Picks up pineapple*] I've always adored
pineapple juice. [*Squeezes pineapple*] Now let me see.
I don't see how Rose got the strength to squeeze this
every morning. Oh dear, now what can I have? Oh, I
know—I'd like a nice hot cup of tea. What I need is hot
water. Oh yes, hot water. [*Looks around*] We don't
seem to have any hot water. Oh well, I'll scramble an
egg. [*She shakes the egg in her hand.*] That ought to be
scrambled enough. I hope there's bacon in this egg.
[*Door bell rings.*]

Ah, there's the door bell. Yes, darling? What is it,
darling? You want to sell me a vacuum cleaner? Oh
well, we don't have any dirty vacuums. Oh, it cleans
rugs, furniture and drapes, darling? We don't use a vacuum cleaner for that. We use a maid! Oh, a special
inducement with every vacuum cleaner! Well, makes
it interesting, darling. You've got a sale! Oh, you give
away an encyclopedia, darling. All there is to know
about life. Plagiarist! That's in *my* book!

Now what shall I do? Oh, I know what I'll have!
Toast! That's what I'll have! Some toast! [*Takes a loaf
of bread from the shelf*] Oh that silly girl forgot to get
toast. She only got white bread.
[*The telephone rings. She answers it.*]

Hello. Yes, darling. Yes, this is Miss Bankhead's res-
idence. What do you mean? Is this the man of the
house? Who is this? Max, the butcher? The butcher?
Oh, how do you do, darling. I am very glad to know
you. What is it, dear? Oh, you called to get my meat

order for today. Oh, that's very considerate of you, darling. Well, I tell you, I think I will have a steak. Well done, bernaise sauce, au gratin potatoes and a chef's salad. What do you mean, you only sell raw meat? Look darling, this is Tallulah not Tarzan.

[*Hangs up phone and picks up the egg, drops it—it breaks*]

Oh, I wounded it. Ooooooo—it's messy. Go away . . . go away. What am I to do? I suppose I have to sell my home. I am so hungry, too. Just starving! What can I have to eat? All right, I'll have *bread* and *water*.

[*Takes bread and water. Tastes*]

Why, it's delicious! And they said I couldn't cook!

BLACKOUT

COFFEE
a relativity

by Herbert Hartig and Lois Balk Korey

First produced in *Shoestring '57*, at the Barbizon Plaza Theatre, on November 5, 1956, with the following cast:

NICE-LOOKING YOUNG MAN Paul Mazursky
PRETTY GIRL Patricia Hammerlee

SCENE: *A diner.* COUNTERMAN *looking through newspaper, elbows on the counter at which sit four stools. From left to right these stools are occupied by* [1] *a* FAT TRUCK-DRIVER, [2] *nothing,* (3) *a* PRETTY GIRL, (4) *a suitcase. The* FAT TRUCK-DRIVER *is eating from a plate mountainous with food, the* PRETTY GIRL *sips coffee, the suitcase sits. Coffee simmers broodingly in a nickeled urn. Enter a* NICE-LOOKING YOUNG MAN. *That is the only way one would describe him: he is a* NICE-LOOKING YOUNG MAN. *Slightly paler than most, perhaps, but that's all. This* NICE-LOOKING YOUNG MAN, *after looking for a stool that is vacant, speaks to the* PRETTY GIRL.

NICE-LOOKING YOUNG MAN: This seat taken, Miss?

PRETTY GIRL: Oh. No. I'm sorry.

[*She removes the suitcase, and he sits down. The* COUNTERMAN *comes over.*]

NICE-LOOKING YOUNG MAN: Coffee, please. [*The* COUNTERMAN *goes to fetch it. To the* PRETTY GIRL] Uh ... what are you, going someplace?

[*Referring to the suitcase*]

PRETTY GIRL: [*Pleasantly*] No, just arrived. From San Francisco.

[*The while, the* COUNTERMAN *has brought the* NICE-LOOKING YOUNG MAN's *coffee, and retired to his paper.*]

NICE-LOOKING YOUNG MAN: Oh. I hear San Francisco is nice.

PRETTY GIRL: Yes, it is. Very.

[*The* NICE-LOOKING YOUNG MAN *nods, smiling. He sips*

427

his coffee, stretches, seems to unwind considerably. His face appears to have taken on color.]

NICE-LOOKING YOUNG MAN: This is nice, too. Y'know? . . . Having coffee . . . with someone . . . without all these Sick Complications . . .

[*She looks up at him, slightly startled.*]

Because the important thing in a Human Relationship is for two people to feel Free . . . to come and go . . . and not Make Demands, or have to Explain, or feel Guilt. Y'know?

PRETTY GIRL: [*She is somewhat taken aback by this quickly Significant Talk, coming as it has out of nowhere; but she does agree.*] Why, I—uh—yes, I think that's very tr—

FAT TRUCK-DRIVER: [*Speaking with his mouth full*] Lady, woo ja pleaj pajda kejjup?

[*The* PRETTY GIRL *pushes the bottle to him, with barely a glance in his direction. But it is enough; when she turns back to the* NICE-LOOKING YOUNG MAN *there is a difference. She isn't aware of it at first, because, although he has stiffened and withdrawn, on the surface he is by might of will keeping the air of amiability. And it is with that air that he asks—*]

NICE-LOOKING YOUNG MAN: You . . . known him long?

PRETTY GIRL: Who?

NICE-LOOKING YOUNG MAN: [*With a jerk of his head*] Him. Your—boyfriend. [*The word has stuck in his gorge. He looks sick.*] I think that's disgusting!

PRETTY GIRL: [*Bewildered, but with charming equanimity*] I don't know him at all. Would you like some sugar for your cof—

[*As she offers him the sugarbowl, he, with an abrupt, violent movement, knocks the bowl out of her hands. She recoils in shock.*]

NICE-LOOKING YOUNG MAN: What do you take me for? You just got into town, huh? Just got into town. Oh, you're good. You're *Good!* And I'm supposed to *believe* you? How *can* I believe you? How can I believe anything you say after this? Already Looking for the Next One! And the coffee not even cold in the cup! And how many were there Before Me? Huh? Well? *Answer me!!!*

[*The* COUNTERMAN *comes over, to investigate all the shouting.*]

COUNTERMAN: This guy bothering you, lady?

PRETTY GIRL: No, it's . . . all right.

[*But she has misgivings about the wisdom of her reply. The* COUNTERMAN, *shrugging, goes back to his paper.*]

NICE-LOOKING YOUNG MAN: [*Pointing a horrified finger*] How do you know *him?*

PRETTY GIRL: Who? The *counterman???* Oh, come *on!*

NICE-LOOKING YOUNG MAN: [*Fighting the panic*] Oh my God, my God! Must it always be like this? Look, I—I knew there must have been Others, but here—now—there should be Just Us Two, but something's—*Wrong*, something's—*Honey:* [*He seizes her shoulders; she looks very frightened.*] Honey, what are we Doing To Each Other? We're Tense, we're Saying All The Wrong Things, it—it isn't us, it's—This Place! Let's get out of here. We'll have dinner, see a show, we'll—[*He breaks it off. His face falls. He sees.*] You *don't want* to see me tonight, do you? Why don't you say it? Why Pretend? It's Over, isn't it, what we had. It's Finished. But *Where?* Where did it *Go Wrong?* Is there Someone Else? Do I know him? Is he Nice? I promise I won't Make Any Scenes. Just tell me. [*Wringing his hands in soul-agony, Steig-like*] The horrible thing is I feel like such a Fool! I know I shouldn't behave like this, I know it doesn't Do Any Good Now, but I Can't Help Myself. You can't just Go Like This—[*He grabs her wrist without looking. She has been reaching slowly down for her suitcase. She looks now like a cornered rat.*] We can't Leave It This Way. Give me a Few Minutes. After All We've Meant To Each Other you can give me A Few Minutes! Before you go to *Him!* You *Owe Me* that! Please! Wait? At least—you—? [*Reaching wildly for a means of detaining her*] you—want another cup of coffee . . . or . . . ?

[*He waits, breathing heavily, for her response; barely daring to hope. It is a long time coming. When it does, she doesn't look at him; she looks at her coffee-cup. She puts it down in its saucer very carefully, still holding it with both hands, however. She begins then, slowly and quietly, to speak.*]

PRETTY GIRL: "Another cup of Coffee." Do I want
"Another Cup of Coffee?" ... It's so easy, isn't it? Al-
ways so easy for the man. The woman is supposed to
Forgive and Forget The Hurt, and be content with
"Another Cup of Coffee" ... [*Screams*] WELL, IT'S
NOT ENOUGH!!! [*She slams down the cup, smashing
it to smithereens.*] COFFEE—COFFEE—COFFEE!!!!!
Sure—Buy the girl Coffee!—*She* won't know the dif-
ference! Make her Completely Dependent on you and
your Coffee! And *you* call *that* a "Human Relation-
ship?" Always *your* Needs! *My* Needs didn't matter!
I—offered—you—Sugar. But you Rejected me. You
Shut Me Out. Well ... I knew; I Knew—when you
Rejected My Sugar—that that was the way it would
Always Be With Us. You showed me Oh So Clearly.
For which I *Thank* you. No—Don't—Touch Me! [*He
hasn't moved. He just sits there, receiving this diatribe
thunderstruck.*] I'm Tired of it. I Don't Want Any More.
You did this. *You*. I want you to Remember, Always,
and Live With It: *You* ... took something Fine and
Beautiful ... and *Destroyed* it with your Nasty *Suspi-
cions!!!* ... I *had* this Warmth for you ... My Normal
Impulse was to Reach Out to you ... [*In the spell of
remembrance she has cradled his head gently in her
bosom.*] But now ... ? I just [*She thrusts his head
violently from her, in flat and final rejection.*]
BLOOOOOOOORGHHH!!! No! Don't Plead with me,
don't try to Follow Me or Look Me Up. It's Over. *Over*.
And I· *Tried*. GOD KNOWS I Tried! But now ... ?
[*Snatching up her suitcase*] I'm going to take The Little
I Have Left ... and spend the Rest Of My Life ...
trying to forget the Bitterness You've Made Me Feel
In My Heart For *You!*
[*She exits, noble with tears. He sits there. He doesn't
know what hit him. He just sits there. A* SECOND
PRETTY GIRL *enters, and takes the stool just vacated
by the first. The* COUNTERMAN *comes over.*]
SECOND PRETTY GIRL: I'd like a cup of coffee, please.
NICE-LOOKING YOUNG MAN: [*To himself, aloud*] What was
the matter with *her?* Why did she go like that? *Boy!*
[*The* COUNTERMAN *brings her coffee and retires.*]

NICE-LOOKING YOUNG MAN: [*To shake the sickness of heart; to the* GIRL] They have good coffee here.

SECOND PRETTY GIRL: [*Sipping it*] Mm, yes, they do.

NICE-LOOKING YOUNG MAN: It's nice having coffee like *this*, ... y'know? Without all these ... [*With a meaningful jerk of his head toward the door*] Sick Complications ... Y'know? [*As she turns in pleasant inquiry, he leans toward her slightly. The lights begin to dim.*] Because the important thing in a Human Relationship ... etc.

[*The lights fade to black.*]

DOUBLE-O OR NOTHING

by William F. Brown

First produced in *Baker's Dozen* at the Plaza 9 in the Plaza Hotel, on January 9, 1964, with the following cast:

HOST Gerry Matthews
BOND Jamie Ross
MILKY Ruth Buzzi
MR. IF Nagle Jackson

HOST: He was the top secret agent in the most secret of British secret intelligence agencies. His name was James Bond, and he was too much. This was his first vacation in twelve books, and except for the slight bulge beneath his coat that marked the Walther PPK in a soft leather holster slung under his left armpit for a quick cross-draw, his disguise was perfect ... dark glasses and a putty nose in which was hidden a miniature Leica camera Bond could trigger merely by sniffing, in case anything *did* come up. Bond felt secure no one could possibly penetrate his disguise, since he had registered under a checked-out alias of Thomas Dylan, antique dealer from Great Barrington. And so he felt at peace with the world, despite the fact the man to his right nervously fingered the trigger of a Schmeisser pointed at Bond's head. Bond's attention was focused on the girl to his left, playing solitaire. After an hour or so, Bond decided to speak, because he wondered if the girl knew that from her back there protruded the hilt of a knife.

BOND: Black ten doesn't go on the black jack, miss. Not the way we play it at the casino.

GIRL: You're James Bond, aren't you?

HOST: The confrontation called for bluff and steady self-assurance.

BOND: If you check the register, you'll find I'm listed as Thomas Dylan, antique dealer from Great Barrington, New Hampshire, or Vermont, or wherever it's supposed to be.

GIRL: Thomas Dylan from Great Barrington doesn't carry a Walther PPK in a soft leather holster slung under his left armpit for a quick cross-draw. [*Pause*] Why are you taking pictures of me through your nose?

HOST: Instinctively, Bond knew this was no ordinary blonde with a knife in her back. He ran his hand casually through his hair, which he had freshly washed that very morning with Pinaud Elixir, just after a breakfast of scrambled *oeufs* and a glass of ten-year-old Calvados. Bond was not only a connoisseur, he was also a bit of a lush.

BOND: Despite that, you'll fall in love with me. But first, do you know you have a knife in your back?

GIRL: Yes. What do you make of it?

BOND: Offhand, I'd say it was a Wilkinson, Model 23Q, hollow-ground steel. Marvelous for chopping rascasse, the tender flesh of the scorpion fish.

GIRL: That's what it feels like.

BOND: But it's no excuse for putting a red three on a red four, miss ... uh ... what *is* your name?

GIRL: Galaxy. Milky Way Galaxy. My father named me after a candy bar.

BOND: I don't know. I think Milky Way is a lovely name for a galaxy.

MAN: That'll be just about enough out of you, Mr. James Bond.

HOST: Bond's hair-trigger responses responded the instant he felt the muzzle of the Schmeisser in his ear. Bond instinctively knew the man had been sent to kill him. He also knew the muzzle velocity of the Schmeisser was twenty-five hundred feet per second, ten feet per second too fast for him to substitute his false head, which he carried in a plastic bag in his breast pocket.

BOND: [*To* MAN] I like your style, but I'm in no mood to be trifled with when I'm about to remove a knife from Milky here.

GIRL: [*Pensively*] Remove ... the ... knife?

HOST: Bond looked into the girl's eyes and saw hate, fear, love, desire, anguish, pride, and prejudice. She looked back into his eyes and saw a reflection of herself in his dark glasses. It was enough.

GIRL: Don't touch me!

BOND: Why not?

GIRL: Because I'm a living bomb and I love you!

HOST: Instinctively, Bond sensed the girl had been sent to kill him too. He phrased his next question carefully.

BOND: Oh?

GIRL: Yes. I've been wired so that when you remove the knife, we both blow up.

BOND: Why did you let them do this to you?

GIRL: I needed the money.

HOST: Bond knew if he wished, he could disarm the girl with the miniature bomb-disposal kit he always carried screwed into his navel.

BOND: In a moment, I shall make you . . .

GIRL: [*Eagerly*] Yes?

BOND: . . . safe.

GIRL: [*Disappointed*] Oh.

BOND: But first, I must know more, because it sounds like the work of SPECTRE! [*To* GIRL] Tell me, who did this to you?

GIRL: He said he was Thomas Dylan, an antique dealer from Great Barrington.

BOND: There's been a leak somewhere.

MAN: I can't wait any longer, Bond. Whatever the girl's game is, I picked up a lower number than she did at the kill counter, so I get to kill you first.

HOST: To Bond, the next question was always the most important he ever asked his would-be killer.

BOND: How?

MAN: I'm coming to that. But let me warn you, I do nice work.

HOST: Bond wondered why everyone always wanted to kill him, when he would much rather be left alone at the wheel of his Continental Bentley, with the "R"-type chassis, the big-6 engine, and the thirteen-forty back-axle ratio that only rally-class drivers could handle well, tooling along the English countryside, chasing broads. Someday he would find out. Meanwhile, he sighed and removed his nose cone.

GIRL: Why, James! Without your nose, you're beautiful!

MAN: Yes! Really quite striking.

BOND: [*To* MAN] You keep out of this. I'm working *her* side of the street!

GIRL: [*Leaning across and resting her head on his chest*] Oh, James!

HOST: The girl's soft body felt warm and willing. Bond wondered how he felt to her.

GIRL: [*To* HOST] Lumpy.

[*She sits back in her place again.*]

HOST: Bond's mind flashed back to the simple lunch he had picked up at Maxim's the day before: half a roast pheasant, turbot poché, and sauce mousseline. The sauce had been lumpy too. Was the girl trying to tell him something? How could he discreetly find out if there was a connection?

BOND: [*To* GIRL] Is there a connection?

MAN: It's too late for a fix now, Bond. In three minutes a boat will arrive with a single Thompson engine in its flattened stern. You will be bound, gagged, blindfolded, and all stuck up with special delivery stamps. You will be dragged behind the boat slowly, over turquoise shoal waters to a cave where a giant squid lurks. He's on my side. At a given signal, the squid will grapple you to the bottom and deposit you at the door of an underground chamber. You will be sucked in through an air vent and placed in an electrified, insulated, soundproofed room. I will be waiting there for you. I'll hit you on the head with a pipe.

BOND: An amusing notion.

GIRL: Oh, James, I know this next little while may be trying, but what of us?

HOST: The girl's eyes filled with tears, shorting her wire mechanism. She was no longer a threat. Bond used the momentary distraction to reach slowly beneath the table for his left shoe, the heel of which contained a cleverly-concealed bow and arrow which no one knew about except Bond and his secret service cobbler.

MAN: I wouldn't go for that bow and arrow if I were you, Bond.

BOND: That impertinence sealed your doom ... Mr. *If!*

MAN: How did you know my name?

BOND: You could be no one else. I remember hearing about you when I solved my most famous case. The one about the madman in Jamaica with the underground laboratory who was planning to steal Palm Beach. What was his name? Doctor . . . ?

MAN: No?

BOND: Yes!

MAN: He was like a father to me.

BOND: You mean he was your analyst?

MAN: No. My mother.

HOST: A boat hove into view on the horizon, its Thompson engine in the flattened stern creaming up a wake that reminded Bond very much of a rich cream sauce he had had the night before, of wine and mushrooms, evenly spread over thinly-sliced filet of sole that . . .

GIRL: [*To* BOND] Food, glorious food, but James, what about us? What are we to do?

BOND: First, let's put the black five on the red six where it belongs.

GIRL: Yes? And then what?

HOST: Bond paused. His keen ears picked up the sound of a missing cylinder in the oncoming boat. He knew the engine would fail some seven hundred yards offshore, leaving the craft to sink on a reef. That left only the man to deal with.

GIRL: [*Impatiently*] Yes, James? And then what?

BOND: [*To* GIRL] You'll notice Mr. If has a slight Hapsburg lip, which means he's probably a hemophiliac and will bleed to death at the slightest scratch. I'm wearing my scratchy cuff-links for just such an occasion. But I'll have to play it cool. [*To* MAN] Say, old chap, before I die, would you like to have your back scratched?

MAN: Thanks. You're too kind.

HOST: One scratch and it was done. Mr. If fell to the floor, writhing in agony, his Schmeisser going off wildly, missing Bond completely as it harmlessly drilled the girl. Bond observed them both coolly.

BOND: [*To* MAN] You've got three seconds to live. [*To* GIRL] And you, my playful pussycat, possibly four. [*To* BOTH] But before you go, may I ask why you both came here to kill me?

MAN: [*Gasping*] Because you know too much.

BOND: About what?

GIRL: [*Gasping*] Everything.

BOND: [*Innocently*] But . . .

GIRL: [*Gasping*] Don't you see, my dear erudite James . . .

MAN: [*Gasping*] . . . *nobody* likes a smart-ass!

BLACKOUT

AUTHORS AND THEIR CONTRIBUTIONS

Arnold Auerbach
  The Army Way
George Axelrod
  I Could Write a Book (with Max Wilk)
Alan Baxter
  Chin Up
  The Dead Cow (with Harold Johnsrud)
Robert Benchley
  The Treasurer's Report
Donald Blackwell
  In Marbled Halls (with William Miles)
Mel Brooks
  Of Fathers and Sons
Lew Brown
  The Feud (with Billy K. Wells and George White)
William F. Brown
  Double-O or Nothing
Abe Burrows
  Highlights from the World of Sports
Betty Comden and Adolph Green
  Space Brigade
  Triangle
Howard Dietz
  For Good Old Nectar (with George S. Kaufman)
  Lost in a Crowd (with Charles Sherman)
  On the American Plan (with George S. Kaufman)
  The Audience Waits

The Gigolo Business
The Great Warburton Mystery (with George S. Kaufman)
The Pride of the Claghornes (with George S. Kaufman)
The Surgeon's Debut

W.C. Fields
  School Days
  Stolen Bonds

David Freedman
  A Day at the Brokers'
  A Smoking Car
  Baby Snooks Goes Hollywood
  Dr. Fradler's Dilemma
  Speed
  Sweepstakes Ticket
  Taxes! Taxes!!
  The Petrified Elevator
  The Reading of the Play

Frank Gabrielson
  Home of the Brave (with David Lesan)

Charles Gaynor
  Do It Yourself

Will Glickman
  I Never Felt Better (with Joseph Stein)

Lee Goodman
  Buck and Bobby (with James Kirkwood)

Moss Hart
  Better Luck Next Time
  Franklin D. Roosevelt to Be Inaugurated To-morrow
  Gone with the Revolution (with George S. Kaufman
  World's Wealthiest Man Celebrates Ninety-fourth Birthday

Herbert Hartig
  Coffee (with Lois Balk Korey)
  Sell, Sell, Sell (with Herbert Reich)

Harold Johnsrud
  The Dead Cow (with Alan Baxter)

George S. Kaufman
  For Good Old Nectar (with Howard Dietz)

Ira Wallach
  Upper Birth
Billy K. Wells
  My
  Stocks
  The Ambulance Chaser
  The Feud (with Lew Brown and George White)
  The Will
George White
  The Feud (with Lew Brown and Billy K. Wells)
Max Wilk
  I Could Write a Book (with George Axelrod)

CONTENTS BY NUMBER OF CHARACTERS

[NOTE: In many cases the genders are interchangeable and the use of doubling is possible. Check the individual sketch for specific requirements.]

4 CHARACTERS

5 CHARACTERS

6 CHARACTERS

7 CHARACTERS

8 CHARACTERS

9 CHARACTERS

BIOGRAPHIES OF CONTRIBUTING AUTHORS

ARNOLD M. AUERBACH was born in New York City. After graduating from Columbia College, where he wrote several varsity shows, he became a radio comedy-writer. He was one of the authors of the Fred Allen radio show for five years. After service in the Army in WW2, he wrote the Broadway revue, *Call Me Mister*, which was followed by sketches for *Inside U.S.A.* and *Bless You All*. Subsequently he wrote for many leading TV shows, including Milton Berle, Frank Sinatra, *Sgt. Bilko*, etc. He is the author of *Funny Men Don't Laugh*, a memoir of his radio days, and of a novel, *Is That Your Best Offer?*, both published by Doubleday. He has written humorous prose and verse for many leading magazines, including *Saturday Review, Harpers, New York* and others. He also wrote many humorous pieces on show business for the Sunday Arts and Leisure section of the *New York Times*.

GEORGE AXELROD was born in New York in 1922. He started as a radio and television script writer, working for many comedians in the late 1940s. In addition to co-authoring the sketches for the show *Small Wonder*, he wrote the Broadway comedies *The Seven Year Itch, Will Success Spoil Rock Hunter?*, and *Goodbye, Charlie*. He is the author of the screenplays for *Breakfast at Tiffany's, The Manchurian Candidate*, and *How To Murder Your Wife*. He is saving the good parts of his autobiography for the "kiss-and-tell" book he plans to write in his late middle age.

ALAN BAXTER, born in 1908, was a member of George
Pierce Baker's famed 47 Drama Workshop at Yale along
with fellow classmate Elia Kazan. From there, he joined
the Group Theatre in New York, appearing in *Men in
White* among other shows. At the same time his acting
career was flourishing, he wrote sketches for *Life Begins
at 8:40*, *Thumbs Up*, and *Calling All Stars*. His stage
work brought him to Hollywood, where he worked free-
lance for virtually every studio and made more than sixty
movies—from above-the-title billing to small supporting
roles. He died in 1976.

ROBERT BENCHLEY claimed that he was born on the
Isle of Wight, September 15, 1807, shipped as cabin boy
on the *Florence J. Marble* in 1815, wrote *A Tale of Two
Cities* in 1820, married Princess Anastasie of Portugal in
1831 (children: Prince Rupprecht and several little girls),
and was buried in Westminster Abbey in 1871. That is
not strictly true. He was born on September 15, 1889 in
Massachusetts. He went to Phillips Exeter Academy,
where he is still remembered as the author of a paper on
"How to Embalm a Corpse," written after being given an
assignment to write an exposition of how to do something
practical. He received his B.A. from Harvard, where he
was president of the *Lampoon*. After graduation, he
worked under F.P. Adams as associate editor of the New
York *Tribune's* Sunday Magazine and in 1919 he was
hired as the managing editor of *Vanity Fair*, working with
Robert Sherwood and Dorothy Parker. From there he became *Life's* dramatic editor and kept that position until
1929. During those years, he began to write books, among
them *Love Conquers All*, *The Early Worm*, and *20,000
Leagues under the Sea or David Copperfield*. He made
his acting debut in *No, Sirree* (reciting "The Treasurer's
Report"). Hollywood beckoned, and he made over thirty
short subjects for several studios, among them are *The
Love Life of the Polyp*, *How to Vote*, *How to Sleep* (which
won an Academy Award), *An Evening Alone* and *Raising a Baby*, in addition to *The Treasurer's Report*.
Under contract to MGM, he was often called in to supply
a light touch or to bolster failing dialogue for their feature
films. He also played supporting roles in several movies,

including *Foreign Correspondent* and *You'll Never Get Rich*. Although he long fought off attractive radio offers (When a tobacco firm questioned him about his favorite brand of cigarette, he wired back "Marijuana."), in 1938 he was persuaded to take part in an Old Gold program and rated sixth on a national popularity poll. Before his death in 1945 he wrote several more books, telephoned the Kaiser at Doorn—on a sudden impulse to speak German, and left a note to the milkman at Grant's tomb.

DONALD BLACKWELL has been an actor, playwright and director. A graduate of the University of Toronto, he appeared in many shows on Broadway. He was co-author of *Nine Pine Street*, *Going Gay* and *The Distant Shore*. His sketches appeared in *Three's a Crowd*, and several editions of *The Little Show*.

MEL BROOKS, born in Brooklyn, haunted the Broadway theatres and vaudeville houses at an early age. He began doing impressions and was an amateur drummer and pianist. He made his first appearance as an actor in *Golden Boy* in Redbank, New Jersey, and worked as a drummer and comic in the Catskills. He began writing for Sid Caesar for the television show *Broadway Revue* and their association continued for ten years, during which time Brooks worked on the memorable *Your Show of Shows* and *Caesar's Hour*. When Sid Caesar left TV, Brooks teamed with Carl Reiner on *The 2000-Year-Old-Man* comedy albums. In collaboration with Buck Henry, he developed the hit television show *Get Smart*. His short film, *The Critic*, earned him an Academy Award, as did his first feature film, *The Producers*, which brought him the Oscar for his story and screenplay. His subsequent films are *The Twelve Chairs*, *Blazing Saddles*, *Young Frankenstein*, *Silent Movie*, *High Anxiety*, and *The History of the World—Part I*. In addition to *New Faces of 1952*, his other Broadway credits include writing the books for the musicals *Shinbone Alley* and *All American*. He has acted in several of his films and wrote many of the songs in them as well, including the famous "Springtime for Hitler" number in *The Producers*. He is married to actress Anne Bancroft.

LEW BROWN, born in 1893, was part of the famous song-writing team with co-lyricist B.G. DeSylva and composer Ray Henderson. They wrote the scores for *Good News*, *Manhattan Mary*, *Hold Everything*, *Follow Thru*, *Flying High*, and three editions of *George White's Scandals*. After DeSylva left the team, Brown and Henderson wrote the 1931 *Scandals*, *Hot-Cha!*, and *Strike Me Pink*. He died in 1958.

WILLIAM F. BROWN wrote his first cabaret sketch for Julius Monk's 1960 Upstairs at the Downstairs revue, *Seven Come Eleven*. Shortly after that, he wrote his first television sketch for a Max Liebman CBS-TV special, *The American Cowboy*. Since then, he has written for any number of cabaret revues (Monk and otherwise); for over one hundred television shows, including *That Was the Week That Was*, *Love American Style* and *The Jackie Gleason Show*. His first full-length comedy, *The Girl in the Freudian Slip*, was produced on Broadway in 1967. The next year, he was a major sketch contributor to *New Faces of 1968* and was bookwriter for the off-Broadway musical, *How to Steal an Election*. He won a Tony nomination and a Drama Desk Award for writing the book to Broadway's Best Musical of 1975, *The Wiz*. In 1978, he was again represented on Broadway as bookwriter for the Charles Strouse-Lee Adams show, *A Broadway Musical*. He has also written special material for many night club performers including Joan Rivers, Joey Foreman and Georgie Kaye; has written book and lyrics for over forty major live and filmed industrial shows; and is a syndicated cartoonist ("Boomer"). He lives in Connecticut.

ABE BURROWS was born in Manhattan's Lower East Side in 1910. He quit college to take a job on Wall Street, and shortly thereafter had the honor of posting plummeting stock prices during the Crash of '29. By the end of the decade, he was a gag writer, selling jokes to radio and vaudeville comedians. As head writer for the hit radio show *Duffy's Tavern*, he wrote for such guest stars as Tallulah Bankhead, Robert Benchley, Fred Allen, and Milton Berle. He had his own radio show for CBS, *The Abe Burrows Show*, and as a nightclub comedian he played major cities coast to coast. His first Broadway show was *Guys and Dolls*, and as co-author of the book, he won his first Tony award. His other Broadway credits include *Two on the Aisle, Can-Can, Say, Darling,* and *How to Succeed in Business Without Really Trying,* for which he won the Pulitzer Prize. As a play doctor, he helped turn several shows into successes, and that list includes *Make a Wish, Three Wishes for Jamie, Silk Stockings,* and *What Makes Sammy Run?* He directed many of the above shows as well as *Cactus Flower* and *Forty Carats.* His recently published autobiography is entitled *Honest, Abe.*

BETTY COMDEN and ADOLPH GREEN have been together longer than any other writing team in musical theatre or film. They began as performers and writers in a satirical nightclub group, *The Revuers,* which expired in Los Angeles in early 1944 after five years of appearances on both coasts, thirty weeks on NBC Radio nationwide, and a cutting-room floor appearance in a Fox movie musical. The two then collaborated with Leonard Bernstein and Jerome Robbins on what was to be the first show for all of them, *On the Town,* which was directed by George Abbott and opened in New York on December 28, 1944. Subsequent works for the theatre include *Billion Dollar Baby, Wonderful Town, Two on the Aisle, Peter Pan, Bells Are Ringing, Say, Darling, Do Re Mi, Subways Are for Sleeping, Fade Out—Fade In, Hallelujah, Baby!, Applause,* and *On the Twentieth Century.* Among their many movie musicals are *The Band Wagon, On the Town, Bells Are Ringing, It's Always Fair Weather, The Barkleys of Broadway,* and *Singin' in the Rain*— voted one of the ten greatest American films of all times by the American Film Institute. They have received Tony Awards for *Hallelujah, Baby!, Wonderful Town, Applause,* and *On the Twentieth Century;* an Obie Award for *A Party with Betty Comden and Adolph Green;* and Screen Writer's Guild Awards for *On the Town, Singin' in the Rain, The Band Wagon,* and *Bells Are Ringing.* They are not now, nor have they ever been, married to each other. Miss Comden was married to the late Steven Kyle and has two children, Susanna and Alan. Mr. Green is married to Phyllis Newman and also has two children, Adam and Amanda. Betty Comden and Adolph Green plan to keep working together.

HOWARD DIETZ, born in 1896, for over thirty years lived a double life—as lyric and sketch writer for Broadway shows and as Director of Publicity and Advertising for MGM. The songs he wrote with composer Arthur Schwartz, most notably "Dancing in the Dark," "You and the Night and the Music," "Alone Together," "A Shine on Your Shoes," "By Myself," "I Guess I'll Have to Change My Plan," and "That's Entertainment" have become a permanent part of American popular music. Their show, *The Band Wagon*, for which he wrote the lyrics, co-wrote the sketches with George S. Kaufman, and supervised the entire production, is considered to be the finest revue ever produced. A listing of his other shows include *The Little Show, Three's a Crowd, Flying Colors, Revenge with Music, At Home Abroad, Between the Devil, Sadie Thompson, Inside U.S.A., The Gay Life* and *Jennie*. The Metropolitan Opera commissioned him to write new English lyrics for *Die Fledermaus* and *La Boheme*. He is married to designer Lucinda Ballard.

W.C. FIELDS was born in Philadelphia in 1880. After many years of playing in vaudeville, he appeared in seven editions of the *Ziegfeld Follies* between 1915 and 1925 and in the *Earl Carroll Vanities* of 1928. In these shows he wrote many of his sketches and routines. He also contributed scenarios and story ideas to many of his Hollywood films, and these included *Tillie's Punctured Romance, Her Majesty Love, Million Dollar Legs, If I Had a Million, International House, Tillie and Gus, Six of a Kind, The Old-Fashioned Way, It's a Gift, David Copperfield, Mississippi, The Man on the Flying Trapeze, Poppy, The Big Broadcast of 1938, You Can't Cheat an Honest Man, My Little Chickadee, The Bank Dick, Never Give a Sucker an Even Break,* and *Sensations of 1945*. He died in Pasadena, California in 1946.

DAVID FREEDMAN was one of the best and most astonishingly prolific writers of his day. Born in 1898 in

Rumania he came to New York City with his family when he was a year old and grew up on the Lower East Side. From those humble beginnings he graduated Phi Beta Kappa from the College of the City of New York. Out of the experiences of his youth evolved a character of fiction that carried him to fame—Mendel Marantz—first as short stories, then as a novel, then as a play. Through these efforts he met Eddie Cantor for whom Freedman wrote gags and later ghost-wrote several books bearing Cantor's name. In quick succession he wrote sketches for Billy Rose's shows, *Sweet and Low* and *Crazy Quilt*, and contributed sketches to *Strike Me Pink* and the *Ziegfeld Follies of 1934*. Other leading comedians of the era employed him, often simultaneously, to write their jokes. That list included Fannie Brice, Jack Benny, Al Jolson, and George Burns and Gracie Allen. At the time of his sudden death in 1936 he had two shows playing on Broadway, *White Horse Inn* (for which he did the American adaptation) and the *Ziegfeld Follies of 1936* (for which he wrote all the sketches), and another in rehearsal, *The Show Is On.*

FRANK GABRIELSON, born in 1910, graduated Yale University and contributed sketches to several Shubert shows including *Life Begins at 8:40*. In Hollywood, he collaborated on several Carmen Miranda pictures and even worked for a while at the Walt Disney studio. His greatest success came from adapting the Kathryn Forbes novel *Mama's Bank Account* for a radio series, which in turn led him to co-produce and write most of the episodes for the television version, better known as *I Remember Mama*. He died in 1980.

CHARLES GAYNOR made his Broadway debut as author and composer of the hit revue *Lend an Ear*, in which Carol Channing was introduced to Broadway. After graduating from Dartmouth College, where he wrote book, music and lyrics for two varsity shows, he did numbers for the *Sunday Nights at Nine* revues at New York's Barbizon Plaza and created five revues for the Pittsburgh Playhouse before going to war. His war service took him for a period to London where he wrote numbers for the

Hermione Gingold revue *Sweeter and Lower*. He also wrote the sketches, lyrics and music for *Show Girl* starring Miss Channing and contributed songs to Debbie Reynolds' show, *Irene*. Born in 1909, he died in 1975.

WILL GLICKMAN was born in Brooklyn, New York. After graduating from the University of Alabama, he began writing and directing network radio and television, comedy and comedy-variety series, such as *Duffy's Tavern*, and shows for such stars as Jimmy Durante, Perry Como, Jackie Gleason and Dinah Shore. For Broadway, he was the co-author of revues, one play and three musicals, including *Mr. Wonderful* and *Plain & Fancy*. He now resides in San Francisco, where he writes a weekly show-business column for a newspaper.

LEE GOODMAN was a child actor, later half of the comedy team of Kirkwood and Goodman. He has appeared in the National Company of *Sweet Charity* with Chita Rivera and on Broadway in *Dance Me a Song*, *A Funny Thing Happened on the Way to the Forum*, *Carnival in Flanders* and *On the Twentieth Century*. He almost appeared on Broadway in the ill-fated *Miss Moffat*, which starred Bette Davis.

MOSS HART was born in New York in 1904. His first play, written in collaboration with George S. Kaufman, was produced in 1930. *Once in a Lifetime* was its name, and it marked the beginning of a fabulously successful theatrical relationship. Other Hart and Kaufman products include *Merrily We Roll Along*, *You Can't Take It with You* (Pulitzer Prize winner), *I'd Rather Be Right*, *The Fabulous Invalid*, *The American Way*, *The Man Who Came to Dinner*, and *George Washington Slept Here*. His books for musical shows include *Face the Music* and *As Thousands Cheer* (scores by Irving Berlin), *Jubilee* (Cole Porter), and *Lady in the Dark* (Kurt Weill and Ira Gershwin). Plays written by Hart alone are *Winged Victory*, *Christopher Blake*, *Light Up the Sky*, and *The Climate of Eden*. For the movies, he wrote the screenplays for *Gentlemen's Agreement*, *Hans Christian Andersen*, *The Eddie Duchin Story*, *A Star Is Born* (the Judy Garland version), and *Prince of Players*. He won the Antoinette Perry Award for his direction of Lerner and Loewe's record breaking hit, *My Fair Lady*, after which he also staged their musical *Camelot*. At the urging of his wife, Kittly Carlisle, he wrote his autobiography, *Act One*, which was published in 1959 and remained on the best seller list for two years. He died in 1961.

HERBERT HARTIG performed with The Living Theatre in its halcyon days at The Cherry Lane Theatre and then, as half of the comedy team "Igor & H" ("Igor" was Paul Mazursky), in the country's better supper-clubs (The Blue Angel, The Village Vanguard, The Bon Soir, One Fifth Avenue, The Purple Onion, The Crystal Palace), at the same time turning out special material for Dick Shawn, Henry Morgan, Ronny Graham, Imogene Coca, Jules Munshin, Bea Arthur, Kaye Ballard, and many others. He has been a staff writer for NBC and writer-in-residence at Tamiment and Green Mansions. His work has been featured in revues throughout the United States and Europe, and on many TV variety shows, series and specials. He wrote the song Dick Shawn sang in Mel Brooks' film *The Producers*. A serious writer as well, Mr. Hartig supplied the libretto for the jazz opera *Fat Tuesday*, written on a Ford Foundation grant, has translated the lyrics of Brecht and Prevert, and contributed the dramatization of Nathaniel Hawthorne's *Rappaccini's Daughter* to the American Short Story series on PBS.

HAROLD JOHNSRUD was an actor, writer and director. As a director, he worked on the 1932 production of *Americana*. As a writer, his sketches appeared in *Parade*. As an actor, he appeared in numerous productions including *Winterset* and *Key Largo*. It was during the run of the latter that he died tragically in a hotel fire at the age of thirty-five.

GEORGE S. KAUFMAN was born in Pittsburgh, Pennsylvania, in 1889. During his early career as a reporter and drama critic (and eventually drama editor of *The New York Times*), he began to write for the theatre. After 1921, when *Dulcy*, his first collaboration with Marc Connelly appeared, there was rarely a year (until his death in 1961) without a Kaufman play—usually in collaboration. His only full-length plays written alone were *The Butter and Egg Man*, *The Cocoanuts*, and *Hollywood Pinafore*. A master craftsman of the theatre with a brilliant eye for comedy and satire, he was equally adept in almost all varieties of theatrical art—expressionistic satire, as in *Beggar on Horseback* (also with Marc Connelly); social satire, as in *The Late George Apley* (written with John P. Marquand), and *Dinner at Eight* (with Edna Ferber); revues, as in *The Band Wagon* (with Howard Dietz and Arthur Schwartz); musicals, as in the 1931 Pulitzer Prize-winning *Of Thee I Sing* (with Morrie Ryskind, George and Ira Gershwin); and comedies, some of the greatest of the twentieth century theatre, such as *Once in a Lifetime*, *The Man Who Came to Dinner*, and *You Can't Take It with You* (another Pulitzer Prize-winner in 1936—and all three written with Moss Hart), *The Royal Family* (also with Edna Ferber), and *The Solid Gold Cadillac* (with Howard Teichmann). With Morrie Ryskind, he also wrote the screenplays for the Marx Brothers' films: *The Cocoanuts*, *Animal Crackers*, and *A Night at the Opera*. Mr. Kaufman also directed some two dozen of his own plays plus such other hits as *The Front Page*, *Of Mice and Men*, *My Sister Eileen*, and *Guys and Dolls*.

JEAN and WALTER KERR met as teacher and student at Washington's Catholic University. As director of the Drama Department, Walter Kerr wrote and directed several productions, some for Broadway. The first, *Sing Out Sweet Land* with Alfred Drake and Burl Ives, was presented in 1945; the second in 1949, *Touch and Go*. Mrs. Kerr collaborated with her husband in writing the sketches and lyrics for that revue as well as the book and lyrics for the musical *Goldilocks*. She contributed sketches to *John Murray Anderson's Almanac* and is the author of the Broadway comedies *King of Hearts* (with Eleanor Brooke), *Mary, Mary* (which was one of the longest-running comedies in Broadway history), *Poor Richard, Finishing Touches*, and *Lunch Hour*. Her highly successful books include *Please Don't Eat the Daisies*, *The Snake Has All the Lines, Penny Candy* and *How I Got to Be Perfect*. From 1951 to 1966, Mr. Kerr was the drama critic for the *New York Herald Tribune*. Since then, he has written for *The New York Times*. He is the author of the books *How Not to Write a Play, Criticism and Censorship, Pieces at Eight, The Decline of Pleasure, The Theatre in Spite of Itself, Tragedy and Comedy, Thirty Plays Hath November, God on the Gymnasium Floor, The Silent Clowns,* and *Journey to the Center of the Theatre*.

JAMES KIRKWOOD was born in California of theatrical parents, Lila Lee and James Kirkwood, Sr. Before taking up a writing career, he was one half of the popular night-club comedy team of Jim Kirkwood and Lee Goodman. He was also a disc jockey and put in a four-year hitch on a TV soap opera. As an actor he appeared on Broadway and on tour opposite such fascinating ladies as Tallulah Bankhead, Elaine Stritch, Martha Raye, Imogene Coca, Kaye Ballard and many others. He has been consistently praised in superlatives for his novels *Some Kind of Hero, There Must Be a Pony!, Good Times/Bad Times, P.S. Your Cat Is Dead!, Hit Me with a Rainbow*, and one non-fiction book, *American Grotesque*. He is the Pulitzer Prize and Tony Award-winning co-author of *A Chorus Line* and other plays. In the last three years he has written four screenplays, although writing for Hollywood is not his favorite pastime. He spends his time between East Hampton and Key West and is currently working on his seventh book as well as a new musical for Broadway.

LOIS BALK (later KOREY), with the ink barely dry on her diploma from New York University, had already secured herself a staff writing job for Steve Allen's *Tonight Show*. She went on to write *The Ernie Kovacs Show, The George Gobel Show,* The NBC Sunday-Night *Comedy Hour*, and, on radio, simultaneously *The Peter Lind Hayes–Mary Healy Show* and *The Andy Griffith Show*, both of them across-the-board, requiring her to turn out ten scripts a week for a period of a year! She is at present Creative Director for Needham, Harper & Steers advertising agency.

RING LARDNER, short story writer and humorist, was born in 1885 at Niles, Michigan, and died in 1933 at East Hampton, New York. He was a sports writer and daily columnist in Chicago for fifteen years, during the last five of which he also became famous for his magazine stories. In 1920 he moved to the New York area with his wife and four sons. His books include *You Know Me Al* (1916), *Gullible's Travels* (1917), *The Big Town* (1921), *How to Write Short Stories* (1924) and *Roundup* (1929). He contributed sketches to the *Ziegfeld Follies of 1922* and collaborated with George S. Kaufman on the play *June Moon*, a Broadway hit of the 1929-30 season.

DAVID LESAN was a producer and writer who, after graduating from the Yale Drama School, contributed to such shows as *Parade, Sing for Your Supper*, and *The Illustrator's Show*. He also wrote for radio and television, and among those credits are *Young Doctor Malone, The Guiding Light*, and *Search for Tomorrow*. He died in 1974 at the age of 64.

JACK McGOWAN began his career in vaudeville and burlesque where he wrote many of the songs and jokes used in the shows and by 1916 signed a three-year contract (as a performer) with Florenz Ziegfeld. He soon grew tired of simply being a background singer to Ziegfeld's beautiful girls, and, in order to break his contract, enlisted in the army. When his army service ended in 1918, he went back to Broadway and appeared in many musicals while in the off-time continuing to develop his writing. He subsequently wrote many Broadway shows and is best known as the co-author of *Hold Everything, Heads Up, Flying High* and *Girl Crazy*. Born in 1894, he died in 1977.

WILLIAM MILES was a graduate of the Yale Drama School. After many stage appearances, he contributed sketches to *The Second Little Show* and *Three's a Crowd*. He achieved great success as the manager-director of the Berkshire Playhouse, at Stockbridge, Massachusetts.

HERBERT REICH boasts of being "a man of many parts, some of which are missing." He has been ("not necessarily sequentially") a candy butcher, market researcher, musician, airport planner, statistician, and all-around good joe. He broke into TV in its early days on *Broadway Open House*, the first late-night show, with Jerry Lester and Dagmar, and went on to write for Milton Berle's *Texaco Star Theatre*, *The NBC Comedy Hour*, *The Red Buttons Show*, *The Jan Murray Show*, Olsen & Johnson, Morey Amsterdam—and Howdy Doody. He was one of the editors of *The Random House Dictionary of the English Language*, and is at present senior editor at John Wiley & Sons, the distinguished New York publishing house.

CHARLES SHERMAN, born in 1898, was a Broadway producer, playwright and writer. He was associated with more than forty plays and revues. Among these were *Earl Carroll's Sketch Book*, in 1935, *Streets of Paris*, in 1939, *All in Fun, Seven Lively Arts, Bright Lights, Along Fifth Avenue*, and *Two's Company*, which starred Bette Davis. He died in Hollywood in 1975 where he had been living while writing for films and television.

DANNY SIMON started writing comedy professionally with his brother, Neil, in 1947. In partnership, they wrote special material for such stand-up comics as Buddy Hackett, Milton Berle, Jan Murray, Phil Foster, Dick Shawn, Victor Borge, Joey Adams and many others. Then they went to summer stock in the Poconos at a place called Tamiment where they wrote the sketches for two summers. Then came the Robert Q. Lewis radio show and from there they were hired by Max Liebman to write for the Sid Caesar show. After that came the Red Buttons show and along the way there was *Broadway Open House*, and shows for Phil Silvers, Jackie Gleason and more. After nine years in partnership, the brothers split up and Danny wrote his first play which was produced on the *United States Steel Hour*, starring Gertrude Berg. This was seen by Danny Thomas and Sheldon Leonard, who brought him to Hollywood to become the head writer for *The Danny Thomas Show*. Since then he also wrote and/or was head writer for *The Ann Sothern Show*, *The Real McCoys*, *Bachelor Father*, *My Three Sons*, *Pete & Gladys*, *The Jerry Lewis Show*, *The Jimmy Durante Show*, *One Day at a Time*, *The Facts of Life*, and others. In between, he was head writer and comedy stager for *The Kraft Music Hall* for three years; he produced and staged the NBC special, *Neil Simon's The Trouble with People*, was the first comedy director for the long running *Carol Burnett Show*, as well as *Love, American Style*, *What's Happening?* and others. For the past fifteen years, he has directed for the legitimate theatre, having staged dozens of plays featuring such stars as Jose Ferrer, Milton Berle, George Hamilton, Vivien Vance, Barbara Bel Geddes, E.G. Marshall, and half the membership of the Actor's Guild. For the past year and a half he has been teaching a course in comedy writing at the University of Southern California, the University of Hawaii, the University of California at Santa Barbara, the University of British Columbia at Vancouver, and in many other cities in the United States. In addition, he is also rewriting his play, *The Convertible Girl* into a novel and is nearing completion of a book on the craft of comedy writing.

NEIL SIMON began his writing career in television, creating material for such performers as Tallulah Bankhead, Sid Caesar, Phil Silvers and Garry Moore. He contributed sketches to revues at Tamiment and, with his brother Danny, wrote sketches for *Catch a Star* and *New Faces of 1956* on Broadway. Since 1960, a Broadway season without a Neil Simon comedy or musical has been a rare one. During the 1966-67 season, *Barefoot in the Park*, *The Odd Couple*, *Sweet Charity* and *The Star-Spangled Girl* were all running simultaneously; in the 1970-71 season, Broadway theatre-goers had their choice of *Plaza Suite*, *Last of the Red Hot Lovers* and *Promises, Promises*. Next came *The Gingerbread Lady*, *The Prisoner of Second Avenue*, *The Sunshine Boys*, *The Good Doctor*, *God's Favorite*, *California Suite*, *Chapter Two*, *They're Playing Our Song*, *I Oughta Be in Pictures*, and *Fools*. He has also written the screen adaptations of *Barefoot in the Park, The Odd Couple, Plaza Suite, The Prisoner of Second Avenue, The Sunshine Boys, California Suite* and *Chapter Two.* Other screenplays he has written include *The Out-of-Towners, The Heartbreak Kid, Murder by Death, The Goodbye Girl, The Cheap Detective,* and *Seems Like Old Times.* He lives in California with his wife, actress Marsha Mason.

PAUL GERARD SMITH, born in 1895, was one of the great comedy writers in the heyday of vaudeville. He was most prolific in writing sketches and comedy material for nearly all Keith-Albee-Orpheum headliners and lesser variety performers. For Broadway, his credits include *Keep Kool, Padlocks of 1927, Funny Face,* the *1928 Earl Carroll Vanities, Murray Anderson's Almanac* of 1929, *Heads Up!,* and the *Nine Fifteen Revue.* He died in 1968 in California, where he settled after retiring from the Broadway scene.

JOSEPH STEIN is the author of the musical *Fiddler on the Roof,* which won him the Tony and Drama Critics Circle Awards. His other Broadway works include *Plain and Fancy, Mr. Wonderful, Take Me Along, Juno, Zorba, King of Hearts, Carmelina* and *Enter Laughing.* He wrote the screenplays for both *Enter Laughing* and *Fiddler on the Roof.*

IRA WALLACH is the author of a number of plays, including *Drink to Me Only* (with A.S. Ginnes), and *The Absence of a Cello.* He also wrote sketches for many revues, the most well-known of which is *Phoenix '55,* starring Nancy Walker. His screenplays include *The Wheeler Dealers* (with George Goodman), and *Hot Millions,* for which he received an Academy Award nomination and the Writers Guild of Great Britain's award for the best British comedy screenplay. His nine published books include *Hopalong-Freud, Muscle Beach,* and *5,000 Years of Foreplay.*

BILLY K. WELLS was born in Yorkville, New York, in 1886. He started his career in vaudeville as a young teenager with his original act impersonating a middle-aged Dutch bearded character called "The Orator." He became well-known for his glib repartee and keen sense of comic timing and while still in his teens was sought after to write for other performers and producers. In his lifetime he wrote hundreds of headline vaudeville and burlesque acts, musical comedy sketches, radio and television shows and nightclub acts for the outstanding comedy stars of his day. His Broadway credits include the writing of most of the sketches for thirteen editions of *George White's Scandals* and the script for the show, *Manhattan Mary*. For the movies, he wrote the dialogue for the film that became the greatest box office hit at the Roxy Theatre, *The Cockeyed World*. From his original radio program, *Modern Baron Munchausen*, came the still-quoted line, "Vas you dere, Sharlie?" and for television, he wrote for the famous Milton Berle Texaco show. In the 1930s, he was cited as being the highest-paid comedy writer. In France, he was known as the "American Moliere," and Parnell of Australia called him the "International Dean of Comedy." When he died in 1956, he was working on his first book, his autobiography, entitled *From Tent Show to Television*.

GEORGE WHITE, born in 1890, began his career as a dancer in the *Ziegfeld Follies*, and in 1919 produced the first of what was to be an annual revue series, the *Scandals*. He also directed the shows, wrote sketches for them and even sporadically appeared in them. In all, there were thirteen editions of the *Scandals*, the last one in 1939. Among the other shows he produced were *Manhattan Mary* and *Flying High*.

MAX WILK was born in New York City. He studied at the Berkshire School and received a B.A. degree from Yale University, where he majored in playwriting. He contributed sketches to the Broadway revue, *Small Wonder*, and has also written for television and the movies. He is the author of eleven novels and several works of non-fiction including four nostalgia memoirs of the entertainment world: *The Wit and Wisdom of Hollywood*, *They're Playing Our Song*, *Memory Lane*, and *Every*

Day's a Matinee. His most recent novels are *Moving Picture Boys* and *Get Out and Get Under,* and he has co-authored Audrey Wood's memoirs, entitled *I Sell Plays.* Mr. Wilk is married and has three children. He lives in Westport, Connecticut, and London.

COPYRIGHT NOTICES

For stock and amateur performance rights of the
sketch as part of a revue entitled *The Best of
Broadway,* contact The Dramatic Publishing
Company, 163 Main Street, Westport, Connecticut
06880. For all other inquiries, contact Brooksfilms
Limited, 10201 West Pico Boulevard, Los Angeles,
California 90035.

UPPER BIRTH
Copyright © 1955 by Ira Wallach
Copyright © 1957 by Ira Wallach.
All inquiries regarding rights should be addressed to
Samuel French, Inc., 25 West 45 Street, New York,
N. Y. 10036

SELL, SELL, SELL
Copyright © 1982 by Herbert Hartig and Herbert
Reich
For any inquiries, contact Mr. Hartig, c/o The
Dramatists Guild, 234 West 44th Street, New York,
N. Y. 10036.

TALLULAH FINDS HER KITCHEN
Copyright © 1982 by Neil Simon, Danny Simon, and
Joseph Stein
All inquiries concerning rights should be addressed to
Albert I. DaSilva, 521 Park Avenue, New York, N. Y.
10021

COFFEE
Copyright © 1961 by Herbert Hartig and Lois Balk

◢ BARD BOOKS
DISTINGUISHED DRAMA

BENT, Martin Sherman	75754	2.50
BIZARRE BEHAVIOR:		
SIX PLAYS BY INNAURATO		
Albert Innaurato	75903	3.50
EQUUS, Peter Shaffer	51797	2.50
FANTASTICKS, Jones/Schmidt	54007	2.50
FIVE PLAYS BY RONALD RIBMAN		
Ronald Ribman	40006	2.95
GAY PLAYS: THE FIRST COLLECTION		
William H. Hoffman, Ed.	77263	3.95
GETTING OUT, Marsha Norman	75184	2.50
GREAT JEWISH PLAYS		
Joseph C. Landis, Ed.	51573	3.50
HISTORY OF THE AMERICAN FILM		
Christopher Durang	39271	1.95
IMPORTANCE OF BEING EARNEST		
Oscar Wilde	77404	1.95
MASS APPEAL, Bill Davis	77396	2.50
MEMOIR, John Murrell	38521	1.95
MISS JULIE, August Strindberg	77412	1.75
MISS MARGARIDA'S WAY		
Roberto Athayde	40568	1.95
PIPPIN		
Roger O. Hirson & Stephen Schwartz	45740	2.25
PLAYS BY AMERICAN WOMEN:		
THE EARLY YEARS, Judith Barlow, Ed.	76620	3.95
RUNNER STUMBLES, Milan Stitt	44719	2.25
SHADOW BOX, Michael Cristofer	46839	2.25
UNCOMMON WOMEN AND OTHERS		
Wendy Wasserstein	45997	2.25
WAKEFIELD PLAYS, Israel Horovitz	42903	3.50
WHOSE LIFE IS IT ANYWAY?		
Brian Clark	52407	2.50

AV⬗N Paperback